IN THE **BEST** INTEREST OF **STUDENTS**

Staying True to What Works in the ELA Classroom

Kelly Gallagher

Stenhouse Publishers

Portland, Maine

Stenhouse Publishers
www.stenhouse.com

Credits

Figure 2.3: Republished with permission of University of California Press, from "NASA History and the Challenge of Keeping the Contemporary Past" by Roger D. Launius, *The Public Historian*, Vol. 21, Issue 3, Summer 1999; permission conveyed through Copyright Clearance Center, Inc.

Figure 2.11: By Gaia Russo, published in *Russia Beyond the Headlines*.

Figure 2.16: Edward Hopper, *Nighthawks*, 1942, Oil on Canvas, 84.1 x 152.4 cm (33 1/8 x 60 in.), Friends of American Art Collection, 1942.51, The Art Institute of Chicago.

Figure 4.2: Courtesy of *ESPN the Magazine*.

Figure 4.5: George Strock/The LIFE Picture Collection/Getty Images

Figure 4.6: From *The New York Times*, 9/2/2012 © 2012 The New York Times. All rights reserved. Used by permission and protected by the Copyright Laws of the United States. The printing, copying, redistribution, or retransmission of this Content without express written permission is prohibited.

Chapter 4, pages 97-98: "A Few Disclaimers on the Fourth Amendment" by Leonard Pitts Jr.: From *The Miami Herald*, January 14, 2014 © 2014 McClatchy. All rights reserved. Used by permission and protected by the Copyright Laws of the United States. The printing, copying, redistribution, or retransmission of this Content without express written permission is prohibited.

Chapter 6, page 135: "A Hundred Words to Talk of Death" by Neil Gaiman: Copyright © Neil Gaiman 2006.

Figure 6.2: © The *New Yorker* Magazine/Barry Blitt/Conde Nast

Figure 6.3: Associated Press/Sue Ogrocki

Figure 6.5: © Tom Cheney/The *New Yorker* Magazine/Conde Nast

Figure 7.1: From THE NEW YORK TIMES UPFRONT. Copyright © by Scholastic Inc. Reprinted by permission of Scholastic Inc.

Figure 8.1: Reprinted with permission of the National Center for Public Policy and Higher Education and the Southern Regional Education Board.

Figure 8.2: "Reading by age group" reprinted courtesy of Vox Media, Inc., Vox.com.

Library of Congress Cataloging-in-Publication Data

Gallagher, Kelly, 1958-
  In the best interest of students : staying true to what works in the ELA classroom / Kelly Gallagher.
    pages cm
  Includes bibliographical references and index.
  ISBN 978-1-62531-044-6 (pbk. : alk. paper) -- ISBN 978-1-62531-045-3 (ebook)
  1. Language arts (Elementary)--Standards--United States. 2. Language arts (Secondary)--Standards--United States. 3. Educational accountability--United States. 4. United States. No Child Left Behind Act of 2001. I. Title.
  LB1576.G295 2015
  372.6--dc23
                              2014033956

Cover and interior design by Lucian Burg, Lu Design Studios, Portland, ME www.ludesignstudios.com

Manufactured in the United States of America

PRINTED ON 30% PCW
RECYCLED PAPER

21 20 19 18 17 16 15   9 8 7 6 5 4 3 2 1

IN THE **BEST** INTEREST OF **STUDENTS**

For Big Jim

CONTENTS

Acknowledgments

Watching the Major League Baseball All-Star game this week made me appreciative of the all-star team who helped to make this book possible. The lineup:

Owner: Philippa Stratton, for being the Abner Doubleday of education publishing.

General Manager: Dan Tobin, for his expert guidance of the franchise.

Front Office: Rebecca Eaton, Chuck Lerch, Chris Downey, Jay Kilburn, Jill Cooley, Nate "the Great" Butler, Chandra Lowe, Zsofia McMullin, Pam King, Lise Wood, Elaine Cyr, and anyone else behind the scenes at Stenhouse for their work in supporting this book. Special kudos as well to Lucian Burg for his design of this book and to Erin Trainer for her keen copyediting skills.

My agent: my wife, Kristin, whose immeasurable behind-the-scenes support, as always, keeps me up and running. No way this book happens without her. My love to Caitlin and Devin as well.

Manager: Bill Varner, my editor at Stenhouse, for making the right moves on our sixth book together.

Pitcher: Penny Kittle, for her persistent "pitches" from afar, which motivated me to start writing again, and for her wise feedback on some early sections of this book. "Nulla Dies Sine Linea."

Catcher: Deborah Kenny, founder of the Harlem Village Academies, for carrying on the fight despite all the problems thrown at her—and for inviting me to work with her teachers.

1B: Ariella Diamond, principal of Harlem Village Academy East Middle, for her enthusiastic support. Ariella, if you are wondering why I placed you at first base, ask Jess.

2B: Jeff Anderson, for no other reason than that I once promised him I would always mention him in my books.

SS: Robert Cunard, principal of Magnolia High School in Anaheim, California, for his slick fielding of my leave of absence request. My appreciation goes to the Education Division of the AUHSD as well.

3B: Jason Epting, principal of Harlem Village Academy West Middle, for his ability to handle anything hit his way, as well as for his graciousness and overall awesomeness.

LF: Donna Santman, for challenging my thinking, and for the deep influence she has had in the writing of this book. Donna, I remain awed by your intellect and courage. You should almost be listed as coauthor of this book. Almost.

CF: Julie Wright, for agreeing to eat at Applebee's, but more importantly, for helping me when I got stuck while writing this book, and for occasionally helping me to bring Donna Santman in from deep left field.

RF: Tom Newkirk, for the e-mail you sent encouraging me to start writing again. That meant a lot. And don't feel bad playing right field; that's where Tony Conigliaro and Dwight Evans played.

DH: My students, both in California and in New York, for repeatedly stepping up to the plate.

Bullpen: Tiffany DiPeralta, Rachael Dolan, Dave Hibler, Anna Knutson, Ashley LoTempio, Gavin Nangle, Martin Palamore, John Sharkey, Henry Wellington III, and Isabel Yalouris for allowing me to spend a year in your classrooms. Your students' work grace these pages.

Coaches: Richard Allington, Harvey and Elaine Daniels, Shelley Harwayne, George Hillocks, Carol Jago, Penny Kittle, Stephen Krashen, Judith Langer, Tom Newkirk, Erik Palmer, Grant Wiggins, Maja Wilson, Maryanne Wolf, and Yong Zhao, for their wisdom.

My gratitude to everyone on this team is deep and lasting—and for those of you who were worried about me, rest assured that living in New York did not turn me into a Yankees fan.

CHAPTER 1

Our Students' Best Interest Does Not Always Align with the Current Standards Movement

Years ago, when the No Child Left Behind (NCLB) legislation went into effect, teachers and administrators overreacted, so panicked by these new federal requirements that many states turned to shallow exams as a means of demonstrating student "progress." This was tragic, for although many states had rich standards in place, they often chose assessments that valued lower-level thinking. And as we now know, instruction was not driven by what standards were adopted; instead, instruction was driven by shallow assessments.

Many negative consequences spawned from the NCLB era. Writing, for example, wasn't even mentioned under NCLB guidelines, and, as a result, it got short shrift in many states when it came time to develop the new NCLB-aligned assessments (more on this in a moment). Because recreational reading was seen as "soft," it got kicked to the curb. Because surface-level thinking was demanded, it became the norm. (The 2012 SAT reading scores, for example, were the lowest scores in four decades. The juniors and seniors who took that test were in kindergarten and in first grade when NCLB began, thus becoming the first group of students whose entire school experience was shaped by NCLB-driven instruction.) Because of their allegiance to these new tests, schools started churning out memorizers instead of thinkers. We produced fewer students who could write coherent extended pieces. More students left our schools hating to read. And teaching students how to think deeply—to analyze, to synthesize, to evaluate—became a much more arduous task.

Looking back at the NCLB movement, it is easy to see how the testing pressures led schools away from those practices proven to be in the best interest of developing literate, well-rounded students. Those pressures were real—often with teachers' jobs on the line—and teaching to the test became the laser-like focus at many schools. I can remember conducting workshops for the various schools in my district where teachers spent hours discussing, breaking down, and prioritizing newly adopted state standards. We spent inordinate amounts of time sifting the new standards into categories: Which of these standards should be designated as "power standards"? Which of these standards were most likely to be tested? Which of these standards should receive less attention? We felt a need to prioritize the standards because we realized immediately that there were too many of them, that it was impossible to meaningfully teach all of them. (Marzano and Kendall [1998] studied the standards implemented in states across the country and came to the conclusion that we would have to change K–12 to K–22 to have enough time to properly teach the standards adopted by most states.) As teachers, we were panicked because we realized there was simply not enough time to do what we were being asked to do. Worse, we came to the realization that some of the most valued standards (e.g., the ability to write a multi-draft essay) were not going to be tested at all. Teachers were thus stuck in No Man's Land: should we provide our students with the deep writing experiences we know they need, or should we gear our instruction toward raising test scores? With pressure from administrators and from the public, many teachers chose the latter approach.

Regardless of the instructional approaches taken, not having enough time to teach the standards that would be tested exacerbated the situation. To make sure students were ready for the tests in the spring, schools rushed to develop a series of benchmark exams. We began testing students to see if they were ready to take even more tests. School benchmarks. District benchmarks. State benchmarks. I remember joking that if my boss demanded just a couple more tests, I'd have the easiest (and most boring) job in the world—I could stop teaching altogether and simply be a test monitor. Kind of funny until you consider the teacher in Texas who told me that to meet her school district's testing demands, she had to spend fifty-five days of her school year either directly testing her students or preparing her students for tests. Fifty-five days she was not teaching. Fifty-five days her students were not learning (that's nearly one-third of a school year where her students are not receiving instruction). So at a time when teachers desperately needed extra time to teach the standards, time was taken away so students could have extra test prep time. The results, by now, are well known: reading instruction shifted to an over-emphasis on surface-level understanding. Writing instruction was radically reduced (and in some schools, all but eliminated). And in the middle of all this madness we lost sight of what was in the best interest of our students.

The Common Core State Standards (and other new standards movements like the Next Generation Science Standards) are now here and I am afraid it is starting to feel like déjà vu. We are consumed by talk of a new wave of onerous testing. We are concerned that top-down reform will not work. We find ourselves incredulous at talk of evaluating teachers through one-time test scores. We are offended that the teaching of kids from all kinds of backgrounds (who possess a vast array of ability levels) is characterized as a "Race to the Top."

These concerns raise a new concern: that the issues swirling around the adoption of the newest set of standards, much like the issues generated by the NCLB era, have again diverted our focus from the best practices of literacy instruction. The pressures generated by NCLB, for example, clouded the judgment of many teachers and administrators, veering instruction away from best practices and leading to an over-emphasis on multiple-choice exam preparation. I am concerned that the pressures generated by the latest rounds of new standards and new testing are tempting teachers to abandon what they know is best for their children, sending both teachers and students down similar destructive instructional paths.

To avoid repeating some of the mistakes made during previous reform movements, and to ensure that quality instruction remains at the forefront of our classrooms, educators would be best served to keep three key lessons in mind:

> Lesson 1: Avoid falling in love with these standards. They won't be here forever.

> Lesson 2: Recognize that the standards by themselves are necessary but insufficient.

> Lesson 3: Remember that good teaching is not about "covering" a new list of standards; good teaching is grounded in practices proven to sharpen our students' literacy skills.

Let's take a brief look at each of these lessons.

Lesson 1: Avoid falling in love with these standards. They won't be here forever.

In any era of new standards, we should remind ourselves that new sets of standards come and new sets of standards go. And though the Common Core State Standards (CCSS), for example, are in some ways a marked improvement from the standards of previous movements, the CCSS, too, have their share of shortcomings (more on this later). Before we myopically fixate on any set of new standards, teachers and administrators would be well served to remind themselves two things about the new standards: (1) teachers who religiously follow them are being asked to do things that are not in the best interest of our students, and (2) these new standards will one day be ushered out the door to make room for the next generation of "improved" standards. When first introduced, new standards come with a certain gravitas—a gravitas, however, that is unlikely to persist. One study, *How Well Are American Students Learning? The 2012 Brown Center Report on American Education*, notes that "standards with real consequences are most popular when they are first proposed. Their popularity steadily declines from there, reaching a nadir when tests are given and consequences kick in. Just as the glow of consensus surrounding NCLB faded after a few years, cracks are now appearing in the wall of support for the Common Core" (Loveless 2012,

14). These cracks are evident and widening: some outlier states—Wisconsin, Oklahoma, North Carolina, Indiana—have either opted out of the CCSS entirely, or are on the road to doing so. At least five other states have opted not to offer the online assessments designed to measure students' progress in meeting the standards. As the *Brown Center Report* reminds us, a new and "better" approach is always around the next corner. To steal the words of Laertes in *Hamlet*, it might be helpful to see any set of new standards as "forward, not permanent, sweet, not lasting" (Shakespeare 1997). What is now sexy to policy makers will not be sexy to policy makers in a few years. All standards movements come and go, and the standards currently in favor in your state will be no exception. Don't fall in love with them, because one day they are going to leave you.

Lesson 2: Recognize that the standards by themselves are necessary but insufficient.

In California, where I have taught for twenty-nine years, students had to pass the California High School Exit Exam (CAHSEE) as a prerequisite for receiving a high school diploma. On the language arts section of the exam, students were asked to read a number of passages and to answer questions, and they were required to demonstrate writing proficiency by responding to an on-demand writing prompt. Every student in the state took the CAHSEE, so, in theory, you could compare the literacy level of a student in San Diego with the literacy level of a student in San Francisco. In theory.

But things begin to go sideways when one considers how the CAHSEE was scored. Because the powers that be were deeply concerned that too many students would fail if the bar for passing the exam was set too high, they set the language passing rate at a mere 60 percent (and even more ridiculously, the bar to pass the math section of the exam was set at 55 percent). And it got worse. Though the CAHSEE required students to produce an essay to demonstrate writing proficiency, the essays themselves were weighted lightly into the students' final scores. In fact, because the essay section was factored so minimally, a student could actually score a zero on the written portion and still pass the exam. That's right—a student could pass the CAHSEE without demonstrating the ability to write a single sentence. (When a state tells its teachers that writing is literally worth zero, is it any wonder teachers abandon writing and turn their classrooms into multiple-choice test-prep factories?) To the public, however, a reading of the published test scores looked like many of our students were exiting the system as proficient, but to those of us in the classroom, we knew that it was an illusion created by a simple lowering of the proficiency bar.

This manipulation to make more students appear proficient was not an issue limited to California. As the *Brown Report* notes, many "states have undermined their own credibility when it comes to measuring student learning. Accounts of dumbed-down and poorly-written state tests, manipulation of cut scores to artificially boost the number of students in higher performance levels, and assessments on which students can get fewer than 50% of items correct and yet score 'proficient' fuel the belief that states individually cannot be trusted to give the public an accurate estimate of how American education is doing" (Loveless 2012, 7). In many cases state test scores rose, and as a result many schools *looked* better on paper, yet if one were to take a closer look at national scores—scores that were not influenced by local manipulation of what defines proficiency—alarm bells went off. As mentioned earlier in this chapter, the 2012 reading SAT scores, for example—a national assessment—were the lowest in four decades. (I intentionally chose the 2012 scores because they measured the first set of students whose entire K–12 education was shaped by NCLB.) What I did not mention is that the 2013 scores remained equally as bad—test results that "put a punctuation mark on a gradual decline in the ability of college-bound teens to read passages and answer questions about sentence structure, vocabulary and meaning on the college entrance exam" (Layton and Brown 2012).

I understand and empathize with the philosophy of giving each state the right to develop its own standards and testing program—our country was indeed founded on the notion of states' rights—but giving states this freedom has far too often led to shenanigans (artificially cut scores, ridiculously low passing rates) that undermine our students' education. As the *Brown Report* notes, some states have proven that they cannot be trusted when it comes to determining student proficiency.

I also understand and empathize with the notion of adopting a national set of standards. (This should not be misunderstood as an endorsement of all the over-the-top testing that accompanies the new standards. More on that later.) Students who cannot write should never be deemed "proficient." In addition, a student who is deemed "proficient" in Mississippi should be held to the same standard as a student who is deemed "proficient" in Massachusetts. Adopting a national set of standards is a necessary step toward ensuring that the notion of "proficient" means the same thing, regardless of where you teach. It is my hope that the adoption of national standards will help to eliminate the shameless manipulation of tests scores, thus enabling valid comparisons to be made.

Though adopting a national set of standards may help eliminate some of the problems that occur when states operate independently, let's be really clear about two things: first, that even though the new standards are almost universally markedly better than the standards that drove previous eras of education, the new standards *still do not always serve the best interest of our students*. They are better, but imperfect. They contain blind spots and shortcomings. And second, let's not forget that the adoption of any set of standards, no matter how strong they may be, does not ensure that teaching gets any better. The standards simply indicate *what* should be taught; they do not discuss *how* they should be taught. But, of course, as we know, *how* the standards are taught is the critical component to elevating our students' literacy skills. As the *Brown Report* states, it might be best to consider the new standards "as aspirational, and like a strict diet or prudent plan to save money for the future, they represent good intentions that are not often realized—it is an intended curriculum, and the intent does not necessarily mean results" (Loveless 2012, 13). Later in this book I will examine how these new Common Core standards, despite being a step up from the standards used in the NCLB years, have continued in many cases, despite good intentions, to drive bad teaching.

When thinking about raising student achievement, a strong set of standards is a necessary starting point, but it's just that—a starting point. When considering the possible impact new standards might have on student learning, the *Brown Report* analyzed states' past experiences with adopting new, rigorous standards. The study asked a central question: Did the quality of state standards lead to greater student achievement? The answer, they found, was no. Simply creating and adopting new standards did not raise student performance. This does not bode well for the implementation of the CCSS, for as the study notes, "The empirical evidence suggests that the Common Core will have little effect on American students' achievement. Despite all the money and effort devoted to developing the Common Core State Standards—not to mention the simmering controversy over their adoption in several states—the study foresees very little impact on student learning" (Loveless 2012, 12).

The *Brown Report* also examined another interesting question: Did raising the rigor (the cut points for determining proficiency) drive better student achievement? Once again, the answer was no. The study found that "states with weak content standards score about the same on NAEP as those with strong standards" (Loveless 2012, 12). (NAEP is a national assessment that has been in place since 1969 and is the main source of data for a report known as the "Nation's Report Card." NAEP is generally considered to be the gold standard of national assessments. For more on NAEP, go to http://nces.ed.gov/nationsreportcard.)

So let's review these two key findings by the Brown Center: Simply adopting new standards does not raise student achievement, and simply increasing the rigor by raising the "proficiency" bar does not work, either. Merely spelling out what students should be learning does not equal results. This is not to suggest, however, that the Common Core and other recently-adopted standards are worthless. On the contrary, I believe many of the new standards provide a target for good instruction. But I also believe, as I will discuss in subsequent chapters, that some of the new Common Core standards are misguided, thus leading to practices that are not in our students' best interests. This is why hitching your wagon blindly to any standards movement is rarely a good idea.

Lesson 3: Remember that good teaching is not about "covering" a new list of standards; good teaching is grounded in practices proven to sharpen our students' literacy skills.

There is a scene in the film *Bowling for Columbine* where Michael Moore (2002) approaches a Los Angeles police officer at the site of a petty crime and asks him if he has instead considered arresting anyone for the smog that is blanketing the city. The smog, he says, is sure to harm way more people than the minor crime currently being investigated. Moore's question is a joke, but underlying the joke is a genuine concern: Sometimes we get so wrapped up in the trivial that we lose sight of the bigger picture; the minutia clouds what is most important.

I am often reminded of this scene from *Bowling for Columbine* when I conduct workshops for teachers on how to get reluctant students up and writing. In these workshops, I review the writing demands inherent in the Common Core standards, and I make the point that, generally, students are not getting enough writing practice in our schools. This declaration often makes teachers a bit uncomfortable, and during these workshops, I am invariably asked the same question: "How do you fit in all this writing around the new standards?"

This question is a red flag. The fact that I have been asked this question numerous times lends me to believe that teachers are again becoming so overly focused on the standards that they are losing sight of the bigger picture. The teaching of writing should never be seen as an activity to be "fit in" around the standards. Writing instruction should be a nonnegotiable, core value in any classroom, and teachers should not have to be concerned with fitting it in. The question "How do you fit in writing instruction around the new standards?" is the wrong question. The correct question should be, "How do you fit in all of the standards around your writing instruction?" Like the police officer who is chasing the petty crime instead of seeing the bigger picture, I am afraid that teachers are becoming so hung up on teaching every new standard that they are losing sight of the core literacy needs of our students. Teaching is not an exercise in checking items off a list of standards, and any teacher who cuts writing instruction short simply to ensure every standard is addressed is doing his or her students a terrible disservice. What does it matter if teachers sprint through all the standards if at the end of the year their students still cannot write well?

⊢————————————⊣

Enter a new wave of standards, an attempt to change what was done over the previous decade. The good news is that they have arrived. The bad news is that they have arrived. Let me explain, first by discussing the good news that comes with the latest wave of new standards.

The Good News: Opportunity Knocks

Clearly, it's time to try a different approach, and, though I have already acknowledged that simply handing teachers new standards will not drive meaningful change, I hold out hope that teaching to a set of new, deeper standards might be a necessary first step in reversing this "gradual decline" found in many of our students. What fuels this hope that the new standards might present an opportunity to strengthen instruction in our schools? Why might the new standards be a good thing? Two reasons.

Reason 1: By valuing rigor, the new standards raise the bar of what it means to be literate.

Instruction in the NCLB era was driven by the flurry of testing that accompanied it, and, unfortunately, those tests put a premium on surface-level, multiple-choice thinking. As mentioned earlier, writing was often ignored completely, and as a result, writing was devalued in schools across the country. (I don't think this observation that writing was devalued in schools across the country is hyperbole. It is based on countless conversations I have had with teachers throughout the United States.) We raised a generation of memorizers who have trouble thinking deeply and who can't read and write well.

My hope that new standards will be a catalyst in driving more rigor into our classrooms reminds me of the time I found myself on a flight sitting next to the president of a large computer software company. At that time my oldest daughter had just graduated from UCLA and was looking for work in a very bad economy, so I asked the businessman sitting next to me what he looks for when he recruits new employees. He matter-of-factly told me that when hiring, his firm looks for the smartest people in the world, often searching for candidates from top American universities, from India, from China. The conversation continued as follows:

"How is your search for qualified applicants going?" I asked.

"Not so well," he replied.

"Why is that?"

"It's still easy to find smart people, but it is getting really hard to find smart people who can think."

An interesting idea, isn't it? That our schools are producing smart students who cannot think. At a time when literacy demands increased globally, the NCLB lowered the literacy bar. Teachers drilled their students with multiple choice test preparation materials. Instruction broadened and often stayed in the shallow end of the pool. Rigor was sacrificed, and schools became a lot more boring. One recent study, *Do Schools Challenge Our Students?* found that even students believe that school has become too easy:

You might think that the nation's teenagers are drowning in schoolwork. Images of sullen students buried in textbooks often grace the covers of popular parenting magazines, while well-heeled suburban teenagers often complain they have to work the hours of a corporate lawyer in order to finish their school projects and homework assignments. But when we recently examined a federal survey of students in elementary and high schools around the country, we found the opposite: Many students are not being challenged in school.

Consider, for instance, that 37 percent of fourth-graders say that their math work is too easy. More than a third of high-school seniors report that they hardly ever write about what they read in class. In a competitive global economy where the mastery of science is increasingly crucial, 72 percent of eighth-grade science students say they aren't being taught engineering and technology, according to our analysis of a federal database. (Boser and Rosenthal 2012, 1)

When students say that school is too easy, you know educational reform is headed in the wrong direction. My experience leads me to believe that the above study is half right: I have found that kids who are in the honors track are asked to work hard, but that the bar remains too low for the wide majority of students.

No one is accusing the latest set of standards of being too easy. On the contrary, when it comes to teaching reading and writing, the new standards raise the bar of what it means to be literate. These standards have reintroduced rigor, and that is good. No one rises to low expectations. As Smokey Daniels once said to me, "You can have rigor without the mortis." I am hoping the new standards will help bring this rigor back into all classrooms, and in doing so, redefine what is meant when a student is defined as "literate."

Reason 2: This deepening of reading expectations and renewed emphasis on writing across the curriculum may drive deeper instruction.

To prepare for the demands of the CCSS, participating states have aligned with assessments developed by either the Partnership for Assessment of Readiness for College and Career (PARCC) or the SMARTER Balanced Assessment Consortium (SBAC). These new assessments require much more from students than the assessments that drove the NCLB era, and the pressure generated by these new tests presents an opportunity. For example, the new assessments require students across the curriculum to demonstrate their thinking via writing. This renewed emphasis on writing has already prompted teachers from all content areas at my school to come together to discuss ways writing can be infused into their curricula. Some of these teachers are known for not having their students write very much, but since the new assessments value writing, and since the feet of these teachers are being held to this new testing fire, they are beginning to explore ways to bring more writing into their classrooms. It is true that teachers like you or me do not need to have a test held over our heads to prompt more writing in our classes; if every test was taken away tomorrow, we would still have our students write daily. But, sadly, this is not the case with all teachers. There are a number of teachers out there who need the threat of published test scores to nudge them into bringing more writing into their classrooms. At my own school, I have seen evidence that the pressures of this new testing are beginning to drive more writing across the curriculum. The new standards demand writing; student writing is going to be scored; and the results will be published. New writing accountability is driving more writing across the curriculum, and this is a good thing.

The Bad News: The New Standards Are Here

So the good news is that the new standards raise the bar of what it means to be literate, and in doing so, often encourage richer and deeper instruction. But along with the new standards come some new concerns.

Sequencing of Skills

Though increased rigor may prove to be beneficial, the new standards raise questions about how they are sequenced. P. David Pearson, internationally-known reading researcher from the University of California at Berkeley, wonders how the sequence of skills from one grade level to the next in the Common Core standards was determined. How was it decided, for example, that a particular skill is introduced in the fourth grade instead of in the fifth grade? Who determined these sequencing of skills, and are they developmentally appropriate? "Are they researched-based?" Pearson wonders. "Do they come from tradition? From professional consensus? Best guesses?" Rather than accept this sequencing as gospel, Pearson suggests that "teachers in grade-alike bands get together and assess the logic and the practicality of the progressions that they see in the current standards" (Pearson 2014).

Negative Top-Down Effect on Our Youngest Students

Shelley Harwayne, who in her forty years in education has been a codirector of the Teachers College Writing Project at Columbia University as well as a superintendent of District 2 in New York City, worries that the top-down approach favored by the Common Core of making students more college and career ready has negatively affected children in the early grades, particularly in kindergarten. Harwayne notes that we don't really have kindergarten anymore, that what used to be first grade has become kindergarten, and what was once kindergarten—a time for socialization, a time for play, a time for developing wonder and creativity—has all but been eliminated. Harwayne also laments that not all five-year-olds are developmentally ready for the academic rigor of the kindergarten standards, and to force those standards on all five-year-olds is educational malpractice (2013). More on this concern can be found in Chapter 3.

Heading Down the Path (Again!) of Too Much Testing

With a new set of standards comes a new set of tests. One of the problems with NCLB was that it tested our students into oblivion, and many are concerned that the same thing will happen with the adoption of the CCSS (or with the standards adopted by the previously mentioned outlier states). Stephen Krashen, professor emeritus at the University of Southern California and internationally-recognized expert in second language acquisition, notes that "the common core is calling for more standardized testing than we have ever seen on this planet, far more than the already excessive amount required by No Child Left Behind. In addition to final tests, there will be interim tests given throughout the year and perhaps even pretests in the fall. Instead of only testing math and reading in grades 3 through 8 and once in high-school, the common core will test more subjects and more grades. I estimate at least a 20-fold increase in standardized testing. The common core will not help prepare students for anything except tests" (Krashen 2012).

Though I disagree with Krashen's assessment that the latest standards will do nothing but prepare students for tests—as stated earlier, I believe, for example, the new standards will drive more writing into our schools—I do share his concern that our students will be massively over-tested. The standards themselves are not the issue here; the problem lies in how much instructional time will be diverted to make students "test ready" for the PARCC and SBAC assessments. Those of us who work with below-grade-level students know that every instructional day is crucial, and we also recognize that every day our students spend taking or preparing for a test is a lost instructional day. Worse, I am concerned that teachers' overattention to the exams will once again drive them into an over-the-top test-prep mode, eliminating additional instructional days while increasing the danger of classrooms turning into worksheet factories.

But perhaps the biggest worry that emanates from the new round of tests comes from how the tests already appear to be shaping instruction in a way that is not in the best interest of our students. One example: the tests that assess the new CCSS value argumentative writing over narrative writing; therefore, teaching students how to craft a good story is being placed on the back burner (more on why this is a bad trend is found in Chapter 5). On the reading side, nonfiction is overvalued, and when the tests favor nonfiction, I am concerned that the curriculum and instruction will be tilted so that our students will be given less practice reading novels and poetry. The new Common Core reading and writing anchor standards may be better *on paper*, but the tests that states have adopted to accompany the new standards do not treat all the standards equally. Some standards are more valued than others. Take the skill of close reading, for example. Because close reading of short passages is valued by the tests, some teachers are overdoing having students analyze short passages. Conversely, the tests do not measure a student's ability to hold his or her thinking across 300 pages, so less emphasis is placed on having students analyze longer works. In this case, the new tests are already driving instruction that is not in our students' best interest. (The close reading example is just one example of how the new tests adversely affect instruction. There are other cases as well, as discussed in subsequent chapters in this book.) If teachers teach religiously to these exams, their students' literacy development will be harmed. This is not hyperbolic, especially if you consider one recent study that looked at the effects of top-down federal education policies such as Race to the Top and No Child Left Behind. The study focused on the reform movement in Washington D.C., New York City, and Chicago. These districts were chosen "because all enjoyed the benefit of mayoral control, produce reliable district-level test score data from the National Assessment of Educational Progress (NAEP), and were led by vocal proponents who implemented versions of this reform agenda" (Weiss and Long 2013, 3). What is the big take-away from this study? That these reform movements "delivered few benefits and in some cases harmed the students they purported to help" (3). Specifically, the report found the following:

- Test scores increased less, and achievement gaps grew more, in "reform" cities than in other urban districts.
- Reported successes for targeted students evaporated upon closer inspection.
- Test-based accountability contributed to thinning the ranks of experienced teachers, but not necessarily bad teachers.
- School closures did not send students to better schools or save districts money.
- Charter schools further disrupted the districts while providing mixed benefits, particularly for the highest-needs students.
- Emphasis on widely touted market-reform [test-based teacher evaluation, increased school choice, and the closure of "underperforming" schools] drew attention and resources from initiatives with greater promise.
- The reform missed a critical factor driving the achievement gaps: the influence of poverty on academic performance.
- Real, sustained change requires strategies that are more realistic, patient, and multi-pronged. (3)

In the Best Interest of Students

When it comes to enabling our students to deepen their literacy skills, there is little evidence that top-down federal education policies such as Race to the Top and No Child Left Behind work, so instead of dragging teachers down another new road that is likely to end in yet another dead end, this book suggests an alternate path: Let's step away from the politics and madness that have accompanied yet another new educational movement. Let's step away from the pendulum that has swung once again. Let's step away from teaching to another series of tests that narrow our instruction. Instead, let's direct our focus on what we know works when it comes to teaching students how to read, write, listen, and speak. Let's focus on what is in the best interest of students.

CHAPTER 2

Staying True to What Works in the Teaching of Reading

I was pumped as my seniors walked into class one Monday morning. This was the day that they would begin reading *1984*, one of my favorite novels to teach. After a few introductory comments explaining the concept of a dystopia and hinting at the book's relevance to today's world, I paused and asked a question to get the conversation started:

"Does anyone have an idea why we will be reading this book?" I asked, hopeful that someone in the room would make a connection to today's surveillance-heavy world, to Edward Snowden, to the NSA, to Kim Jong Un, to contemporary propaganda . . . to anything.

"Cuz you want us to write an essay?" asked Antonio.

The worst part about Antonio's response was that I truly could not tell if he was being sarcastic. But, really, does it matter? If he was being sarcastic, then his comment can certainly be interpreted as a stinging indictment of what he has come to believe reading to be. If he was not being sarcastic, then his comment can also certainly be interpreted as a stinging indictment of what he has come to believe reading to be. Either way, not good. For Antonio, and I suspect for many of his classmates, great works of literature have been turned into ten weeks of worksheets, culminating in the writing of dry, teacher-directed essays.

When considering what might be a more effective approach to the teaching of reading, it will be helpful to start by examining the ten Common Core anchor reading standards. Yes, I know not all states have adopted the CCSS, but I do believe all teachers will benefit from a close examination of the Common Core anchor reading standards. As mentioned in Chapter 1, the new reading standards by themselves are necessary but insufficient. They get many things right, and they get some things wrong. Examining what they get right and what they get wrong will be beneficial for all teachers of reading, whether your state has adopted the CCSS or not.

In this chapter, we examine what the standards get right about the teaching of reading and how teaching to students' strengths will make them better readers. In Chapter 3, we examine where the anchor reading standards miss the mark and how we might adjust our instruction to overcome their shortcomings.

First, let's look at the Common Core reading standards:

CCSS English Language Arts Anchor Standards for Reading

Key Ideas and Details

CCSS.ELA-Literacy.CCRA.R.1 Read closely to determine what the text says explicitly and to make logical inferences from it; cite specific textual evidence when writing or speaking to support conclusions drawn from the text.

CCSS.ELA-Literacy.CCRA.R.2 Determine central ideas or themes of a text and analyze their development; summarize the key supporting details and ideas.

CCSS.ELA-Literacy.CCRA.R.3 Analyze how and why individuals, events, or ideas develop and interact over the course of a text.

Craft and Structure

CCSS.ELA-Literacy.CCRA.R.4 Interpret words and phrases as they are used in a text, including determining technical, connotative, and figurative meanings, and analyze how specific word choices shape meaning or tone.

CCSS.ELA-Literacy.CCRA.R.5 Analyze the structure of texts, including how specific sentences, paragraphs, and larger portions of the text (e.g., a section, chapter, scene, or stanza) relate to each other and the whole.

CCSS.ELA-Literacy.CCRA.R.6 Assess how point of view or purpose shapes the content and style of a text.

Integration of Knowledge and Ideas

CCSS.ELA-Literacy.CCRA.R.7 Integrate and evaluate content presented in diverse media and formats, including visually and quantitatively, as well as in words.

CCSS.ELA-Literacy.CCRA.R.8 Delineate and evaluate the argument and specific claims in a text, including the validity of the reasoning as well as the relevance and sufficiency of the evidence.

CCSS.ELA-Literacy.CCRA.R.9 Analyze how two or more texts address similar themes or topics in order to build knowledge or to compare the approaches the authors take.

Range of Reading and Level of Text Complexity

> CCSS.ELA-Literacy.CCRA.R.10 Read and comprehend complex literary and informational texts independently and proficiently.
> (NGA/CCSSO 2010a)

Reading through these standards reminds me that they are a marked improvement over the reading standards adopted in most states during the NCLB era. They ask our students to do deeper, closer reading of rigorous, high-quality literature and nonfiction. This is a move in the right direction.

In looking at what the anchor standards get right, let's chunk them into three major sections. As P. David Pearson notes, each chunk has a separate reading focus:

STANDARDS	FOCUS OF THE STANDARDS
Standards 1–3: Key Ideas and Details	In standards 1–3, the essential question is **what does the text say?**
Standards: 4–6: Craft and Structure	In standards 4–6, the essential question is **what does the text do?**
Standards 7–9: Integration of Knowledge and Ideas	In standards 7–9, the essential question is **what does the text mean?**

Source: P. David Pearson 2014

Being able to answer these questions—What does the text say? What does the text do? What does the text mean?—is an essential reading skill. Let's look at how we might work these skills into our classroom.

What Does the Text Say?

First we'll review anchor reading standards one through three, categorized as "Key Ideas and Details."

Key Ideas and Details

> CCSS.ELA-Literacy.CCRA.R.1 Read closely to determine what the text says explicitly and to make logical inferences from it; cite specific textual evidence when writing or speaking to support conclusions drawn from the text.

CCSS.ELA-Literacy.CCRA.R.2 Determine central ideas or themes of a text and analyze their development; summarize the key supporting details and ideas.

CCSS.ELA-Literacy.CCRA.R.3 Analyze how and why individuals, events, or ideas develop and interact over the course of a text.

Deeper reading starts with a literal understanding of the text. If students cannot figure out what the text is saying—if they cannot retell what is happening—then moving into closer reading and deeper understanding will be impossible. You have to recognize who is a Capulet and who is a Montague before any rich understanding of *Romeo and Juliet* can take place.

When it comes to making sure my students know what the text says, I start by introducing a series of summary activities. The ability to write summaries is an often overlooked and underrated skill. They are hard to fake, and they give me a quick, formative assessment of what my students understand (and what they are missing in their initial reading). When introducing the skill of summarizing, I start very simply and scaffold my students up from there. Here are some activities I have my students do to sharpen their summary skills:

17-Word Summaries

My students were just beginning to read *Lord of the Flies* (Golding 1962). I walked them into Chapter 1 by reading the first few pages of the chapter to them and then asked them to complete the reading of the chapter on their own. Before we really dove into the later chapters of the novel, I wanted to see if they understood what was happening in Chapter 1, so I chose a student at random and asked her to pick a number between ten and twenty. She chose seventeen, so I asked my students to write seventeen-word summaries of the chapter. Not eighteen words. Not sixteen words. Seventeen, and exactly seventeen words. Here are some of their responses:

Ralph and Piggy are stranded, but with the help of a conch shell, they discover more kids.

—Alicia

Because of a plane crash, a group of kids are stranded on an island with no adults.

—Miguel

Ralph, who's "fair," becomes leader of the plane-crash survivors after uniting them by blowing on the conch.

—Karen

A plane crashes on an island; the kids will have to learn how to survive without groups.

—Jessica

I like this activity on a number of levels. It not only teaches them to summarize but also teaches them to pay very close attention to sentence structure and to word choice. In the preceding examples, notice the "moves" the writers have to make to exactly hit the seventeen-word target. Karen uses a hyphen, and Jessica employs a semicolon as a way of avoiding the use of a coordinating conjunction. This activity requires students to pay attention to their sentence construction, and, better yet, I can read their responses very quickly and get an instant sense of who understands the text and who does not.

Write a Headline

To help students refine their summary skills, I have them create headlines for actual newspaper stories. I usually start lightly, often sharing actual headlines that are unintentionally funny. Here are some actual headlines that overstate the obvious:

"Missippi's Literacy Program Shows Improvement" (note misspelling)

"City Council Runs Out of Time to Discuss Shorter Meetings"

"Man Accused of Killing Attorney Receives New Lawyer"

"Homicide Victims Rarely Talk to the Police"

"Healthy Diet Lowers Death Risk"

"Pregnant Girls are Vulnerable to Weight Gain"

"Most Earthquake Damage is Done by Shaking"

"Tight End Returns After Colon Surgery"

Source: Huffington Post 2012

Okay, maybe I would not share the last one with ninth graders, but you get the idea. Once students are warmed up a bit, we have a brief discussion of what makes an effective headline. I then give students newspaper stories with the headlines removed and ask them to supply headlines of their own. In Figure 2.1, you will see an example from Alejandra, a ninth-grade student.

Guess the headline:

Blizzard traps East Coast

Amid a mix of rain, sleet and snow, plows and electricity-repair crews across the Northeast continued their efforts to clean up the remains of the blizzard of 2013 with transportation issues remaining a key concern.

The morning commute in many areas remained slow on Monday as key roads continued to be closed. Mass transit was returning to service but slowly. The Long Island Expressway, a key commuter roadway in suburban New York, reopened for business, Gov. Andrew Cuomo announced Monday morning, days after hundreds of vehicles were caught by the blizzard, trapping drivers and passengers overnight Friday and, in some cases, well into Saturday.

The storm dropped more than two feet of snow across the region and in some parts, notably central Connecticut and Rhode Island, more than three feet. Many smaller roads in Connecticut remained impassable, slowing recovery efforts, while the icy rain spread a patina of pain on other thoroughfares. Police closed parts of Interstate 91 from Windsor, Conn., to the Massachusetts state line on Monday.

In the Boston area, freezing rain and hail made commutes sluggish and dangerous as people trying to get back to work found themselves stuck in traffic for two or three times the usual period of time. Essential routes such as Storrow Drive and the Mass Pike in Boston were not moving, and giant excavators and bulldozers slowed traffic at many intersections, still clearing snow. Pedestrians forced onto streets by snow piles six feet high in some places contended for space with the cars spitting up mushy, brown slush.

School was still canceled in many Massachusetts towns, including Boston. Schools in Providence, R.I., and the eastern end of Long Island were also closed.

At the height of the blizzard, more than 5,300 flights were canceled and airports from New York to Boston were closed. All of the airports reopened on Saturday, but operations were still slow to return to normal.

Guess the headline:

Healthcare coverage but not enough doctors

SACRAMENTO — As the state moves to expand healthcare coverage to millions of Californians under President Obama's healthcare law, it faces a major obstacle: There aren't enough doctors to treat a crush of newly insured patients.

Some lawmakers want to fill the gap by redefining who can provide healthcare. They are working on proposals that would allow physician assistants to treat more patients and nurse practitioners to set up independent practices. Pharmacists and optometrists could act as primary care providers, diagnosing and managing some chronic illnesses, such as diabetes and high-blood pressure.

"We're going to be mandating that every single person in this state have insurance," said state Sen. Ed Hernandez (D-West Covina), chairman of the Senate Health Committee and leader of the effort to expand professional boundaries. "What good is it if they are going to have a health insurance card but no access to doctors?"

Hernandez's proposed changes, which would dramatically shake up the medical establishment in California, have set off a turf war with physicians that could contribute to the success or failure of the federal Affordable Care Act in California.

Figure 2.1 Alejandra's newspaper headlines

Fahrenheit 451
The Sieve and the Sand pp. 71-110

What percentage of the reading did you do? 100%

Write a headline for this section of the book:

Montag has an epiphany.

Explain your headline: Montag, in the beginning only wanted to
burn books. His ambitions now
are to save them. Montag realized

Explain the significance of the following: the importance of books, how
they could change society. He thought
of how people spent an immense

Faber   amount of time to write a book
Montag goes to Faber to   for him to only burn in
help him understand the Bible.   minutes. He wanted his culture
Faber says it could possibly   to prevail or avenge itself. The
be the last copy and gives   first step, him.
him an earpiece to communicate
and help Montag understand the
Bible. I think Faber is going
to either influence Montag to do
a tremendous act of valor, or he
will re-
publish the   "I voted last election...I laid it on the line for President Noble. I think he's one of the
bible.   nicest-looking men ever became president."

The significance of this quote is to show the
ignorance. The society's vote is determined by the
looks of the candidate rather than his morals.
Ambitions of the President mean nothing, but what
they wear does.

"Why...we have stopped in front of my house."

Beatty and Montag are driving to burn a house down due
to a call saying it contained books. Montag stops in front
of his house. I think this foreshadows that Montag, like
the girl, will stay in his house and burn with his
books. Montag has realized the importance of books, and he
will die with them.

Figure 2.2 Ricardo's headline for *Fahrenheit 451* reading

Once my students get the knack of writing newspaper headlines, I have them apply this skill to the literature they are reading by having them write headlines for assigned chunks of the novels. Recently I assigned a section of *Fahrenheit 451* (Bradbury 1953) to be read, and as part of a reading check, I began class by having students write a headline for that particular chunk. Along with the headline, I ask for a brief response explaining why the headline they wrote is appropriate. In Figure 2.2, you will see that Ricardo wrote "Montag has an epiphany" as his headline, and then follows by explaining how the character has come to realize the importance of books. Also, notice how I expand the reading check by asking students to explain the significance of both a character (Faber) and of a passage found in the assigned reading.

Window Quotes

Often in longer magazine articles the editor will choose a key line or quotation and feature it in a window quote, a box placed in the article so that the text of the article wraps around it (see Figure 2.3). The purpose of the window quote is to lure the reader into the piece by highlighting something interesting from the article; in doing so, the window quote often captures a big idea of the piece as well.

Efforts to guard against NASA court history notwithstanding, I also point out to my academic colleagues what I consider a great naiveté among many professors that they are somehow impartial and can "tell the truth" (whatever that is, and if it really does exist) in their historical discourses without having to satisfy some client. After all, academic historians writing without a contract on virtually any topic imaginable are still serving a clientele—their peers, and identity group of some type, a publisher and its review board—that has certain perspectives on the past. Generally speaking, those historians tell the group for which they write pretty much what they want to believe about the history. That clientele might be other academic specialists in whatever field is under investigation; it might be groups bound together by religion, ethnicity, or labor; or it might be any number of identifiable groups that have an interest in the subject.

I also point out to my academic colleagues what I consider a great naiveté among many professors that they are somehow impartial and can "tell the truth"

These need not be monolithic groups, either. My point is that consciously or unconsciously, historians—even if they have not been formally hired to prepare histories for the group—shape their discourses to provide understanding about the past in relationship to ideas already present among those with an interest in the subject. If they stray too far afield from the major streams of understanding about the subject, historians may be unable to find an outlet for publication, may be censured in reviews, may have their livelihood destroyed by not receiving tenure, or may lose whatever reputation they had. All of that is possible, without serving some formal client who may have a vested interest in ensuring that a historian tells a story in a certain way. While we must be endlessly diligent to ensure that NASA not produce court history, those occupying the chief historian position have long labored to ensure that historians working for NASA have latitude in presenting their findings as great as those in academia.

Figure 2.3 This magazine page contains a window quote that highlights a key point of the article.

I have students practice writing window quotes in their article of the week (AoW) assignment. (For those unfamiliar with the AoW assignment, I give my students an article to read every Monday. More details on the AoW assignment can be found in my book *Readicide* [Gallagher 2009].) In Figure 2.4, you will see an example of a window quote written from an AoW that explains that the postal service is awash in red ink and is considering curtailing Saturday mail delivery.

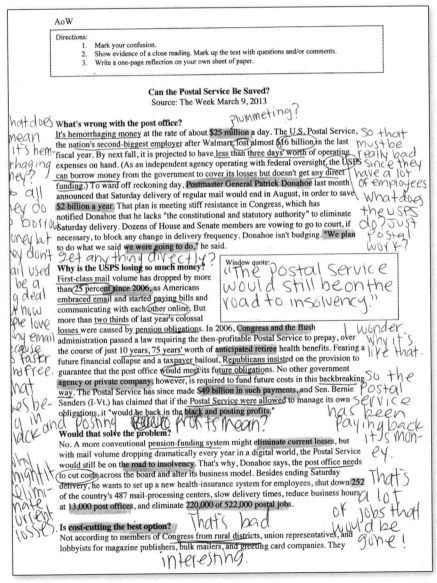

Figure 2.4 This student's annotated AoW includes a window quote selected by the student.

Digital Text Summaries

Another way of helping our students sharpen their summary skills is to move them beyond the printed page and have them work with digital text. I use a series of Ted Talk video clips to do this, starting with a brief lecture by Jimmy Wales (2005), the cofounder of Wikipedia. Before I show this clip, I simply ask students to listen carefully to the lecture and to write down the key points. I know this is not the best teaching, but I intentionally underteach because I want to see what kind of listening and note-taking abilities students possess prior to any support from me. Upon completion of the TED Talk video clip, I collect the students' notes, pick a couple of models that show students seem to have captured the gist, and use them to generate whole-class discussion on what makes an effective summary (see Figure 2.5 for Javier's notes).

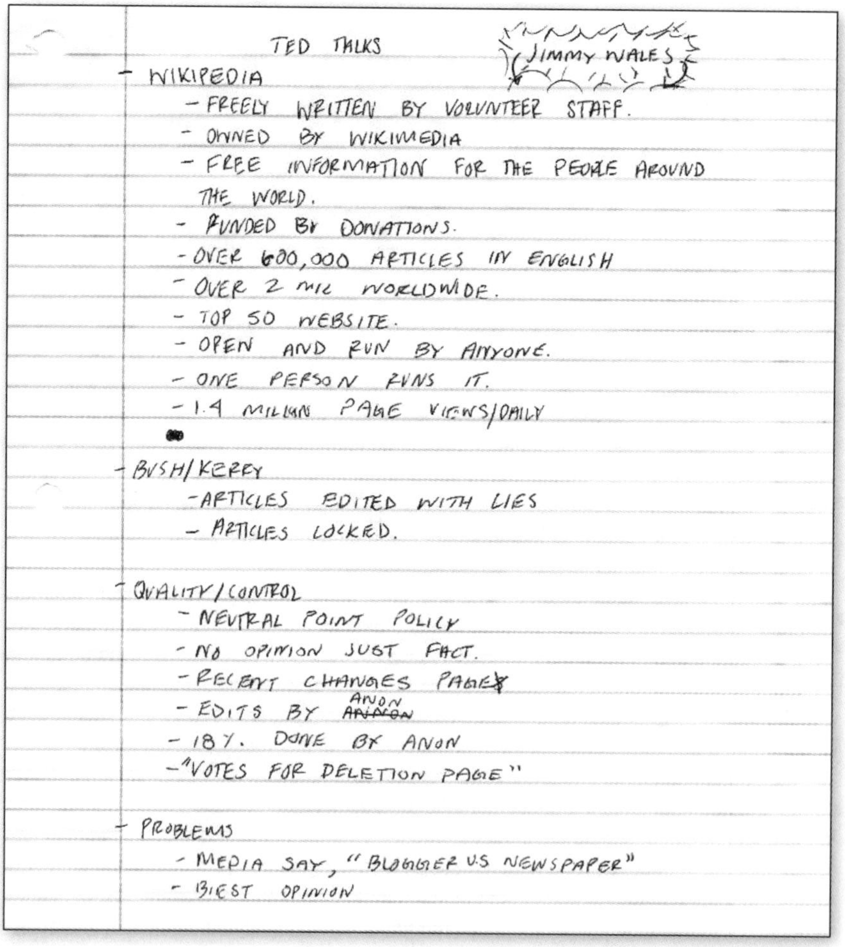
TED TALKS
JIMMY WALES
- WIKIPEDIA
- FREELY WRITTEN BY VOLUNTEER STAFF.
- OWNED BY WIKIMEDIA
- FREE INFORMATION FOR THE PEOPLE AROUND THE WORLD.
- FUNDED BY DONATIONS.
- OVER 600,000 ARTICLES IN ENGLISH
- OVER 2 MIL WORLDWIDE.
- TOP 50 WEBSITE.
- OPEN AND RUN BY ANYONE.
- ONE PERSON RUNS IT.
- 1.4 MILLION PAGE VIEWS/DAILY
- BUSH/KERRY
- ARTICLES EDITED WITH LIES
- ARTICLES LOCKED.
- QUALITY/CONTROL
- NEUTRAL POINT POLICY
- NO OPINION JUST FACT.
- RECENT CHANGES PAGE
- EDITS BY ~~ANNON~~ ANON
- 18% DONE BY ANON
- "VOTES FOR DELETION PAGE"
- PROBLEMS
- MEDIA SAY, "BLOGGER VS NEWSPAPER"
- BIEST OPINION

Figure 2.5 Javier's notes on a TED Talk

I find consistently that, without any instruction on how to take notes, many of my students follow the approach found in Figure 2.5—a very linear, step-by-step retelling of the text. There is nothing wrong with this particular approach, but I want my students to know there are other ways to take notes. To get them thinking in other directions, I show them the notes I took of the Wikipedia speech—notes I intentionally crafted in a nonlinear fashion (see Figure 2.6). I then choose another TED Talk for students to "read" and I ask them to emulate this nonlinear note-taking technique.

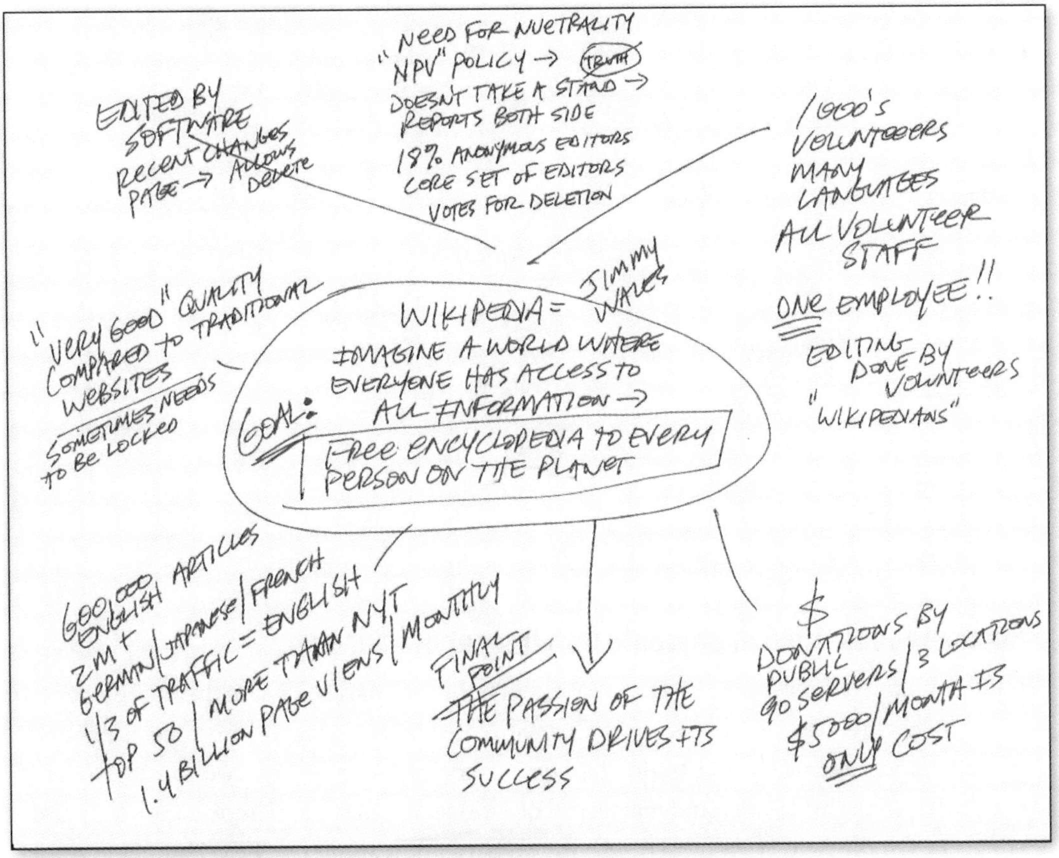

Figure 2.6 I show students this sample of my nonlinear notes.

Group Summaries

After my students have created individual notes from watching any TED Talk, I often put them in groups and give them a few moments to compare their summaries. Once they've had a little time to identify the similarities and differences between their notes, I give them ten minutes to compile all of their notes and turn them into a single-paragraph group summary.

This activity requires students to reconsider what is truly important in their individual notes, and, in doing so, generates good discussion on what should stay in and what should be removed from the group paragraph. See Figure 2.7 for a group summary my students composed after watching and comparing their notes on the TED Talk on Wikipedia.

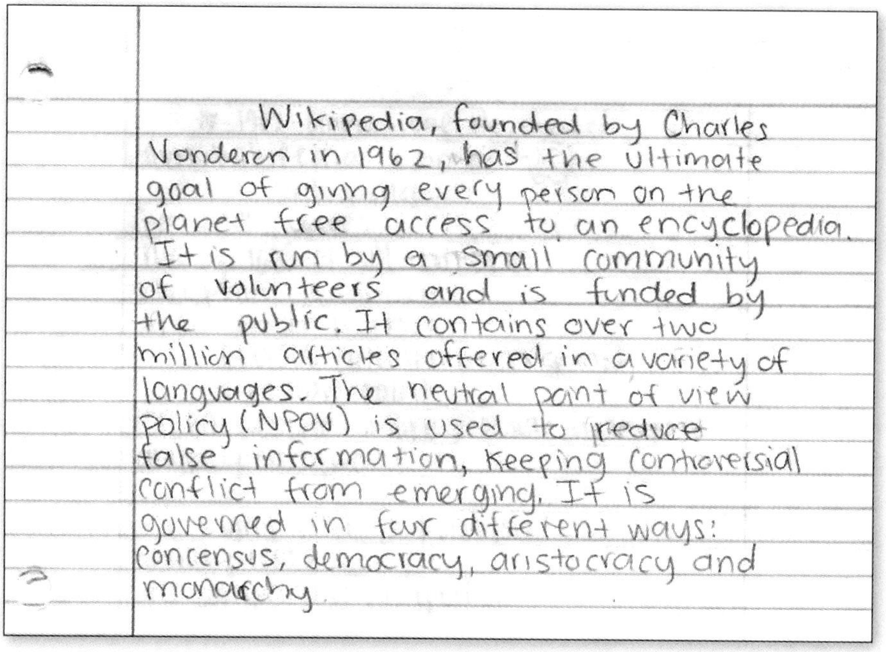

Wikipedia, founded by Charles Vonderen in 1962, has the ultimate goal of giving every person on the planet free access to an encyclopedia. It is run by a small community of volunteers and is funded by the public. It contains over two million articles offered in a variety of languages. The neutral point of view policy (NPOV) is used to reduce false information, keeping controversial conflict from emerging. It is governed in four different ways: concensus, democracy, aristocracy and monarchy.

Figure 2.7 A small-group summary based on students' notes

Summary Plus: Moving Students into Deeper Thinking

Once my students get some practice creating straight summaries, I move them into deeper water by having them do a version of Cornell Notes. I ask them to turn their notebook pages to landscape mode and to divide their papers into a one-third/two-thirds T-chart. On the left (one-third) side, students record questions, key ideas, and important words and concepts. On the right (two-thirds) side, they record notes about the TED Talk.

In Figure 2.8, you will see Jocelyn's notes from watching Sir Ken Robinson's TED Talk titled "How Schools Kill Creativity" (2006). When, in the left-hand column, Jocelyn asks questions like "What if great ideas weren't cherished?" and "How did the humanities and arts lose their value as education?" she is moving beyond summary and getting into deeper levels of cognition.

Questions / Key words / ideas

+ A life's worth of education?
+ epifany - sudden realization
+ unavailable condition
+ more to think (Glen Lynn)
+ gift of human imagination
+ what if great ideas weren't cherished?
+ How is creativity being destroyed?
+ what do schools do to digrade this creativity?
+ Are the teachers to blame? who is?
+ All children are born artists
+ How did humanities and arts lose their value as education?
+ what countries have the most
+ musically inclined
+ wrong is important

higharchy   + Nurture
                   creativity
Howard Gardner
↳ 7 intelligences
– verbal
– visual
– physical
– musical
– mathematical
– introspective
– interpersonal

Notes

- Everybody has interesting education
★ - creativity as imp. as literacy
- If you're not prepared to be wrong there would be no originality
- every education on earth has the same

- art and music @ the bottom
- produce university professors + purpose of public education
- whole system created to meet industrialism — ⎧
- whole world ingulfed in revolution
- in the next 30 more people will be graduating next year than the whole exordium of history
- academic inflation ————————→ degree walves ↑↓
- 3 things of education   4 year = hs diplome
  · diverse · dynamic · distinct   degree
    dif.   ongoing
              changes
- woman are better @ multitasking
- our education has mined our mind
- rethink fundimentals to which we educate our children   Principles of School
↳How? creative compacities to the richness they are
- A person will ever be creative if they are afraid of being wrong.
   No chance of being creative

              ————
              ARTS ↓

   Smart is not what you are
   Smart is what you become.

2. academic ability

Figure 2.8 Jocelyn's notes on a TED Talk

When students have finished their Cornell Notes, I want them to share and discuss them, but instead of simply having them turn and talk, I find that I will get much more meaningful talk if I have the students first do five minutes of private reflection via writing. Sometimes, students need to think before they can think, and giving them time to discover what they are thinking via writing leads to a much richer discussion when the quick-write is over. In Figure 2.9, you will find the reflection Jocelyn wrote before joining the group discussion. (You'll notice that Jocelyn references the Puente Project, a University of California outreach program designed to help underrepresented students make it into a four-year university. She is a Puente student.) Five minutes of writing time positioned Jocelyn to be a better participant when the subsequent conversation began.

The purpose of the Puente Program is to have its students attend four-year universities. What will its purpose be ten years from now when a BA or BS isn't high up in the food chain due to the increasing academic inflation? Will it remain the same?

In the next thirty years more people, worldwide, will be graduating through education than since the exordium of history. It is definitly discouraging to think that the four years that it used to take to earn a degree, won't be much of beneficial investment in the years to come.

It's not the first time hearing about it: that having a degree has lost its rarity. The topic was very briefly discussed at the Puente night when we had the meeting at the district. However, I had not seen it from the angle that was utilized in the form Sir Ken Robinson did – as an academic inflation. The simple use and format of those two words being embilized to represent a possible stilling point in the futures education outlook, is quite frightening. I see kids slacking off here in this high schools environment, I smeerdy can't imagine these same kids striving from a BA or BS when it's basically the tantamount to a high school diploma.

Figure 2.9 Jocelyn's private reflection writing

What Is Left Out?

Another strategy that reinforces summary skills but also moves students into deeper thinking is to ask students what has been left out. I discuss this strategy in *Deeper Reading* (2004), but here I apply it to the reading of digital text. I show my students Jill Bolte Taylor's TED Talk titled "Stroke of Insight" (2008). In this video clip, Taylor, a scientist who specializes in brain disorders, describes what she learned when she herself suffered (and recovered from) a stroke. Before my students view the clip, I preview some key difficult vocabulary, which the students take notes on. Below the vocabulary in their notebooks, the students create a T-chart where on the left side they record what the text says and on the right side they record what is not said in the clip. (See Figure 2.10 for Licci's chart.) Capturing what is said helps strengthen my students' summary skills, and capturing what is not said (what is left out) drives them to think about the text at deeper levels (in this case the "text" is a video clip).

"How it feels to have a stroke."

vocab

schizophrenia → mental illness / hallucinations

kinesthetic → motion/body

nirvana → heaven/beautiful place

what she says?	what she leaves out?
· studies mental illness	· how exactly can you get a stroke
· blood vessel exploded on left brain	· what caused her to have a stroke
· no walk, talk, write, move, or recall	· why did it take 8 years to recover
· right = parallel processor	· how did she recover, what did she do during those 8 years
· two hemospheres are completely separate	· what was she able to do
· right = present	· what wasn't she able to do.
· left = serial processor	· how was the pain
· left = past and future, thinks in language	· did the stroke affect any part of her body or any part of her life
· pounding pain behind eye	· how did she get better, did her brain process back?
· thought she looked weird	is there a danger of the stroke
· everything in her body slowed down	re-occurring again.
· atoms/molecules in body blended with the wall	· what happen to her brother
· felt enormous/expansive	· how does that help
· body surrendered	
· sounds were loud	
· 8 years to recover	

Figure 2.10 Licci's notes list both what is said and what is not said in a text.

Having students "read" digital clips creates an added bonus in that it helps students sharpen their ability to listen closely, a skill many of my students lack. (For more on sharpening listening skills, see Chapter 7.)

If students do not understand the text at a surface level, they are not going to develop their deeper reading skills. All the strategies mentioned in this chapter thus far (17-Word Summaries, Write a Headline, Window Quotes, Digital Text Summaries, Group Summaries, Summary Plus, and What Is Left Out?) are designed to help students answer the question, "What does the text say?" Once this is established, it's time to move students into the kind of reading demanded by the Common Core reading standards that relate to the question, "What does the text do?"

What Does the Text Do?

Let's look at anchor reading standards four through six, categorized as "Craft and Structure."

Craft and Structure

CCSS.ELA-Literacy.CCRA.R.4 Interpret words and phrases as they are used in a text, including determining technical, connotative, and figurative meanings, and analyze how specific word choices shape meaning or tone.

CCSS.ELA-Literacy.CCRA.R.5 Analyze the structure of texts, including how specific sentences, paragraphs, and larger portions of the text (e.g., a section, chapter, scene, or stanza) relate to each other and the whole.

CCSS.ELA-Literacy.CCRA.R.6 Assess how point of view or purpose shapes the content and style of a text.

When we think about how to move our students into deeper levels of reading, it is helpful to remember an expression that has been used for years at National Writing Project sites: "Students need to read like writers and they need to write like readers." The first half of that statement—"Students need to read like writers"—is especially true when it comes to getting students to recognize what a text does.

To better understand this notion of reading like a writer, read the following passage from Martin Luther's King Jr.'s famous "Letter from Birmingham City Jail":

> I guess it is easy for those who have never felt the stinging darts of segregation to say wait. But when you have seen vicious mobs lynch your mothers and fathers at will and drown your sisters and brothers at whim; when you have seen hate-filled policemen curse, kick, brutalize, and even kill your black brothers and sisters with impunity; when you see the vast majority of your 20 million Negro brothers

smothering in an airtight cage of poverty in the midst of an affluent society; when you suddenly find your tongue twisted and your speech stammering as you seek to explain to your six-year-old daughter why she can't go to the public amusement park that has just been advertised on television, and see the tears welling up in her little eyes when she is told that Funtown is closed to colored children, and see the depressing clouds of inferiority begin to form in her little mental sky, and see her begin to distort her little personality by unconsciously developing a bitterness toward white people; when you have to concoct an answer for a five-year-old son who is asking in agonizing pathos: "Daddy, why do white people treat colored people so mean?" when you take a cross country drive and find it necessary to sleep night after night in the uncomfortable corners of your automobile because no motel will accept you; when you are humiliated day in and day out by nagging signs reading "white" men and "colored" when your first name becomes "nigger" and your middle name becomes "boy" (however old you are) and your last name becomes "John," and when your wife and mother are never given the respected title of "Mrs." when you are harried by day and haunted by night by the fact that you are a Negro, living constantly at tip-toe stance, never quite knowing what to expect next, and plagued with inner fears and outer resentments; when you are forever fighting a degenerating sense of "nobodiness"—then you will understand why we find it difficult to wait. There comes a time when the cup of endurance runs over, and men are no longer willing to be plunged into an abyss of injustice where they experience the bleakness of corroding despair. I hope, sirs, you can understand our legitimate and unavoidable impatience. (1963)

In a traditional, NCLB-influenced classroom, students might be asked to read this passage and respond to traditional questions such as the following:

> List three things that Dr. King rails against.
>
> Explain what Dr. King means by "nobodiness."
>
> What is Dr. King's central claim in this piece?
>
> What evidence supports this claim?

These questions are designed to see if the students have gained a surface-level understanding of the text (What does the text say?). But if we want to encourage our students to read like writers, we might, instead, start by asking some of the following questions:

> What makes this an effective piece of writing?
>
> What techniques are used by the writer that elevates the writing?
>
> What "moves" does the writer make?

What does he do here? What does he do there?

This is a different line of questioning than many of our students are used to answering. "Reading like a writer" means we want the students to move beyond telling us what the text says and to recognize the "moves" the writer is making. In the excerpt from "Letter from Birmingham City Jail," for example, we might want our students to recognize King's use of intentional repetition ("when you . . . when you . . . when you . . ."), or his techniques of using semicolons to separate long items in a series, or of his infusing an anecdote about his own daughter as a way to forge a connection with the reader. When we ask students to read like writers, we are not asking them to recognize *what* the text says; we are asking them to recognize *how* the text is said.

When my students were reading *All Quiet on the Western Front* (Remarque 1929), I brought in passages from Kevin Powers's *The Yellow Birds*, a brilliant novel that follows Bartle, an American soldier, through the Iraq War. Near the end of the novel, Bartle has come home and is suffering from PTSD. He can't stop his mind from recounting the horrors of the war, and as a result, he has become suicidal. I asked my students to read the following passage like writers. I invite you to do the same. What do you notice? What makes this an effective piece of writing?

> Or I should have said I wanted to die, not in the sense of wanting to throw myself off the train bridge over there, but more like wanting to be asleep forever because there isn't any making up for the killing of women or even watching women get killed, or for that matter killing men and shooting them in the back and shooting them more times than necessary to actually kill them and it was like trying to kill everything you saw sometimes because it felt like there was acid seeping down into your soul and then your soul is gone and knowing from being taught your whole life that there is no making up for what you are doing, you're taught that your whole life, but that even your mother is so happy and so proud because you lined up your sight posts and made people crumble and they were not getting up ever and yeah they might have been trying to kill you too, so you say, What are you gonna do?, but really it doesn't matter because by the end you failed at the one good thing you could have done, the one person you promised would live is dead, and you have seen all things die in more manners than you'd like to recall and for a while the whole thing f***ing ravaged your spirit like some deep-down sh*t, man, that you didn't even realize you had until only the animals made you sad, the husks of dogs filled with explosives and old arty shells and the f***ing guts and everything stinking like metal and burning garbage and you walk around and the smell is so deep down into you now and you say, How can metal be so on fire? and even back home you're getting whiffs of it and then

that thing you started to notice slipping away is gone and now it's becoming inverted, like you have bottomed out in your spirit but yet a deeper hole is being dug because everybody is so f***ing happy to see you, the murderer, the f***ing accomplice, the at-bare-minimum bearer of some f***ing responsibility, and everybody wants to slap you on the back and you want to start to burn the whole god**n country down, you want to burn every god**n yellow ribbon in sight, and you can't explain it but it's just, like F**k you, but then you signed up to go so it's all your fault, really, because you went on purpose, so you are in the end doubly f**ked, so why not just find a spot and curl up and die and let's make it as painless as possible because you are a coward and, really, cowardice got you into this mess because you wanted to be a man and people made fun of you and pushed you around in the cafeteria and the hallways in high school because you liked to read books and poems sometimes and they'd call you fag and really deep down you know you went because you wanted to be a man and that's never gonna happen now and you're too much of a coward to be a man and get it over with so why not find a clean, dry place and wait it out with it hurting as little as possible and just wait to go to sleep and not wake up and f**k 'em all. (Powers 2012, 144)

What did you notice? What techniques does the writer employ? My students are a little taken aback when they realize that this entire passage is one massive run-on sentence. Obviously, Kevin Powers knows he has broken a major writing rule; his flagrant disregard for sentence boundaries is intentional. Why he broke the run-on rule, and what effect he was hoping this might have on the reader, generates interesting classroom discussion. As in the Kevin Powers passage above, it is important that my students recognize that proper punctuation is not simply an editing concern; I want them to recognize that punctuation can be manipulated to bring additional *meaning* to the piece, that a writer can punctuate for reasons beyond correctness. To illustrate this point, I share the following sentence I have written:

If they ask, I will not do it.

And then I share how I revised this sentence:

If they ask, I. Will. Not. Do. It!

How would you characterize the moves I made in the revised sentence? Are they editing moves? Or are they revision moves? Are they both? Editing is not just a process to make sentences correct. Editing is often done to add *meaning* to what I am trying to say. Good writers often edit for effect.

One way to help students pay attention to writers' moves is to have students carefully consider the choices that poets make, particularly when it comes to deciding where line breaks should be placed. I could, for example, take the mentor sentence from above and write it poetically more than one way:

If they ask,

I will not do it.

... has a different feeling than ...

If they ask,

I will not do

It.

After having students consider how a single line might be divided in different ways, I might choose a stanza from another poem for them to analyze. For example, consider the following from Alfred Lord Tennyson's "Charge of the Light Brigade," where the poem describes soldiers storming into battle on horseback:

Cannon to right of them,
Cannon to left of them,
Cannon in front of them
Volley'd and thunder'd;
Storm'd at with shot and shell,
Boldly they rode and well,
Into the jaws of Death,
Into the mouth of Hell
Rode the six hundred.
   (1998, 408)

In this stanza, Tennyson doesn't just describe the rush into battle. If you read it aloud, you can hear a rhythm woven into the poem—a meter that enables the reader to actually *hear* the horses' hooves as they gallop into battle. The *way* the poem is written adds depth to one's understanding of the intensity of the battle.

Another way, via poetry, to teach students to pay attention to an author's craft comes from W.D. Snodgrass's *De/Compositions: 101 Good Poems Gone Wrong*, where he rewrites original poems to make them deliberately worse. For example, here is the first stanza of Emily Dickinson's "I Heard a Fly Buzz—When I Died":

I heard a Fly buzz—when I died—
The Stillness in the Room
Was like the Stillness in the Air—
Between the Heaves of Storm—
   (Dickinson 1976, 223)

Here is Snodgrass's revision of the stanza:

A fly got in, the day I died;
The calm in my bedroom
Was like the quiet in the air
Between the blasts of storm
   (2001, 85)

Snodgrass reads the original stanza and then has the students read the rewritten version. When they have finished, Snodgrass asks them to identify the most "scandalous" thing he has done to the poem. Why, for example, is the use of the word "Stillness" in the original poem a better choice of diction than the word "calm" in the second version? And why did Dickinson choose to capitalize "Stillness" (when "calm" is not capitalized)? Having students pay attention to the differences between the two poems pushes them to sharpen their close reading skills.

Teaching students to recognize what a writer is doing is a major step in having students actually *do* what the writer is doing (as I demonstrate in Chapter 6). Noticing what a writer does, of course, requires the reader to read closely—a skill valued by the CCSS, as seen in the following statement by the Partnership for Assessment of Readiness for College and Careers (PARCC):

> Close, analytic reading stresses engaging with a text of sufficient complexity directly and examining meaning thoroughly and methodically, encouraging students to read and reread deliberately. Directing student attention on the text itself empowers students to understand the central ideas and key supporting details. It also enables students to reflect on the meanings of individual words and sentences; the order in which sentences unfold; and the development of ideas over the course of the text, which ultimately leads students to arrive at an understanding of the text as a whole. (PARCC 2012, 7)

We want our students to develop the habits of mind associated with close reading, and getting them to do so requires careful practice. Teaching students to read closely makes them better readers and writers, and a large part of developing close-reading skills begins by being able to recognize the author's craft.

Let's recognize a potential problem that comes with the renewed emphasis on close reading, which has become the "it" thing to teach in many language arts classes. Many schools have put "close reading" on the front burner, and as a result, students are being asked to dissect everything they read. And when students are asked to dissect everything they read, bad things occur: the art and beauty of the work gets lost in a sea of sticky notes and marginalia, the book gets turned into a ten-week worksheet, and the joy of reading gets killed.

Let's be aware of the tension that exists between giving our students enough practice so they will acquire close reading skills versus overdoing the practice in a way that leads to the reader dying a slow, painful death. Students need close reading practice, but too much practice of anything can be a bad thing. Find the balance.

What Does the Text Mean?

So far, we have looked at anchor standards 1–3, which ask "What does the text say?" and anchor standards 4–6, which ask "What does the text do?" We now turn our attention to anchor standards 7–9, titled "Integration of Knowledge and Ideas," which essentially ask for a third kind of reading: "What does the text mean?"

Integration of Knowledge and Ideas

> CCSS.ELA-Literacy.CCRA.R.7 Integrate and evaluate content presented in diverse media and formats, including visually and quantitatively, as well as in words.

> CCSS.ELA-Literacy.CCRA.R.8 Delineate and evaluate the argument and specific claims in a text, including the validity of the reasoning as well as the relevance and sufficiency of the evidence.

> CCSS.ELA-Literacy.CCRA.R.9 Analyze how two or more texts address similar themes or topics in order to build knowledge or to compare the approaches the authors take.

Answering "What does the text mean?" requires the reader to move beyond the literal interpretation and to start to think inferentially. To do so, students must be taught how to make claims from the text. To help my students to develop this skill, I start small. I begin by using factoids taken from the "Harper's Index," a one-page collection of statistics found in every edition of *Harper's* magazine. Here is an example of one factoid:

> Percentage change since 1996 in the number of U.S. children living in poverty: +12
> (*Harper's* 2013)

Students are asked to make a claim based on this factoid. To help them, I ask what can be inferred from the factoid. Here are some of their responses:

The economy is bad. There are fewer jobs.

More people are being laid off than in 1996.

Salaries have been cut. Even people who have jobs are making less.

Things cost more than they used to.

From there, I will give students a pair of factoids and ask them to create a claim that addresses both of them:

Portion of U.S. public-school students who are Latino: 1/4

Portion of U.S children's books published annually that are by or about Latinos: 1/50
   (*Harper's* 2013)

Their responses:

History books do not tell the full story.

Book publishers are missing a large market.

Racism still exists.

This imbalance may change soon as the Latino population grows.

From "Harper's Index," I move students into making claims from visual texts. As Carol Jago notes,

> Our students are bombarded by visual images yet rarely stop to analyze them. I'm not talking only of advertising. Media study units are popular components in many English syllabi. What isn't much in evidence in the secondary English curriculum are rhetorical readings of visual texts. (Jago 2013, 1)

Jago is right. Using visual texts is an excellent way to enable students to deepen their reading skills (and important given the amount of visual texts our students will read in their lives). I begin with having my students wrestle with infographics, starting with "Readers round the world" found on The Digital Reader website (Hoffelder 2013; see Figure 2.11).

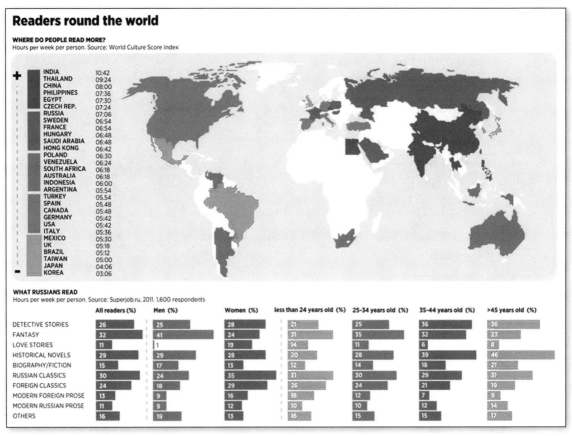

Figure 2.11 Students examine infographics like this one to deepen reading skills.

I place students in groups and give them a few minutes to read and discuss the image; I eventually bring it back to a whole-class discussion, making sure they understand the image on a literal level. Then I ask them to begin inferring claims. "According to this infographic, people in India read more than anyone else in the world," I say. "Why might that be?"

Their responses (claims):

There are fewer technological distractions for children growing up in India.

Kids in India do more reading in school.

Their school days are longer.

India has more bookstores.

Students in India have more digital access.

Maybe the graphic is wrong. Who is the source?

It is possible that some of these claims are incorrect. I don't know, for example, if Indian children have fewer technological distractions. I have to remind myself that making numerous incorrect assumptions is necessary before students can begin making correct assumptions. It is important to keep in mind that even as adults, we often make incorrect inferences. How do we get better at inferring? By doing it. We are better than our students in applying inference skills because we are more experienced in doing so. Building strong inferential skills takes practice.

From "Readers round the world" I ask my students to interpret two more infographics. The first provides data on urban life in the United States, including statistics about life expectancy, demographics, and possible advantages. The second infographic is about American voting trends, citing voter turnout percentages based on classifications such as race, gender, and income level. While reading these, I ask students (1) to make a list of what they have learned by reading the infographics and (2) to generate claims from what they've learned. In Figure 2.12, you'll find Alicia's response to the infographic about the growth of cities, and Figure 2.13 shows her response to the voting trends infographic.

If you want to slip in a message that reading is important, you might have students analyze Janet Neyer's infographic, "Why Read?" (Figure 2.14). This infographic can be downloaded by selecting "Instructional Materials" in the "Resources" section of my website, kellygallagher.org.

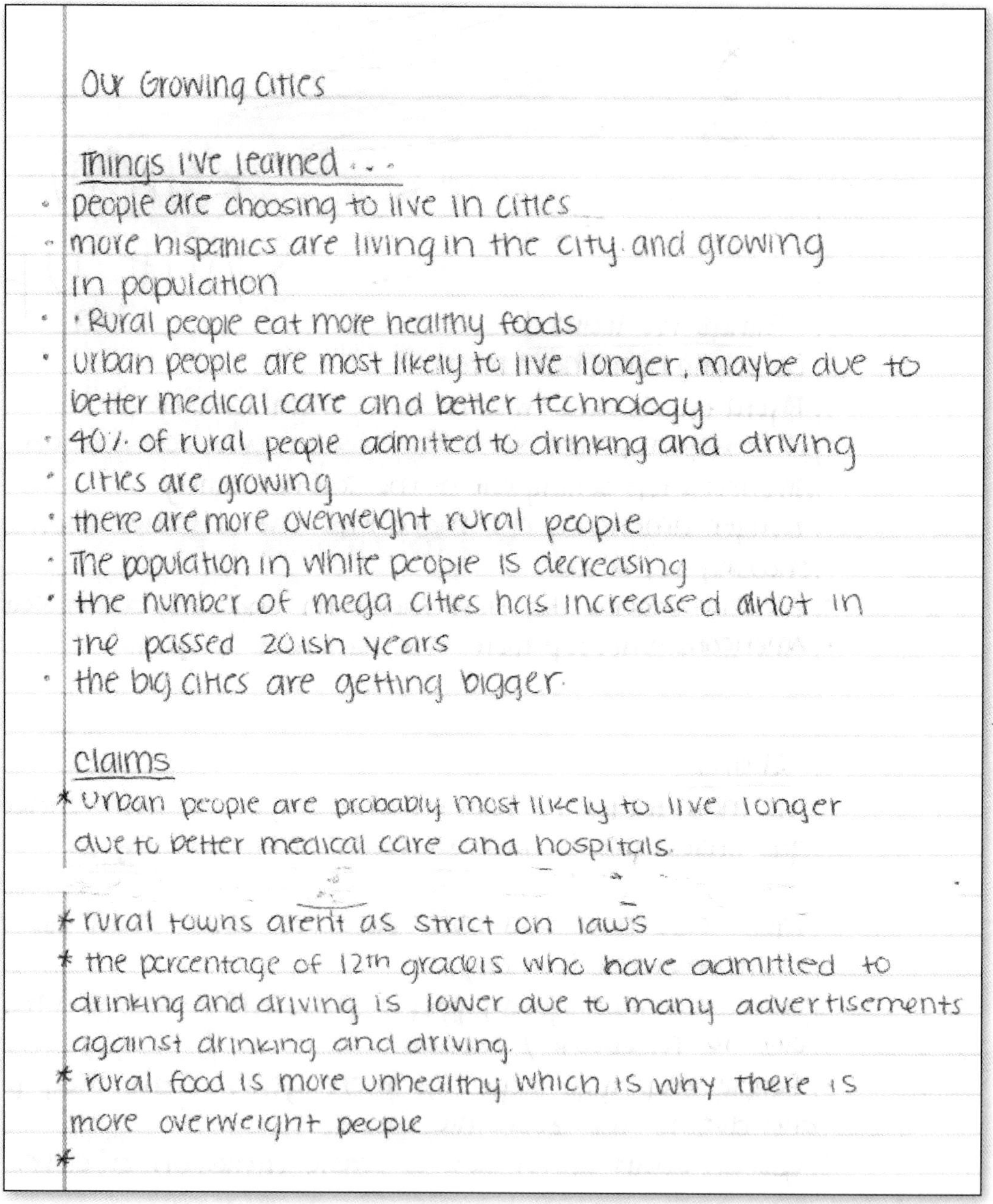

Our Growing Cities

Things I've learned...
- people are choosing to live in cities
- more hispanics are living in the city and growing in population
- Rural people eat more healthy foods
- urban people are most likely to live longer, maybe due to better medical care and better technology
- 40% of rural people admitted to drinking and driving
- cities are growing
- there are more overweight rural people
- The population in white people is decreasing
- the number of mega cities has increased alot in the passed 20ish years
- the big cities are getting bigger.

Claims
* urban people are probably most likely to live longer due to better medical care and hospitals.

* rural towns aren't as strict on laws
* the percentage of 12th graders who have admitted to drinking and driving is lower due to many advertisements against drinking and driving.
* rural food is more unhealthy which is why there is more overweight people
*

Figure 2.12 Alicia's response to an infographic about the trend toward urban living in the United States

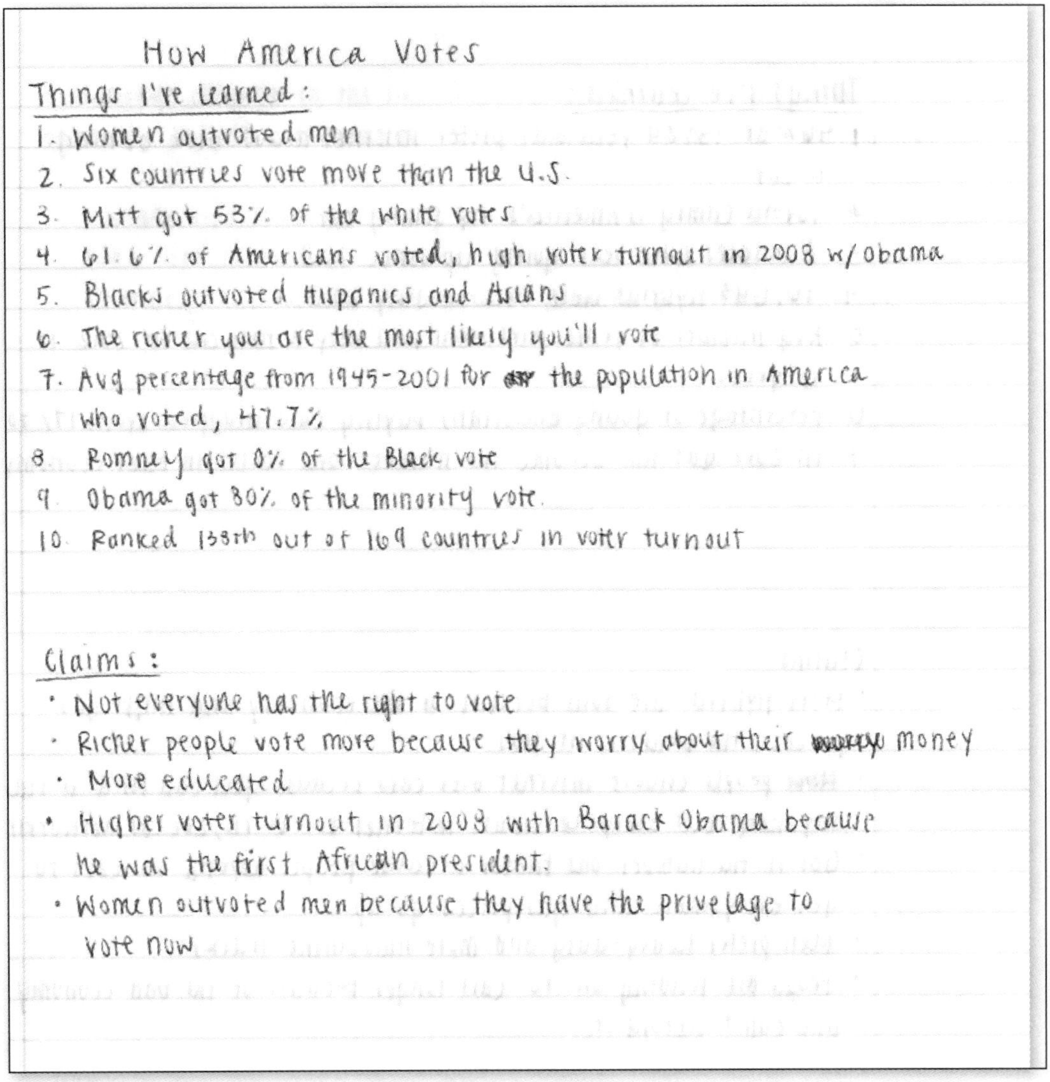

How America Votes

Things I've Learned:

1. Women outvoted men
2. Six countries vote more than the U.S.
3. Mitt got 53% of the white voters
4. 61.6% of Americans voted, high voter turnout in 2008 w/ Obama
5. Blacks outvoted Hispanics and Asians
6. The richer you are the most likely you'll vote
7. Avg percentage from 1945-2001 for ~~the~~ the population in America who voted, 47.7%
8. Romney got 0% of the Black vote
9. Obama got 80% of the minority vote.
10. Ranked 138th out of 169 countries in voter turnout

Claims:

• Not everyone has the right to vote
• Richer people vote more because they worry about their ~~worry~~ money
• More educated
• Higher voter turnout in 2008 with Barack Obama because he was the first African president.
• Women outvoted men because they have the privelage to vote now

Figure 2.13 Alicia's response to an infographic about how America votes

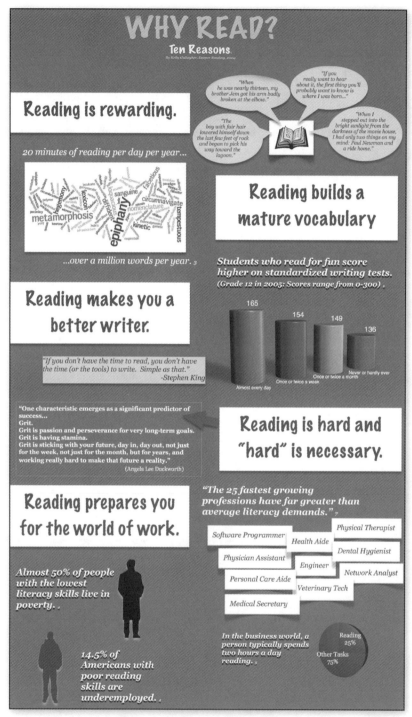

Figure 2.14 "Why Read?" infographic by Janet Neyer

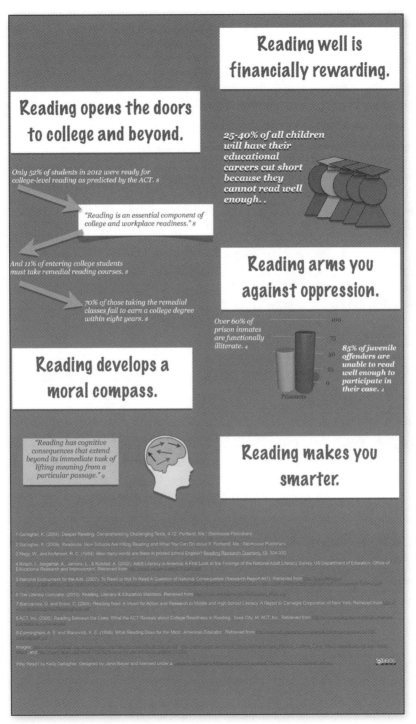

Figure 2.14 (Continued) "Why Read?" infographic by Janet Neyer

Recognizing Audience and Purpose

When trying to move my students beyond surface-level thinking, I move them past infographics and into analyzing photographs. I start with selections from Life's *100 Photographs That Changed the World*, choosing photos that provoke the reader (Sullivan 2003). In Figure 2.15, for example, you will see Dorothea Lange's *Migrant Mother*, which captures a thirty-two-year old California farmworker who scavenged vegetables and hunted wild birds in a desperate attempt to feed her seven kids.

Figure 2.15 Dorothea Lange's *Migrant Mother*

I ask the students to first consider what the text "says," asking them to read the photograph carefully. I have them list what they notice. One group's responses:

The woman looks sad/worried.

The children have buried their faces away from the photographer.

Their clothes are dirty and torn.

They appear very poor.

The wall behind them looks dirty. Are they in a tent?

Even without a working knowledge of the Dust Bowl, students are able to discern what the text "says." They understand, on a literal level, that the photo puts the spotlight on poverty.

Once the initial understanding of the photograph is established, I introduce Lange's work, telling the students that she was famous for documenting the poor during the Great Depression. I then ask the students a different set of questions; here is a recorded classroom conversation:

"What was the photographer's purpose in taking this photo?" I asked.

"She was trying to show poor people to the rest of the world," Brianna said.

"Why?"

"So they would understand how hard it is to be poor."

"That's it? To show others what poverty looks like? Any other reason?"

"To show people she had skills as a photographer?" Michael offered.

"C'mon. Really? What might be a deeper purpose for sharing this photo?"

"Maybe she thought the photo might get people to do something about it," Alex jumped in.

"Like what?"

"I don't know. Send food or money."

"Well, that brings up another interesting question: Who did Dorothea Lange hope would see her photo?"

"Rich people," Samuel offered.

"Okay. But Alex said that maybe the photo would spur people to do something about it. Can you think of others besides rich people who might be in a position to do something about it?"

(*Pause.*)

"People who make the laws?" Alicia offered.

"Politicians," Elias added.

"People who vote," said Ricky.

These students have moved beyond literal understanding and into consideration of what the photo *means*. Once they understand that a single photograph can lead to creating real change in the world, I give them other influential photographs to consider. You might try George Strock's photo that depicts dead American soldiers washed up on the beaches of Papua New Guinea during World War II. (This photo is easily found by searching Google images.) *Life* magazine published this controversial photo "in concert with government wishes" because Franklin D. Roosevelt "was convinced that Americans had grown too complacent about the war" (Sullivan 2003). This photo had the desired effect: "The public, shocked by combat's grim realities, was instilled with yet greater resolve to win the war" (Sullivan 2003). Or try Charles Moore's *Birmingham*, which shows water hoses being turned on African Americans in Alabama in 1963. This iconic photograph is famous for rallying public support for the plight of African Americans in the early days of the civil rights movement. This photograph is easily found by Googling both the author's name and the name of the photograph.

After analyzing photographs, students can easily transfer that skill to the reading of paintings. I start with Edward Hopper's well-known *Nighthawks*, which depicts three people sitting at a diner counter at night (see Figure 2.16). In their initial readings of the painting, I make sure students pay attention to Hopper's unusual use of perspective, color, and light. Once they wrestle with the painting a bit, I shift their thinking by asking them to consider the painter's claim, to consider what he might be trying to say in this painting. Many of my students focus on the solitary figure at the center of the painting and suggest that Hopper is saying something about loneliness and isolation. I also like introducing my students to *Nighthawks* because it is one of the most recognizable paintings in American art, and I want them to have this piece of cultural literacy (this will enable them, for example, to understand the reference when they see Homer sitting at the same lunch counter in an episode of *The Simpsons*).

Figure 2.16 Edward Hopper's *Nighthawks*

Fiction/Nonfiction Weave

In her books, Barbara Greenwood weaves fiction and nonfiction together to help the reader make sense of historical events. In *A Pioneer Sampler: The Daily Life of a Pioneer Family in 1840*, for example, she chronicles a year in the life of the fictional Robinson pioneer family, and to demonstrate these hardships, Greenwood weaves in nonfictional artifacts throughout the book (1994). When the Robinson family builds a log cabin, Greenwood provides the reader with a visual cut-out that demonstrates how a log cabin is constructed. To demonstrate life at home, Greenwood interrupts the narrative with instructions on how to make maple syrup. As the reader works through the book, he or she encounters a number of real artifacts that lend authenticity to the fictional story.

In another Greenwood book, *Factory Girl*, we meet young Emily Watson, who works eleven hours a day clipping threads from blouses in the Acme Garment factory (2007). Emily's story, though fictional, is grounded in the real-life hardships of children working in sweatshops in the early 1900s. Throughout Emily's tale, Greenwood sprinkles in advertisements for the various clothing styles that were in vogue at the time along with a number of photographs that depict life in the factories. Through the weaving of fiction and nonfiction, Greenwood gives students a richer understanding of history.

My colleague Donna Santman suggests that students be instructed to use Greenwood's approach with the novels they are reading in class. A student reading *Lord of the Flies*, for example, should be asked to consider what nonfiction artifacts he or she would use throughout the text to deepen the readers' understanding of the novel. The student might include the following nonfiction examples:

- Survival tips on how to survive a plane crash
- A chart identifying which plants are edible and which plants are poisonous
- Directions on how to start a fire from scratch
- Information on conch (and other) shells
- A diagram on how to build a thatch hut

Deciding which artifacts compliment the reading of the book is only half the job; once the artifacts are created, the student must then decide *where* to strategically place them in the novel. Students are asked to share their thinking behind the placement of the artifacts. How do these placements heighten the readers' understanding of the book?

Greenwood's idea of weaving nonfiction artifacts into works of fiction can be used with any novel or play.

Good News

When we have students read speeches, paintings, novels, works of nonfiction, magazines, and TED Talks and other digital texts, we are not just teaching them reading skills. We are deepening their understanding of the world, which, in turn, makes them better readers. As the CCSS rightly recognize, teaching students to recognize what a "text" says, does, and means is vitally important to developing literate citizens. These standards are rich, they are necessary, but as I said earlier in this chapter, they, alone, are insufficient. To examine where these reading standards fall short, turn this page.

CHAPTER 3

Where the Common Core Reading Standards Fall Short

In Chapter 2, we focused on important core values behind the teaching of reading, and in doing so, we looked at some of the things that the Common Core anchor reading standards get right. Let's now turn our attention to what they get wrong. When it comes to the teaching of reading, the new standards raise numerous major concerns:

Concern 1: Readers should not be confined to stay "within the four corners of the text."

David Coleman and Susan Pimentel, two of the principal architects of the CCSS, have said on a number of occasions that when reading, students should "stay within the four corners of the text" (Wilson and Newkirk 2011, 1). By this, they mean that readers should focus entirely on what the author is saying and what the author is doing, and there should be little or no emphasis on connecting the reading passage to the outside world. This poem (or novel, or play), they stress, is really not about your grandmother, so we should stop allowing our students' interpretations to lead them far away from the printed page. Instead, Coleman argues, our students would be better off if the students studied the text on "its own terms."

To put it bluntly, this is ludicrous. To illustrate just how so, I ask you to read the following sentence without venturing outside the four corners of the text:

> Syria missed an important deadline this week, failing to turn over all its chemical weapons.

How'd you do? My guess is that you can tell me what the text says without straying from the four corners (Syria missed its deadline to turn over chemical weapons). I am sure you can also tell me what the writer does (stylistically, the author connects an independent clause as an "end branch" to the sentence). But can you tell me what the text means without activating your thinking beyond the four corners of the text? No, because deeply comprehending this sentence is impossible without considering the following:

What do you know about Syria?

Where is Syria located?

Who is president of Syria?

What is the history of the current conflict in Syria?

Why has Syria been told to turn over its chemical weapons?

Who has demanded that Syria turn over its chemical weapons?

When and why did Syria agree to do so?

Based on other examples in recent history, what might happen if Syria refuses to comply?

Given the current regime in Syria, how do we interpret this missed deadline?

When my students read of the genocide occurring in Syria, are they not to connect their thinking to their previous studies of Anne Frank's diary or to Elie Wiesel's memoir? When my students read the arguments for and against the Affordable Care Act are they not to think about the health histories of their families or their neighbors? When my students read a website "news" story on Fox or MSNBC, are they not to consider the history of these organizations and how these histories might influence the veracity of what they are reading?

Of course I want my students to be able to tell me what a text says. Of course I want them to be able to recognize what the text does, to understand the techniques employed by the author. Of course I want my students to embrace the wrestling match that comes with making deep sense of challenging texts, to wean themselves from me, their teacher, and to move away from the learned helplessness many of them have acquired. I want my students to do all of these things that Coleman and Pimentel advocate. They are all worthy steps in building deeper readers. But they, alone, are not enough. Stopping inside the four corners of the text limits our students' thinking.

The very reason I want my students to read core works of literature and nonfiction is so that they can eventually get *outside* the four corners of the text and use these reading experiences to think about, to understand, to gain greater insight into the world they are about to inherit. Books worthy of study should be *rehearsals* for the real world. They should be springboards to close examination of what is happening in the here and now. If our students read *The Grapes of Wrath* (Steinbeck 1939) deeply but never use that reading experience to catapult them into an examination of today's immigration debate, or if our students read *Animal Farm* (Orwell 1946) and do not apply their newfound thinking to the propaganda they face in a given day, or if our students read *The Red Badge of Courage* and they do not use the wisdom found in this book to help them better understand the US involvement in Iraq and Afghanistan, then they are simply reading stories. True, they might be great stories that stand on their own terms, but surely these works have more to offer than to teach students to recognize when foreshadowing is evident or to gain an appreciation when an author is intentionally using repetition. I want my students to work through "What does the text say?" and "What does the text mean?" as soon as possible so they can spend as much time as possible applying their newfound thinking toward answering, "How does this book make me smarter about today's world?" I want them to deeply consider what the books *mean in our world and for their future.*

If we teach students to think *only* inside the four corners of the text, we are telling them what not to think. And when we tell students what they cannot think, oppression and hegemony occur.

Concern 2: Prereading activities are undervalued.

One of the concerns addressed by the authors of the Common Core reading standards is that teachers are often doing too much of the work for the students, especially in the prereading stage. I have seen this firsthand: Teachers "frame" the reading so much that the reading has virtually been done for the students. Students quickly learn that they don't have to wrestle with the text because the teacher has done much of the wrestling for them. To address this concern of overscaffolding text, the writers of the CCSS suggest this:

> The scaffolding should not preempt or replace the text by translating its contents for students or telling students what they are going to learn in advance of reading the text; that is, the scaffolding should not become an alternate, simpler source of information that diminishes the need for students to read the text itself carefully. Effective scaffolding aligned with the standards should result in the reader encountering the text on its own terms, with instructions providing helpful directions that focus students on the text. Follow-up support should guide the reader when encountering places in the text where he or she might struggle. (Coleman and Pimentel 2012, 8)

Though I share the concern that many teachers enable their young readers by doing too much of the heavy prereading lifting for them, Coleman and Pimentel's statement is problematic on a number of fronts. Allow me to extract some of this statement in chunks and share my concerns:

> The scaffolding should not preempt or replace the text by translating its contents for students or telling students what they are going to learn in advance of reading the text.

On the contrary, I frequently tell my students what they are going to learn in advance of reading the text. I have consciously stopped teaching all things in all books; I am trying to avoid turning the novel into a ten-week worksheet. Instead, I teach one or two big things in a book and try to take my students deep into those concepts. I am not trying to fool them; I don't want these concepts to be secrets. I want my students to know what I want them to know, and I want them to know this before we get started. I want the focus of study out on the table, and I want it to drive a focused reading of the text.

I am not suggesting that I tell my students how the novel will end before they commence reading; I am suggesting that students will know before chapter 1 that the reading of this novel will help lead us to a deeper understanding of X, and achieving a deeper understanding of X will be driven by a central question. (When reading *1984*, for example, I might frame the reading of the novel around the following central guiding question: How much power should citizens permit their leadership to have?) This essential question drives a focused reading of the text, and students know this before reading chapter 1.

> Effective scaffolding aligned with the standards should result in the reader encountering the text on its own terms. (Coleman and Pimentel 2012, 8)

Let's use a wrestling metaphor to illustrate my concern about this point. If you have little or no experience as a wrestler, asking you to jump in there and to take on the best varsity wrestler in the county is going to be a very difficult, if not impossible, sell. Simply assuring you that it will be good for you to encounter the wrestler on your own terms—that you should take on this formidable opponent without any help (because that is good for your development as a wrestler)—is certainly not going to be enough to sustain you through the difficult experience. Giving you assurance that help will come from your coach *after* the other wrestler kicks your butt could possibly be the worst coaching strategy ever.

If I really want to prepare an inexperienced wrestler to take on a difficult opponent, I would use another approach. First, I would get on the mat with the novice wrestler and model some of the wrestling moves one would need to compete. We would practice these moves repeatedly, together. I would demonstrate them, and then I'd have the student repeat them. I would make sure that the inexperienced wrestler got in the weight room to build up his or her strength and stamina. I would demonstrate how each machine in the weight room worked and how to use them properly. I would watch video of expert wrestlers with the student, making sure the novice analyzed the moves made by the expert wrestlers. I would have the young wrestler adopt many of these moves in numerous practice sessions. When I felt the young wrestler was ready, I would have the novice begin wrestling others in scrimmage situations, where I could stop the action at any time and make suggestions.

Finally, when the wrestler was up to the challenge, I would set up a match with a difficult opponent, thus completing a gradual release that would put the protégé in a place where he or she could encounter this match on his or her own terms.

Students also need to be gradually released into the "wrestling matches" necessary to make sense of difficult texts. Anyone who has ever taught Shakespeare, for example, knows that the beginning of the play is very hard for students to interpret, even at a literal level. The rhythm and the language of the play are very unfamiliar, and the students' frustration level can be very high. If you work with reluctant readers, or readers who are behind grade level, it is entirely unrealistic to hand the play to them and expect them to "encounter the text on its own terms." Though I understand (and empathize) with the goal of having students take ownership of grappling with the complexity of the text, it is wishful thinking that students will initially take on that challenge on their own. Instead, they need to be led there by a teacher who expertly walks them into the work, especially if the work they are about to read is far away from their prior knowledge. The more unfamiliar the work, the more scaffolding will be needed to prepare them for the wrestling match.

Those of us who have taught difficult books also know something else: that somewhere in the middle of the book, the students' ability to understand it vastly improves. If the teacher has done effective scaffolding, the students begin to "settle in" to the language, to the rhythm of the text. This is where the teacher needs to begin to let go, to begin the process of getting out of the way so that the students can take ownership of wrestling with the rest of the text.

> Follow-up support should guide the reader when encountering places in the text where he or she might struggle. (Coleman and Pimentel 2012, 8)

The idea that we should allow students to first "encounter the text on its own terms" before we come in and offer "follow-up support" is backward. Throwing a poor swimmer into the deep end and then tossing him or her a life preserver just prior to the swimmer's drowning is the wrong approach. Let's put our students into the deep end with life preservers to cling to, and then gradually teach them how to swim without them. This is not the same as enabling students by doing all the work for them. There is still plenty of text left for students to encounter on its own terms. They are still going to work very hard. But if you begin the unit by throwing them into the deep end of the pool without any coaching, they will drown.

With this in mind, think about the hardest book that you teach—the one book you know will present a major challenge to your students. Have it in mind? My guess is that the book you picked is really hard for your students because it is really far away from their prior knowledge. Not having important background information is what makes the reading of the book hard. If you handed me a book about the Anaheim Angels, I would not need any support before I began reading. (I have been an Angels fan for decades.) On the other hand, if you handed me a book about the Crimean War, your guidance would be necessary to put me on the path to deeper reading. (Without Google at hand, I could not tell you a thing about this war.)

When prior knowledge is sparse or missing, what the teacher does *before* the kids begin reading is often as important as the actual reading itself. Our job is to ease our students into the difficult reading, to walk them into it. Then, and only then, should the gradual release occur.

Concern 3: Recreational reading is all but ignored.

Have you ever been invited to a wedding, only to find your place card on the worst table in the reception hall? You know that table; it's the one next to the kitchen door, the one where you find yourself sitting between a third cousin of the groom on one side and the bride-doesn't-really-like-him-but-she-must-invite-him-because-she-works-with-him colleague on the other side. At the risk of overdosing this chapter on metaphor, that is the table where recreational reading has been sat.

One visit to the CCSS website will give you a clear indication how little recreational reading is valued (http://www.corestandards.org/the-standards). Recreational reading is not mentioned in the introduction. It is not mentioned in any of the ten anchor reading standards. It is not mentioned in the grade-specific standards for reading literature. It is not mentioned in the grade-specific standards for reading informational texts. It is not mentioned under the discussion of "foundational skills." It is not mentioned in the appendixes. It is not mentioned in any of these places, period.

To find what the authors think about the value of recreational reading, you will have to dig through the "Revised Publishers' Criteria for the Common Core State Standards in Language Arts and Literacy, Grades 3–12" (an obscure guide—the equivalent to the worst table at the back of the wedding reception). In this document, Coleman and Pimentel write this:

> Additional materials aim to increase regular independent reading of texts that appeal to students' interests while developing both their knowledge base and joy in reading. These materials should ensure that all students have daily opportunities to read texts of their choice on their own during and outside of the school day. Students need access to a wide range of materials on a variety of topics and genres both in their classrooms and in their school libraries to ensure that they have opportunities to independently read broadly and widely to build their knowledge, experience, and joy in reading. Materials will need to include texts at students' own reading level as well as texts with complexity levels that will challenge and

motivate students. Texts should also vary in length and density, requiring students to slow down or read more quickly depending on their purpose for reading. In alignment with the standards and to acknowledge the range of students' interests, these materials should include informational texts and literary nonfiction as well as literature. A variety of formats can also engage a wider range of students, such as high-quality newspaper and magazine articles as well as information-rich websites. (2012, 4)

There is a lot to like about this statement. We know that the students who read the most for fun are also the same students who read the best. (We know that students who read the most become our best writers as well.) We also know that the single biggest obstacle to our students becoming proficient readers may be that they simply do not have access to interesting books to read. (For studies that support this claim read Krashen's *The Power of Reading* [2004].)

Though Coleman and Pimentel's statement recognizes the importance of joyful reading, it is buried so far out of the sight of teachers and curriculum directors that it will be all but forgotten. Placing this statement at the equivalent of the back table of the wedding reception is a mistake, because it doesn't matter how good the anchor reading standards are if our students don't read. It doesn't matter how much effort teachers put into teaching the anchor reading standards if our students don't read. And if we don't create environments where our students are reading lots of books, they will never become the kinds of readers we want them to be. They will simply remain test takers (and not very good test takers at that). More on how to increase the amount our students read is discussed in Chapter 8.

Concern 4: There are no reading targets.

The path to lifelong reading begins with lots of early reading, so it is disconcerting that the CCSS do not provide specific grade-level reading targets. Goals are important in developing young readers. There is a strong, undeniable connection between time spent reading and performance on reading assessments, yet recommendations on how much students should read are nowhere to be found in the CCSS. Simply stating which reading skills students should learn without suggesting *how much* students should read sets a dangerous precedent. As we learned in the NCLB era, this approach turned many classrooms into places where drill and skill took precedence, and the overall amount of reading done by many students declined. Teaching skills without establishing reading goals ignores a central tenet to the teaching of reading: *If your students are not reading a lot, it doesn't matter what skills you teach them.* Volume matters.

To ensure my high school students are getting enough reading under their belts, I set a goal that they read one self-selected book a month. These books are in addition to the books we may be reading as a class or in book clubs, and to keep track of their progress, I have each of them complete a "My 10" chart (see Figure 3.1). When a student finishes a book, he or she confers with me and I then initial his or her My 10 chart. I do not score the chart; it is a prerequisite. Failure to keep the chart up to date results in the student's grade being dropped one level on the report card. (I explain this in a letter home to parents and have them sign off on the grading policy.) The My 10 chart creates accountability—but not so much accountability that the reading experience actually ceases to be recreational. (To download a copy of the My 10 chart, go to kellygallagher.org and pull down "Resources" to find "Instructional Materials.")

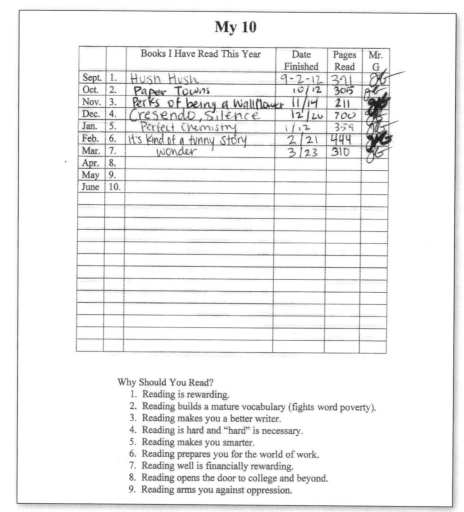

Figure 3.1 "My 10" reading chart

When kids read a lot, their fluency and comprehension improve. They build broad vocabularies (see Figure 3.2). They develop stamina. Reading gets easier, which, in turn, invites more reading. As stated earlier, volume matters. If we know all of this to be true, why didn't the CCSS set reading targets?

The most recent National Assessment of Educational Progress Study (NAEP) found the following:

- Fourth-grade students performing above the 75th percentile in reading comprehension also had the highest average vocabulary score.

- Lower-performing fourth-graders at or below the 25th percentile in reading comprehension had the lowest average vocabulary score.

- Similar differences were found in grade 8 and in grade 12.

- The highest performing 4th graders scored lower in 2011 than the highest scoring 4th graders scored in 2009. The same drop held true with 8th graders.

- The higher the poverty rate, the lower the vocabulary scores, highlighting the importance of providing disadvantaged students with good books to read.

Source: http://nces.ed.gov/pubsearch/pubsinfo.asp?pubid=2013452

Figure 3.2 Results of NAEP study

Concern 5: The reading standards may be developmentally inappropriate.

Kids' brains, which are still developing, are different from adult brains. Renowned developmental psychologist Jean Piaget identified the following stages of intellectual development in children:

Sensorimotor	Birth through ages 18-24 months
Preoperational	18-24 months through early childhood (age 7)
Concrete operational	Ages 7 to 12
Formal operational	Adolescence through adulthood

(WebMD 2012)

At the preoperational stage, the age where students enter kindergarten, children's thinking "is based on intuition and still not completely logical. They cannot yet grasp more complex concepts such as cause and effect, time, and comparison" (WebMD 2012). This is why, for example, you cannot teach algebra to a kindergartner. To understand algebraic concepts, explains child clinical psychologist Megan Koschnick, a student has to be able to reason abstractly, and abstract reasoning doesn't begin to develop in most people until they reach the formal operational stage, which is approximately age 12 (American Principles Project 2013).

This raises serious questions about the standards written for the early grades. When it comes to developing very young writers, for example, the CCSS has students eliciting peer response as a revision technique. But as Koschnick notes, this may be developmentally inappropriate. If one kindergartner in a writing group tells another that his cat should have been black instead of orange, this may stunt the writer's creativity, leading to frustration and tears. At this early age, we should be more concerned with developing the *independence* of young writers. Following a standard that asks students to respond to one another's work may actually hinder the level of independence that we want to foster in our emerging writers.

When it comes to the teaching of reading, Koschnick notes that there are a number of standards that are also developmentally inappropriate (American Principles Project 2013). For example, she cites the following third-grade standard:

> CCSS.ELA-Literacy.L.3.5c: Distinguish shades of meaning among related words that describe states of mind or degrees of certainty (e.g., *knew, believed, suspected, heard, wondered*). (NGA/CCSSO 2010b)

This reading standard asks students to think abstractly at an age when abstract thinking has not been developed. It requires a nuance that most students that age do not yet possess.

The CCSS were written with college and career readiness in mind, and as a result, they were developed backward from young adulthood all the way down to kindergarten. Instead of asking, "What is developmentally appropriate for kindergarten?" and creating standards upward from there, the new standards take a "top-down" approach that has resulted in some new standards that are developmentally inappropriate for some young children. And when you ask students to do things that are developmentally inappropriate, Koschnick notes, bad things happen (American Principles Project 2013). Stress is induced, which causes disengagement from learning. This disengagement, in turn, causes teachers—and parents— to see normally developing students as delayed, which, in turn, may lead to additional problems (for example, this "delay" may prompt educators to recommend the "need" for an IEP when there really is no need for an IEP).

Concern 6: There is a misinterpretation regarding the amount of informational reading.

The CCSS suggest that 30 percent of reading done by students should be literary in nature, while 70 percent of their reading should be informational. This 30/70 split is not a guideline for reading done solely in ELA classes; it is a suggestion for the types of reading that students should be doing *across an entire school day*. But even if the majority of informational reading is done in classes other than English/Language Arts, this still presents a problem for the ELA teacher. Simply, the math doesn't add up. Sandra Stotsky, Professor Emerita of Education Reform at the University of Arkansas, notes that the 30 percent figure

> raises important questions that have not been discussed, never mind answered. Since students typically take 4-5 major subjects in high school and English is therefore responsible for only about 20-25% of what they read (assuming students read something in their science, math, history, and foreign language classes), wouldn't this mean that just about all of the reading instruction in high school English classes should be literary so that students can achieve there most of the 30% quota desired by Common Core? Students would need about 5-10% more literary study somewhere else to satisfy Common Core's quota, although Common Core's architects don't explain where else literary study is to take place or what kind of literary study elsewhere would satisfy their quota, especially if students don't achieve most of the 30% quota in the English class. (2013)

More likely, Stotsky notes, is that this artificial 30/70 division will lead to a reduction of imaginative literary works taught in the ELA classroom.

Giving students fewer literary works to read is not in their best interest. In *Envisioning Literature*, Judith Langer, an internationally known reading scholar, notes that the literary experience is "a profoundly different kind of social and cognitive act, one that engages minds in ways that are essentially different from other disciplines, yet are critically important to the well-developed and highly literate mind" (1995, ix). Reading literature, it turns out, develops the mind in unique ways because the thinking that is generated through the reading of literary works is different from the thinking that is generated by reading in other disciplines. It is through literature, Langer notes, that "students learn to explore possibilities and consider options; they gain connectedness and seek vision. They become the type of literate, as well as creative, thinkers that we'll need to learn well at college, to do well at work, and to shape discussions and find solutions to tomorrow's problems" (1995, 2).

Literature and poetry have always been at the center of a strong ELA program, and they should remain so. No one would dare tell math teachers that they should no longer teach algebra, and no one should be telling ELA teachers to cut back on the reading of literature and poetry. This trend of moving students away from literary reading is antithetical to good ELA instruction. Kids need more literary reading, not less.

Concern 7: CCSS is driving an overemphasis of the teaching of excerpts.

One of the lessons learned in the NCLB era is that the tests started driving what was taught. Those tests valued multiple-choice surface-level thinking, so students were given a lot of practice answering multiple-choice surface-level questions. Those tests did not value writing, so students were not asked to do a lot of writing.

To help prepare students for the type of reading passages valued by the CCSS, many teachers turn to CCSS Appendix B (NGA/CCSSO 2010c), which provides test exemplars and sample performance tasks (see CCSS Appendix B at http://www.corestandards.org/assets/Appendix_B.pdf). The reading passages found in Appendix B are all short excerpts, which, I am afraid, will negatively affect how reading is approached in our classrooms. When excerpts are valued by the exams, the emphasis in many classes will shift to giving students lots of practice reading excerpts. And when the emphasis shifts to reading more excerpts, the emphasis shifts *away* from sustained reading of longer literary works. This approach creates a choppy curriculum, and students don't get the crucial practice needed to develop the ability to stay with extended works of literature.

Recently, I tweeted the concern that the heavy emphasis on excerpts might squeeze out the reading of longer works, and I was immediately bombarded with responses from teachers around the country who told me it is already happening in their schools. As Maryanne Wolf notes in *Proust and the Squid: The Story and Science of the Reading Brain*, when students are not stretched by longer, challenging works, their cognitive windows run the risk of shutting down (2007). Wolf reminds us that the mental acuity required to read an entire novel is a different skill set than the skill set required to simply read an excerpt, and it is important to remember that the ability to read a novel in its entirety comes through the practice of reading novels in their entirety. If the reading of excerpts replaces the reading of novels, students will be denied the opportunity to stretch their capacities at exactly the time when they are in the key stages of brain development.

Concern 8: The exemplars are problematic.

The exemplars found in CCSS Appendix B create another concern: they are not organic (NGA/CCSSO 2010c). They are randomly selected without any intrinsic connection to what is being taught. Sandra Stotsky notes that in the ninth and tenth grade, you'll find the following:

> Patrick Henry's Speech to the Second Virginia Convention, Margaret Chase Smith's Remarks to the Senate in Support of a Declaration of Conscience, and George

Washington's Farewell Address. In fact, most of the "informational" exemplars for English teachers in grades 9/10 are political speeches. Why political speeches, and why these political speeches, as exemplars for English teachers? How many English teachers are apt to understand the historical and political context of these speeches? How did such heavily historically-situated political speeches with few literary qualities come to be viewed as suitable nonfiction reading in an English class? No explanation is given. (Stotsky 2013)

As Stotsky notes, it appears free reign "has been given to people to write standards documents who are, apparently, insufficiently aware of three very important matters: the content of the subjects typically taught in regular public high schools, the academic background of the teachers of these subjects, and the academic level of the courses in a typical secondary curriculum, grade by grade, from 6 to 12" (Stotsky 2013).

These exemplars overlook another concern as well: some of them are too hard to read for those students who are two or three years (or more) behind grade level in reading. There are no tiered texts offered, no differentiation for those readers overmatched at this grade level.

Staying True to What Works

Let's review the big ideas shared in this chapter and in Chapter 2 about the Common Core anchor reading standards.

COMMON CORE ANCHOR READING STANDARDS	
THE STRENGTHS	THE SHORTCOMINGS
1. Students are asked to read rigorous, high-quality literature and nonfiction. 2. Students are asked to determine what a text says, what a text does, and what a text means. 3. Close reading of rigorous text is emphasized.	1. Readers should not be confined to stay "within the four corners of the text." 2. Prereading activities are undervalued. 3. Recreational reading is all but ignored. 4. There are no reading targets in terms of how much students should read. 5. The reading standards may be developmentally inappropriate. 6. There is a misinterpretation regarding the amount of informational reading. 7. CCSS is driving an overemphasis on the teaching of excerpts. 8. The exemplars are problematic in terms of relevance and reading levels.

As P. David Pearson notes, the new reading standards, despite the problems I've listed, "are still the best game in town" (2014). But just because the new reading standards are the best game in town doesn't mean we should adopt them without critically challenging them. Let's not make the same mistake many teachers made when they blindly hitched their wagons to the latest rounds of adopted exams. Let's remain mindful of the concerns listed in the right-hand column of the preceding table. Let's take the best of what the Common Core reading standards have to offer, while remaining acutely aware of their shortcomings. And where the new standards come up short, let's take the steps necessary to ensure that our core values in the teaching of reading are not sacrificed.

Staying True to What Works in the Teaching of Writing

In Chapter 2, we began our discussion about the teaching of reading by first looking at the strengths of the Common Core anchor reading standards. In Chapter 3, we then examined the weaknesses of these standards, keeping in mind that we need to be sure that our reading instruction stays true to what is in the best interest of our students. We now turn our attention to the teaching of writing, and we will follow the same sequence: this chapter, Chapter 4, examines the strengths of the Common Core anchor writing standards, and, in doing so, offers teachers strategies proven to elevate student writing. (Again, I know some states have not adopted the CCSS, but I do believe all teachers will benefit from a close examination of the strengths found in these standards.) Chapter 5 takes a close look at the shortcomings of the new writing standards so that we can ensure that our writing instruction stays true to what is in the best interest of our students.

First, let's look at the Common Core anchor writing standards.

CCSS English Language Arts Anchor Standards for Writing

Text Types and Purposes

CCSS.ELA-Literacy.CCRA.W.1 Write arguments to support claims in an analysis of substantive topics or texts using valid reasoning and relevant and sufficient evidence.

CCSS.ELA-Literacy.CCRA.W.2 Write informative/explanatory texts to examine and convey complex ideas and information clearly and accurately through the effective selection, organization, and analysis of content.

CCSS.ELA-Literacy.CCRA.W.3 Write narratives to develop real or imagined experiences or events using effective technique, well-chosen details, and well-structured event sequences.

Production and Distribution of Writing

CCSS.ELA-Literacy.CCRA.W.4 Produce clear and coherent writing in which the development, organization, and style are appropriate to task, purpose, and audience.

CCSS.ELA-Literacy.CCRA.W.5 Develop and strengthen writing as needed by planning, revising, editing, rewriting, or trying a new approach.

CCSS.ELA-Literacy.CCRA.W.6 Use technology, including the Internet, to produce and publish writing and to interact and collaborate with others.

Research to Build and Present Knowledge

CCSS.ELA-Literacy.CCRA.W.7 Conduct short as well as more sustained research projects based on focused questions, demonstrating understanding of the subject under investigation.

CCSS.ELA-Literacy.CCRA.W.8 Gather relevant information from multiple print and digital sources, assess the credibility and accuracy of each source, and integrate the information while avoiding plagiarism.

CCSS.ELA-Literacy.CCRA.W.9 Draw evidence from literary or informational texts to support analysis, reflection, and research.

Range of Writing

CCSS.ELA-Literacy.CCRA.W.10 Write routinely over extended time frames (time for research, reflection, and revision) and shorter time frames (a single sitting or a day or two) for a range of tasks, purposes, and audiences.
Source: (NGA/CCSSO 2010d)

Following are six strengths found in the anchor writing standards.

Strength 1: The CCSS recognize that reading and writing are interconnected.

Unlike many states' standards in the NCLB era, which virtually ignored writing, the CCSS weave reading and writing together. Figure 4.1 is a sample assessment item released by the Smarter Balanced Assessment Consortium (2014a).

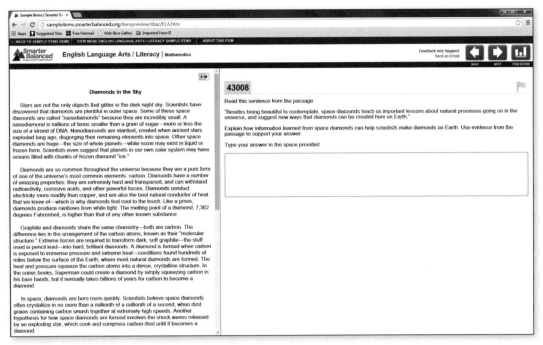

Figure 4.1 "Diamonds in the Sky" assessment item

In the example shown in Figure 4.1, students are first asked to read a passage about space diamonds and then to explain via writing how information learned about space diamonds can help scientists make diamonds on Earth. There are two things worth noting in this example: (1) the reading and writing are science-based, which reinforces the critical idea that teaching students how to better read and write is a shared responsibility among teachers of all content areas (not just English teachers); and (2) the writing required by the prompt is text-dependent, meaning that the students cannot answer it without a close reading of the passage. Gone are the days (at least for now) when students will be asked to write responses to stand-alone prompts. The new standards—and many of the newly adopted tests—require students to weave reading and writing together, and this is a good thing.

Strength 2: The CCSS may drive more writing across the curriculum.

Because the CCSS recognize that reading and writing are interconnected, and because the assessments generated by the CCSS require students to write across various content areas, I remain hopeful that students will be asked to write more in classes other than English. Of course, for many of us this seems silly, for we know the value of having our students write every day. The powers that be could take every assessment away tomorrow and we would still have our students write daily. But the sad truth is that there are teachers out there who need their feet held to the testing fire before writing will occur in their classrooms, and assessments of Common Core standards provide that fire. If a test is what it takes to get some teachers to integrate more writing into their curriculum, this is also a good thing.

Strength 3: The Common Core writing standards value process writing.

Many of my students begin the year as "one-and-done" writers. They write one draft; they are done. They think "revision" means "type it." I am hoping that the CCSS will help students— and teachers—to push past one-and-done writing and into multiple-draft practice. It is important to keep the tenth anchor writing standard in mind, which asks students to "write routinely over extended time frames (time for research, reflection, and revision)" (NGA/ CCSSO 2010d). Our students should wrestle with the cognitive challenges that occur when working on a paper over an extended period of time. Doing so produces a much deeper level of brain exercise than simply writing a single draft and walking away from it.

As I outline in *Write Like This*, the best way to help students to internalize the value of moving beyond one and done is through intensive modeling (Gallagher 2011). We should provide models...

> ...before they begin writing (by outlining and brainstorming).
>
> ...as they begin writing (by writing alongside them and presenting them with mentor texts).
>
> ...when they share and respond to one another's papers (by first responding to the teacher's draft).
>
> ...to demonstrate how revision occurs (by using student and teacher models as examples).
>
> ...that help students properly edit a paper (by using mentor sentences to teach these editing skills).
>
> ...to ensure our students learn proper manuscript guidelines (by using exemplary examples for guidance).

Far from one and done, our modeling should be woven *throughout* the writing process. This level of modeling marks the crucial difference between *assigning* writing and *teaching* writing.

Strength 4: The Common Core writing standards sharpen our students' narrative writing skills.

Narrative writing is one of the big three writing genres of writing valued by the CCSS. This is important since the ability to tell a good story is a skill that resonates well beyond the walls of the English classroom.

In *Write Like This*, I share a number of narrative writing activities I worked through alongside my students (Gallagher 2011). Following are more narrative writing ideas that invite students to write longer pieces. For each of them, you will see my brainstorm of possible writing topics on the left-hand side and the ideas my students brainstormed on the right-hand side.

Moments That Matter

Some moments in our lives matter more than others. For this writing activity, students are asked to consider the moments in their lives that really matter. I share my list, and then students create their own lists, which generate numerous writing possibilities.

MR. GALLAGHER'S MOMENTS THAT MATTERED	STUDENTS' MOMENTS THAT MATTERED
• The start of a friendship • The end of a friendship • Meeting my future wife at a wedding • The birth of each of my children • My parents informing me they were divorcing • The death of my father • Adopting our dog, Scout • Receiving notice that my first book would be published • Dropping out of school (which led me to reconsider my career) • Being told we were moving • An automobile accident • Seeing my sister being arrested • The talk with my grandfather • Hearing Sheridan Blau speak at a teaching conference • Reading *Sophie's Choice*	• That kiss • The Prom • Meeting my best friend • Getting suspended • Moving from Puerto Rico • Making the team • My mom's new boyfriend • Getting my driver's license • Moving in with my dad • Getting hired at Wendy's • Breaking up with my boyfriend • 9/11 • Failing geometry • Attending my first funeral • Saying no to my mom • Stopped smoking weed • When my dog died • Staying home alone for the first time • Being introduced to snowboarding

Stranded

We have all been stranded, physically and/or emotionally.

MR. GALLAGHER'S STRANDED MOMENTS	STUDENTS' STRANDED MOMENTS
• Stuck in O'Hare at midnight with no hotel room or rental car • Locked out of my family home (as a young boy) with everyone gone for the weekend • Living alone in a New York City apartment • Left by my group to finish the high school project • Staring at a blank page when facing a deadline • Standing next to my conked-out VW on the side of the freeway	• Getting lost in the grocery store • My friends moved away • Trying to write an essay the night before it is due • Phone dies while trying to meet someone • Stuck in a jail cell without my parents knowing • Stuck at a friend's house during Hurricane Sandy • Getting suspended • Alone during a blackout • Got lost on the train • Home alone during a thunderstorm

When the Weather Mattered

Students are asked to consider times when weather was a factor.

MR. GALLAGHER'S WEATHER MOMENTS	STUDENTS' WEATHER MOMENTS
• The first time I saw snow fall • Driving through a whiteout in Northern Michigan in a tiny rental car • Golf-ball sized hail in Texas • Tornado warning in Chicago • Drought—everything died • Luggage door of airplane frozen shut in Edmonton. • Siting on my grandmother's porch in Arizona watching the lightning storm • Trying to outrun the storm while boating in the Gulf of Mexico	• Massive snowball fight • Sledding with my family • Airplane turbulence • Hurricane Sandy flooding the subway • Best "snow day" • Sweating in North Carolina • Rain pouring at the funeral • Game suspended due to lightning • Walking in a blizzard • Forgot my jacket • Ice injury

MR. GALLAGHER'S WEATHER MOMENTS (CONTINUED)	STUDENTS' WEATHER MOMENTS (CONTINUED)
• Circling. . . . . . and circling . . . .. . and circling above the storm (and ending up in Cheyenne instead of Denver) • Santa Ana winds knocking neighborhood trees down and starting fires • Trying to sleep on the floor of the Grand Canyon on a 105-degree night • Rams-Vikings 1970 playoff game	• Lost feeling in my hands for hours • Driving through Vegas at 105 degrees • My street flooded • Wind rattles the tree outside my window at night • Slipping on icy sidewalk • Too cold to play the game • Being stuck inside during "recess" on a rainy day • Neighborhood snowball fight • Being way overdressed

A Change

Students are encouraged to write about significant changes in their lives.

MR. GALLAGHER'S SIGNIFICANT CHANGES	STUDENTS' SIGNIFICANT CHANGES
• Introduction to meditation • Hair style • New Year's resolution: no more french fries • Brad after his brain surgery • Quitting an old job and starting a new job • Breaking up with a girlfriend • Disney buying the Anaheim Angels • Moving to New York • Teaching a new grade level • The closing of my favorite breakfast restaurant • Empty nest syndrome: daughters leave home • Jeremy Renner is not Jason Bourne	• Cutting off my braids • From Blackberry to iPhone • Changing jobs • Moving to Harlem • Facebook re-do • Beating my father in pool for the first time • Getting a girlfriend • New grading system • New baby in the family • New zit • Mom losing her job • New friend • Miley Cyrus—what happened? • My father's attitude • New student in our writing group

First Attempt

Students are asked to reflect on attempting something for the first time.

MR. GALLAGHER'S FIRST ATTEMPTS	STUDENTS' FIRST ATTEMPTS
• Driving a stick shift up a hill • Building a skateboard • Learning to ski • Writing a book • Teaching my first class • Eating escargot • Bodysurfing • Creating a website • Navigating the subway system • Trying that yoga pose	• Drinking • Reading a new genre • Working out • Driving a golf cart • Cutting my own hair • First demerit • Getting arrested • Getting "stopped and frisked" • Shaving • Kissing a girl

Unprepared

Students are asked to consider a time they were unprepared.

MR. GALLAGHER'S UNPREPARED	STUDENTS' UNPREPARED
• Job interview(s) • Entering the Fire Academy • Physics exam in college • Giving a speech at a basketball banquet • Teaching a summer school math class • For the ending of the following films: *Planet of the Apes, Gallipoli, Soylent Green, The Sixth Sense, The Crying Game* • News of parents' divorce • Friend's cancer news	• College interview • My uncle coming out • My grandmother dying • Hurricane Sandy • Socratic seminar in social studies • My cousin's pregnancy • SpongeBob getting canceled • Attending my friend's funeral • Stuck outside without an umbrella • Watching *Paranormal Activity*—it freaked me out!

Near Misses

Students are asked to write about near misses they have experienced.

MR. GALLAGHER'S NEAR MISSES	STUDENTS' NEAR MISSES
• Near runway collision • Near barbed wire decapitation • Almost drowned • The shot that would have won the basketball game • Losing control of the car in the ice storm • Rams losing to the Steelers in the 1979 Super Bowl • Seagull poop attack • Sledding accident	• Nearly getting electrocuted • Jennifer Hudson on American Idol • One girl texting me when I was with another girl • Almost got caught cheating on a test • Losing the game by 1 point • Almost falling off a balcony • Getting away with losing my phone • Coming in 2nd in a dance competition

Choosing Sides

Students are asked to discuss a time they had to choose a side.

MR. GALLAGHER'S CHOOSING SIDES	STUDENTS' CHOOSING SIDES
• Coke or Pepsi? • Obama or Romney? • Mom or Dad? • USC or UCLA? • Angels or Dodgers? • United Airlines or American Airlines? • Jimmy: Fallon or Kimmel? • Back in the day: English department versus social science department	• This high school or another high school? • Junk food or healthy food? • Run or fight? • Candace or Bria? • Knicks or Heat? • Play Station or Xbox? • Go out for football or basketball? • Lebron or Melo? • USA or Mexico soccer teams?

You Are a Teacher

Students are asked to write about times when they taught others something.

MR. GALLAGHER'S YOU ARE A TEACHER	STUDENTS' YOU ARE A TEACHER
• Taught my nephew how to spin a basketball on his finger • Taught my daughters to value reading • "The Ethicist" column in the *New York Times* taught my daughters ethics • Training new waiters • Teaching basketball player how to tie a tie	• Taught my sister how to count • Taught my grandma how to use an iPhone • Taught myself to memorize Shakespeare • Taught myself to be a vegetarian • Taught my sister how to cook • Taught my little brother how to call 911 • Taught my mom how to speak English

From A to B

Students are asked to discuss how they got from one place to another.

MR. GALLAGHER'S FROM A TO B	STUDENTS' FROM A TO B
• Walking three miles to junior high every day • First airline flight (ending in disaster) • Endless car trip to Mexico City • Secret midnight horseback riding in Laguna Beach • Skateboarding the Huntington Beach boardwalk • Running the half mile for the track team • My dad giving us wheelbarrow rides • Go-kart racing • Canoeing the Colorado River • Zip line in Cancun • Snorkeling across Honolua Bay • Taking the train to Berlin	• First train ride by myself • Sneaking out through the fire escape • Driving to find the block party • Driving to Florida/Disney World • The cab ride from hell • Crossing state lines • Walking home from the hospital • Riding a garbage can lid in the snow • Six mile walk after car broke down • Swimming in the Gulf of Mexico • The fight on the subway • First ride on the Long Island Ferry • Ditching to take the train to Coney Island • My first solo motorcycle ride • Long car ride: 4 kids/2 seats

MR. GALLAGHER'S FROM A TO B (CONTINUED)	STUDENTS' FROM A TO B (CONTINUED)
• Riding an elephant • Nightmare trip—Orange County to Michigan: 20 hours • Seasick on boat to Catalina Island • Stuck on a BART train underneath San Francisco Bay	• Riding bikes to Chelsea Pier • Riding a scooter in Honduras • Running endlessly in basketball practice • How I went from being a junior to being a senior • Walking from Harlem to the WTC • Going from happy to sad in an instant

Strength 5: The Common Core writing standards will sharpen our students' ability to inform and explain.

The ability to inform and/or explain is a real-world writing skill I want my students to practice. Additionally, it is one of the three types of writing valued by the CCSS and the new generation of tests. With this in mind, the following exercises invite students to write longer pieces in this genre.

Reverse Bucket List

In *Write Like This*, I share a "Bucket List" assignment where my students listed all the things they would like to do before they die (Gallagher 2011). Inspired by Jeffrey Goldberg's column in the *Atlantic*, I now have my students create reverse bucket lists—lists of things they are positive they *never* want to do (2011). I go first:

Mr. Gallagher's Reverse Bucket List

1. Eat sushi
2. See any movie featuring Renee Zellweger
3. See any movie featuring Sarah Jessica Parker
4. See any movie featuring Arnold Schwarzenegger
5. Play Candy Crush
6. Go to a Pit Bull concert
7. Get a job as a telemarketer
8. Play golf
9. Get a pet turtle

10. Hang out in Times Square on New Year's Eve
11. Hang out anywhere on New Year's Eve
12. Join the *Duck Dynasty* fan club
13. Read a Stephenie Meyer book
14. Shop at any mall
15. Run an ultra-marathon
16. Request a middle airline seat
17. Become a Yankees fan
18. Subscribe to *Oprah*
19. Become a dentist
20. Wear a monocle
21. Visit/shop at a pet store
22. Go to Disneyland on a summer day
23. Retire to Florida
24. Write a book about penguins
25. Gather a deep understanding of the US tax code
26. Collect snow globes
27. Get a facial tattoo
28. Pierce my nose
29. Take yodeling lessons
30. Go on a Disney cruise

My students then create their reverse bucket lists. Here is a sampling:

1. Twerk
2. Eat frog legs
3. Become a taxi driver
4. Clean zoo cages
5. Shave my head
6. Work at McDonald's
7. Watch every episode of *Law and Order*
8. Date a girl with less hair than me
9. Get an STD
10. Work as a janitor
11. Sing a Justin Bieber song
12. Go to jail
13. Go back to jail
14. Play ping pong

15. Be at a graveyard at night
16. Open a restaurant
17. Buy a motor scooter
18. Visit Siberia
19. Watch *Vampire Diaries*
20. Make coleslaw
21. Learn how to knit
22. Ride in an ambulance
23. Go on a safari
24. Get hit by pepper spray
25. Give birth
26. Repeat 12th grade
27. Play bridge
28. Study the history of catsup
29. Raise snakes
30. Be featured on YouTube

From their lists, students pick one (or more) and explain in detail why it (or they) made the list.

Six Things You Should Know About . . .

Every issue of *ESPN* magazine has a one-page column titled, "Six Things You Should Know About . . ." In Figure 4.2, you can see an example of six things you should know about playing in the World Cup. Here are other recent topics found in the magazine:

Six Things You Should Know About . . .

. . . being a Pro Gamer.

. . . acting in a Sports Movie.

. . . faith in the Locker Room.

. . . treating NHL Teeth.

. . . owning a NASCAR Team.

. . . dealing at the World Series of Poker.

. . . the Westminster Kennel Club Show.

. . . the upcoming Olympics.

PAGE 2

ESPN THE MAGAZINE

6

THINGS YOU SHOULD KNOW ABOUT PLAYING ON EARTH'S BIGGEST STAGE

BY U.S. CAPTAIN CARLOS BOCANEGRA
(AS TOLD TO LUKE CYPHERS)
PHOTOGRAPH BY PIER NICOLA D'AMICO

1. WE PLAY MULTIPLE MATCHES, YOU KNOW. "Before the game, people made a stink about England. We knew it would be a good test, but we didn't invest all our emotions into that one game. There are two other games that are just as important if we're going to get out of the group. We need to play consistently the whole time. That's one of the harder things to do in a World Cup."

2. IT TAKES A VILLAGE. OR A TEAM. "I was appointed captain three years ago, but we have a group of guys who take on leadership roles. There's a lot of yelling on the field—and not just from our keeper, Tim Howard. My main job is to be a link between the coach and the team. On the field, I try to lead by example and hope that spreads. Off it, if players have issues, I communicate that to the coaches. But for the most part, everybody gets along."

3. THE ALUMS SET THE TONE. "The last generation was cool with us. Claudio Reyna, Brian McBride, Eddie Pope: They knew we were young, eager and full of energy, and they let us have fun. But they made sure we knew how to fit in and when to be serious. I keep that in mind with our new guys. You want to bring them along and make them feel like part of the group. This isn't the NFL. We don't send rookies for snacks, no matter how good doughnuts sound."

4. WE AVOID BOOKS ON THE FIELD, NOT OFF IT. "With all our travel, we have to be good at occupying our time. There are lots of readers on the team. Last year it was sports bios and *The Game*. Jonathan Spector is currently reading *The Dynamic Path*, which Steve Cherundolo says is about him. If Brad Guzan knew how to read, he might be able to offer an opinion."

5. WE'VE LIVED AND LEARNED. "Before the last World Cup, we all discussed whether we'd play in various countries for money, for a certain lifestyle or to be in bigger leagues. Now, with so many of us in Europe, we've been comparing experiences."

6. THE DOWNTIME IS WELCOMED. "During the Cup we're confined to our hotel, but it's fun. We play board games, and this year DJ Hero is big. Our place is nice—it's a lodge. Italy wanted it and couldn't get it because we already had reservations, so we're happy about that."

ALL NEWS On bet, New Hampshire man walks from Boston to New York, wins courtside NBA Finals tix ... Poker star Phil Laak plays for 115 straight hours, breaking world record ...

28

Figure 4.2 Sample "Six Things You Should Know About . . ." article

The examples from *ESPN* magazine are all sports related, but I ask my students to brainstorm topics both inside and outside the world of sports. Here are some topics I modeled, next to some of my students' topics:

Six Things You Should Know About. . . (Mr. Gallagher's List)	Six Things You Should Know About. . . (Students' List)
. . . buying a car.	. . . playing *Grand Theft Auto V*.
. . . renting an apartment.	. . . passing AP biology.
. . . owning a dog.	. . . being a babysitter.
. . . becoming a teacher.	. . . playing varsity football.
. . . being a parent.	. . . being a twin.
. . . writing a book.	. . . the McDonald's menu.
. . . being in an airport.	. . . a Galaxy 7 phone.
. . . being an Angels fan.	. . . being in student government.
. . . coaching high school basketball.	. . . playing soccer.
. . . applying to college.	. . . Instagram.
. . . applying for a job.	. . . Harlem.
. . . our school library.	. . . the subway system.

After we brainstorm, I choose one topic and write a model for my students, noting the formatting of the magazine piece (e.g., each of the "things" is numbered and in bold font). I take students into the computer lab and teach them how to insert a stock photo and how to wrap text around it. In Figure 4.3, you will see the first page of my rough draft of "Six Things You Should Know About Writing a Book." Figure 4.4 shows Alicia's first draft of "Six Things You Should Know About Being a Twin."

Six Things You Should Know About Writing a Book

1. YOU HAVE TO BE A LITTLE CRAZY.

Writing a book is challenging, especially when I am teaching full time. Because I am exhausted after a day of teaching, my only writing time comes in the morning. And when I say "morning," I mean morning. I wrote each of my last two books at 4:00 a.m. While the rest of the world was dreaming pleasant thoughts, I was staring with blurry eyes at my computer screen, trying to come up with something—anything—worth reading. Let me repeat: 4:00 a.m. You have to be a little crazy to do this, right?

2. SOME DAYS IT FLOWS; OTHER DAYS IT DOESN'T.

I haven't figured out why this is true, but some days when I sit down to write the words just flow onto the screen. These are the good writing days. Unfortunately, however, there are days where I find myself with writer's block, and I sit there staring stupidly at a blank screen. I don't know why some days are better writing days than others, but I have come to accept this as part of what it means to be a writer. Knowing this, I don't panic when I am having a bad writing day.

3. WRITING IS EASY; RE-WRITING IS HARD.

As I mentioned, some days the words flow onto the paper. That's the good news. The bad news is that almost all first drafts are lousy. They need revision—sometimes lots of it. I would estimate that when I write a book I spend about 25 percent of my time writing and about 75 percent of my time revising. Though revising is hard, I actually enjoy seeing when a draft moves. Sometimes, it heads in very unexpected directions.

4. YOUR BOOK IS NEVER FINISHED; IT'S JUST DUE.

Revision makes your writing better, but it never makes your writing perfect. There comes a time when you have to believe the draft is good enough to let it go. Sometimes I read something that I have published and think, "Wow, I should have revised that one more time." This always reminds me that drafts are never finished, they are just due.

5. YOU HAVE TO DEVELOP THICK SKIN

The scariest part of writing comes when you allow someone else to read what you have written. Sharing writing is risky. Even though I know deep in my brain that all early drafts are lousy, it is still difficult when someone provides constructive criticism. Whenever I show an early draft to my editor, I am always a bit on edge until I receive the feedback. You have to develop thick skin so you do not take the criticism personally.

6. AS GOOD AS YOUR BOOK IS, SOMEONE IS NOT GOING TO LIKE IT.

I have been fortunate that all of my books have received favorable reviews, but I have come to learn that there are some people out there who will not like what I have written. Sometimes when I read a negative review, I think the person did not read my book closely. Other times, I think we just have an honest disagreement. It helps when I look up authors I love and see that they, too, get the occasional negative blast. It comes with the territory, I guess.

Figure 4.3 The first draft of my "Six Things . . ." piece

Six Things You Should Know About Being a Twin

1. DON'T ANGER EACH OTHER

Twins tend to fight a lot about every little thing! When we're mad at each other we don't talk at all. We just ignore each other. When my sister and I get into a fight things are not fun. We often end up in a huge argument usually over something dumb like a pencil. But we often make up rather quickly. We can't stand being mad at each other. We talk to each other every second of the day. We help each other with projects and other homework. Being mad at each other just ruins our day and doesn't allow me to talk about my other problems with her.

2. YOU HAVE TO LEARN TO SHARE

There's always that moment when you get something and your brother/sister doesn't, right? Like maybe one day your mom buys you something to eat but doesn't buy anything for your sibling. Once I arrived home from the store to find my mom had bought me chips, but she didn't buy any for my sister, so my mom tells me to share. Being a twin, this type of situation happens a lot. For example, I have Internet access on my phone, but my sister doesn't because she has gone over her allowed minutes, so she is always asking me to use my phone. I have learned that sharing causes a lot less trouble.

3. AS A TWIN YOU ARE NEVER ALONE

The good thing about having a twin is you're never alone. You always have someone right by your side. You might have one of those days where you need someone to lean on, and I know my sister is always there. There are moments where you get irritated by being together all day, and all you want is time to yourself. The bad part is that our parents want us together 24/7 or else they start worrying about each of us. On the rare occasion I'm allowed out without her, it's nice, but it's also a nice feeling to know that you are never alone and that you will always have someone by your side.

4. REVENGE IS PART OF BEING A TWIN

Revenge—isn't it a lovely thing? There are moments where I almost want to murder my sister, but you cannot act on these urges without getting into big trouble. The bad thing is that is hard to plan revenge on someone whose mind works just like mine, because she anticipates what I am going to do. One time she ate a bag of my chips, so I planned to drink her Arizona tea. I thought hat was a fair response, but when I went to get it, she hid her drink from me. So I did the next best thing—I put her toothbrush in the toilet.

Figure 4.4 The beginning of the first draft of Alicia's "Six Things . . ." piece

Your Birthday in History

One of my students' favorite writing assignments is to inform the reader of significant moments in history that occurred on their birthdays. There are a number of "This day in history" websites where a student can type in his or her birthday and get a list of important historical occurrences from that day (my favorite site is *www.onthisday.com*). Here, for example, are important historical events that occurred on my birthday, October 9 (http://www.on-this-day.com/onthisday/thedays/alldays/oct09.htm):

> 1781: The last major battle of the American Revolutionary War took place in Yorktown, VA. The American forces, led by George Washington, defeated the British troops under Lord Cornwallis.
>
> 1855: Isaac Singer patented the sewing machine.
>
> 1858: Alexander Graham Bell and Thomas Watson made their longest telephone call to date (two miles).
>
> 1940: St. Paul's Cathedral in London was bombed by the Nazis.
>
> 1940: John Lennon was born.
>
> 1944: Churchill and Stalin conferred.
>
> 1974: Oskar Schindler died in Frankfurt, Germany. Schindler is credited with saving the lives of 1200 Jews during the Holocaust.
>
> 1986: The musical *Phantom of the Opera* by Andrew Lloyd Webber opened in London.
>
> 1994: The U.S. sent troops and warships to the Persian Gulf in response to Saddam Hussein sending thousands of troops and hundreds of tanks toward the Kuwaiti border.

Students choose one event and explain the details of the event to the reader. If teachers want to add another layer to the assignment, they can also ask students to argue why this historical event still matters today.

Photographs That Mattered

As English teachers, we spend a lot of time teaching students the power of words. In generating informative writing, there is value in having students consider the power of photographs as well.

On April 24, 2013, an eight-story commercial building housing garment factory workers collapsed in Bangladesh, killing an estimated 1,129 people and injuring 2,515 others. Taslima Akhter, a photographer, rushed to the scene and took a heartbreaking and haunting photograph of two deceased workers embracing one another in the rubble. (Because of the disturbing nature of the photograph, I chose not to include it in these pages. It can be viewed by searching "Taslima Akhter" online.) Akhter's photograph mattered: it helped spark an outcry that manifested itself in protests and riots, ultimately culminating in labor laws being reformed in Bangladesh.

Figure 4.5 George Strock's famous photograph of dead American soldiers at Buna Beach

Using Akhter's photograph as a starting point, I move to George Strock's famous photograph of dead American soldiers at Buna Beach, which shows the bodies of American serviceman washed up on the beaches on Papua New Guinea (see Figure 4.5). First published in *Life*, this photograph shocked Americans, who were insulated from the grim realities of the war. The editors of *Life* knew that in this case a picture spoke more than a thousand words, and, apparently, so did President Franklin D. Roosevelt, who lifted the ban on images depicting U.S. casualties. Strock's photograph "ended the censorship rule, boosted support for the war and had a lasting effect on photo journalism" (Associated Press 2013). It is also interesting to note that Roosevelt's strategy in releasing the photograph was the opposite of the strategy employed by George W. Bush, who forbade any photographs from being taken of flag-draped coffins returning from Iraq. Both presidents knew the power of photography.

After sharing these photographs by Akhter and Strock (and why they mattered), I ask students to research and find photographs that mattered and, after researching their photographs, to explain why they mattered. One great resource for students to start their searches is *100 Photographs That Changed the World* (Sullivan 2003). (Students can also find Strock's iconic photograph in this book.)

Who Made That?

In the *New York Times Magazine*, published every Sunday, is a column titled, "Who Made That?" This column informs the reader how and where common, everyday items originated. (For example, see Figure 4.6, where the reader learns who first made flip-flops.) In recent weeks, this column has highlighted the people who first made. . .

. . . dog tags.

. . . the home pregnancy test.

. . . Nigerian scams.

. . . the tricycle.

. . . the planetarium.

. . . the corkscrew.

. . . the contact lens.

. . . the food truck.

Figure 4.6 From the *New York Times Magazine*'s "Who Made That?" series

This year, my colleague Isabel Yalouris asked her seventh-grade students to pick common items and to research their origins. In Figure 4.7, you will see how Anaya explains the origin of the woman's handbag.

Who made the handbag?

With so many different trends like the cross-body, clutch, and tote, combined together with millions of different colors and embellishments, plus many brands to choose from, a woman can find lots of good handbags. Even though there was no Michael Kors and Gucci bags back then, handbags still have a long history, starting in ancient Mesopotamia where the first handbag was made.

In ancient Egypt, people needed to walk miles to stores to buy things to properly support their families. They had to bring money to the markets, and people got sick and tired of holding their money. As a result, they decided to make little coin pouches to hold traveling items such as coins, lipstick, tissue and more. They were made with fabric and sewn with colored yarn. The pouches sometimes had detailing of rubies and gems. They were used by men and women and were very useful.

This went on for another generation until the Elizabethan era. In that era, there were no pockets on clothes, so they used tiny bags named griddle pouches. They held cosmetics and became even bigger in the 18th century. Even though clothes had pockets, woman preferred bags. The women of the 18th century used an early sign of today's "clutch." Soon came the Victorian Era, and women were into handbags. Excitedly, fashion began to open up as clutches were turned into totes.

As people continued using handbags, the bags' popularity increased. Women got Dory bags with matching robes and shoes. Getting matching items were popular back then, so when woman started matching handbags to their clothes- it blew up! While WWII took place, women loved the styles of military-inspired items. Women during this time couldn't wait to get their hands on military-inspired items. They thought it showed boldness and not being afraid.

When the 50's dropped by, women loved handbags. Brands like Hermes, Chanel, and Vuitton inspired woman to live through fashion. In result of living through fashion, in the 1960's formal dressing was dropped and casual dressing began. With the fashion change- handbags changed too. They became simpler and they were brighter. The best thing about the fashion change was women were able to express themselves and live through fashion.

In the 60s, 70s, and 80s, the style of "cross-body" bag were invented, which ended 77% of handbag robberies. People became into the punk style back then also. This means people loved the studs and neon colors. They also added tassels and buckles as well. Also people made the designer sports bags and diaper bags. And we cannot forget the beloved Coach bags!

Today handbags are a way for people to express themselves. You don't always have to express yourself through words, religion, race, sexuality, nor appearance. A handbag can say a million words the mouth can't . . . so next time you just so seem to be shopping for a handbag, remember the history that started it all.

"Elegance is not the prerogative of those who have just escaped from adolescence, but those who have already taken possession of their future"

- Coco Chanel

Figure 4.7 Anaya's "Who Made That?"

Last year, my students made a classroom edition of "Who Made That?" by binding all their responses into one booklet and then placing the booklet in the classroom library.

36 Hours in . . .

Another idea taken from the *New York Times* is a column titled "36 Hours in . . . ," which is found in the newspaper's weekend travel section. This column recommends how a person might spend thirty-six hours in a given city, providing suggestions on where to stay, where to eat, what to do, and what to see within a thirty-six-hour time frame. Using this newspaper column as a template, Yalouris had her students emulate the "36 Hours in. . ." format. Hadja, a seventh grader, put together a thirty-six-hour itinerary for a visit to New York City that included the following stops: Times Square, the Barclay Center, a Serendipities ice cream parlor, the Statue of Liberty, Yankee Stadium, the Magic Johnson Theater, Riverside Park (for ice skating), the Bronx Zoo, and the Empire State Building. Each suggested stop was accompanied by a short paragraph giving the potential visitor more information (e.g., hours, cost, why this spot is worth the visit).

Have your students choose locales and have them explain to the reader how best to spend thirty-six hours there.

Theme Newsletter

Another colleague of mine at the Harlem Village Academies, Dave Hibler, had his students create theme newsletters under the umbrella of informational writing. Each student was asked to choose a big topic, and then to generate four informative pieces that fit under the big topic. Hibler, an avid runner, created a model newsletter around the topic of running. He wrote four pieces: (1) suggestions on the best places to run in New York City; (2) ten tips for long-distance running; (3) a biography on a student runner; and (4) a news report on a student track meet. After completing his writing, Hibler taught his students how to lay out the pieces in a newsletter format.

Dave's students then emulated him. Esther, a seventh-grade student, created a newsletter on the topic of reading urban fiction. Her four pieces: (1) an introduction to the genre; (2) an explanation of myths versus facts regarding urban fiction; (3) profiles on prominent authors in the genre; and (4) reviews on three books students might want to read in the genre (see Figure 4.8).

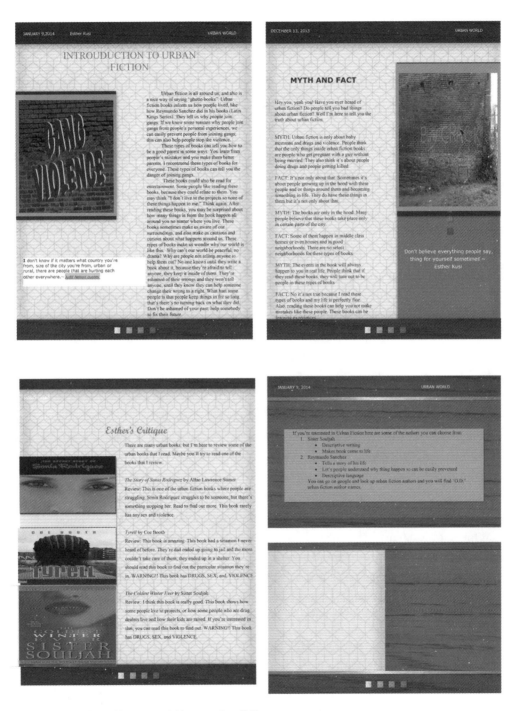

Figure 4.8 Esther's theme newsletter on urban fiction

Have your students choose topics they are passionate about and have them create newsletters containing articles that offer further information and/or explanation to the reader.

Strength 6: The Common Core writing standards will sharpen our students' argumentative writing skills.

Of the three big writing types, the authors of the CCSS place the heaviest emphasis on our students' ability to write effective arguments. The standards suggest that by the end of the twelfth grade, 40 percent of a student's writing done in schools be argumentative in nature. (This 40 percent target also raises some concerns—see Chapter 5.) With such a heavy emphasis on teaching the argument paper, here are five key points to keep in mind.

Key Point 1: There is a difference between persuasion and argument.

To understand the difference between persuasion and argument, one needs to look no further than the Norm Reeves Honda Superstore, a car dealership in Southern California. In an attempt to persuade consumers to visit their dealership, the folks at Norm Reeves promised in advertisements that customers could lease new cars without paying anything up front. This form of persuasion worked in getting people to visit the car lot, as evidenced by the fact that this car dealership is the top-selling Honda dealership in the United States. However, there was one big problem with the ads that lured customers to the car lot: they were untrue. Though the ads claimed that customers could drive off without any down payment, the FTC found that there were "substantial fees and other amounts" hidden in the fine print (LaReau 2014).

As the Norm Reeves example reminds us, persuasion (as opposed to argument) can be dependent on the use of propaganda. In persuasion, style rather than substance is often utilized to detract from the issue at hand. Persuasion can be steeped in falsehood. Think about the last presidential campaign: Were both parties always truthful in their attempts to persuade you to vote for their candidates?

Argument, on the other hand, is grounded in logic and critical thinking. It is reasoned. It is not overly dependent on style; it is rooted in substance. In *Teaching Argument Writing*, George Hillocks recognizes three kinds of arguments:

- Arguments of **fact:** This type of argument dates back to Aristotle and was often taught through syllogisms. For example, start with a major premise: All mortals die. This leads to a minor premise: All men are mortals. Which, in turn, leads to a conclusion: All men will die. But as Hillocks notes, "In most disciplines (with the exception of mathematics and sometimes physics), and in most everyday problems and disputes, we do not have premises that we know to be absolutely true. We have to deal with statements that may be true or that we believe to be true—but are not absolutely true" (2011, xviii). In other words, truth shifts, and, because of this, Hillocks argues we should have our students focus on the other two types of arguments—arguments of judgment and arguments of policy.

- Arguments of **judgment**: Is the president doing a good job? Who is the greatest living baseball player? What makes a good teacher? To argue any of these questions requires judgment on the part of the writer—judgment, of course, that we hope is supported by facts and evidence.
- Arguments of **policy**: As Hillocks notes, arguments of policy "typically make a case to establish, amend, or eliminate rules, procedures, practices, and projects that are believed to affect people's lives" (2011, 67). When a student argues that the school's dress code is unreasonable, or that the Affordable Care Act is good (or bad), the student is making an argument of policy.

Rather than ask students to write "persuasive essays," we should give students practice writing both arguments of judgment and arguments of policy. Hillocks (2011), citing Stephen Toulmin's *The Uses of Argument* (2003), suggests that arguments of judgment and arguments of policy should include the following:

1. A claim: what is the big idea being argued?
2. Evidence that supports the claim. This evidence should be based in data.
3. A warrant: this explains how the evidence supports the claim.
4. Backing supporting the warrants.
5. Qualifications and rebuttals or counterarguments that refute countering claims. (Hillocks 2011, xix)

To understand how these elements fit into an argument, consider the following excerpt from an argumentative essay:

As a high school student, I think it is unfair that we have to wear school uniforms. Therefore, it is time to get rid of mandatory uniforms at this school.

Most students at Valley High agree with me. They believe they are old enough to decide what to wear. They also believe they are being denied their right to express themselves. Denying students the ability to creatively express themselves is wrong. It is time we were treated like adults.

This is a typical excerpt of argumentative writing that I might get from my students. (I say "typical" because I wrote it for demonstration purposes. Believe me, after twenty-nine years, I have seen enough to create an accurate representation of student argument papers.) To show my students the shortcomings of this draft, I have them compare it against this revision:

> *As a high school student, I think it is unfair that we have to wear school uniforms. Therefore, it is time to get rid of mandatory uniforms at this school.*
>
> *Most students at Valley High agree with me, as evidenced by a survey recently conducted through the English classes. When asked if they would support the removal of mandatory school uniforms, 92 percent of students said yes. This is not simply a majority of students who support this position; it is an* overwhelming *majority. Because this anti-uniform sentiment is so widespread, the time has come to take it seriously. When this many students feel this strongly about the uniform issue, the policy is surely overdue for reevaluation. It is possible that the administration may challenge the validity of the survey, but please know that in an attempt to eliminate bias, it was administered to every student in the school (as opposed, for example, to only giving it to seniors). As such, it is an accurate representation of the feelings of this student body, which means the time has come to give students choice when deciding what to wear to school.*

I then have my students notice the elements of the second example:

Claim *What is the big idea being argued?*	"Therefore, it is time to get rid of mandatory uniforms at this school."
Evidence *What evidence (based on data) exists?*	"When asked if they would support the removal of mandatory school uniforms, 92 percent of students said yes."
Warrant *Explains how the evidence supports the claim*	"This is not simply a majority of students who support this position; it is an *overwhelming* majority."
Backing *Support for the warrant*	"Because this anti-uniform sentiment is so widespread, the time has come to take it seriously. When this many students feel this strongly about the uniform issue, the policy is overdue for reevaluation."
Rebuttal of the counterargument *Refute anticipated counterarguments*	"It is possible that the administration may challenge the validity of the survey, but please know that in an attempt to eliminate bias, it was administered to every student in the school (as opposed, for example, to only giving it to seniors). As such, it is an accurate representation of the feelings of this student body."

Having students compare the two models helps to ensure that they will include all of the essential elements of arguments when they write their papers.

Key Point 2: Teachers approach this like there is an argument when there is no argument.

When we ask students to make an argument defending the central theme found in *To Kill a Mockingbird* (Lee 1960), for example, there is not much of an argument there. In effect, the teacher has asked the question "Can you find the main theme in the novel?" and the students dutifully set off in search of evidence to support the answer to the teacher's question. This line of questioning seems artificial, especially when students know they can go to SparkNotes and immediately find an answer(s). When a student makes a claim that "It takes courage to stand up to racism" is a main theme found in *To Kill a Mockingbird*, there is no real argument there. An argument is more compelling *when there are two people actually arguing*.

It's a little thing to answer someone else's argument question; it's a big thing to initiate your own idea and craft an argument from it. This is the kind of argumentative thinking we want our students to develop.

Key Point 3: Argument doesn't start with a claim; argument starts with data.

When crafting an argument, students often begin by forming claims and then set out to find data that supports their claims (as with the aforementioned *To Kill a Mockingbird* example). Hillocks argues that this approach is backward (2011). Instead, he suggests that students should start by reading lots of data, and as they work their way through their reading, they should take note of the interesting claims that begin to emerge.

To consider how this might look in the classroom, let's look at the case of Philip Seymour Hoffman, the Academy Award-winning actor who died two weeks before I wrote this paragraph. In two weeks' time and in a number of newspaper articles, the story of Hoffman's death evolved. Here is the sequence of that evolution:

Philip Seymour Hoffman was found dead in his apartment.

News leaks that he possibly died of a heroin overdose.

Reactions from others pour in.

A video of Hoffman and two men withdrawing money from an ATM surfaces.

Police are trying to find the drug dealer(s). Possible murder charges to be filed.

Obituaries emerge.

Retrospectives of Hoffman's career appear.

Hoffman had reportedly told friends he was afraid he was going to fatally OD.

Tips surface on how to help someone who is addicted to heroin.

Hoffman had fallen out of rehab shortly before dying.

A report surfaces that Hoffman spent $1000 on drugs the night before he died.

A timeline of his final hours emerges.

Stories emerge examining the use of heroin across the country.

Questions are asked: Where is the heroin coming from? Why is its use increasing?

Four arrests are made in Hoffman's case. Identities of the suspects are not revealed.

One of the suspects had Hoffman's phone number on his cell phone.

The suspects' identities are revealed.

The suspects plead not guilty.

Autopsy results are inconclusive. Further tests pending.

News outlets get hold of and publish parts of Hoffman's diary.

Hoffman was allegedly involved in a love triangle.

Backlash over printing excerpts from his diary arises.

While reading through this stream of stories interesting questions begin to arise—questions that may eventually lead to meaningful arguments. As Hillocks notes, teachers should try "to find data sets that require some interpretation and give rise to questions. When the data are curious and do not fit preconceptions, they give rise to questions and genuine thinking. Attempts to answer these questions become hypotheses, possible future thesis statements that we may eventually write about after further investigation. That is to say, *the process of working through an argument is the process of inquiry*" (2011, xxii; emphasis in original). The approach Hillocks suggests is the opposite of the traditional approach to teaching the argument paper, where a student starts with a claim and then begins to find evidence that supports the claim. Instead, Hillocks says that students should start with inquiry. They should "swim" in issues until interesting arguments begin to emerge. For example, given the data generated by the Hoffman story, here are some arguments that emerge that might be worthy of further exploration:

Was Hoffman one of our greatest actors?

Was Hoffman's death preventable?

Do our nation's drug policies need overhaul?

Are more rehabilitation facilities needed?

Is more drug prevention work needed in our schools?

Are the "Just Say No" and Red Ribbon Week campaigns effective?

Why is heroin use increasing?

What might a person do to help a friend with an addiction problem?

Is murder an appropriate (or inappropriate) criminal charge in this case?

Is the attention to Hoffman's case out of proportion?

Do the rich and famous get preferential treatment?

Some of these questions lead to judgment arguments. Others encourage policy arguments. All of the questions were generated after swimming in data (in this case, reading the string of articles published in the days after Hoffman's death).

After I modeled the process of exploring data and then developing possible claims with my students, I had them find developing stories worthy of tracking. Here are some of the stories they tracked this year:

The debate over sanctions on Iran

The Chris Christie bridge controversy

Richard Sherman (of the Seattle Seahawks) ranting on national television

The fight over Michael Jackson's estate

Woody Allen being accused of sexual abuse by his daughter

The disappearance of Malaysia Flight 370

The abduction of 300 teenage girls in Nigeria

All of these developing stories have "legs" and can be tracked over time. Tracking them led my students to write interesting argument papers.

For students who have trouble deciding where to begin searching for interesting data, I have them start with The Learning Network, part of the *New York Times* website. On this site, Learning Network writer Michael Gonchar has posted 200 prompts for argumentative writing under the following broad categories:

Education

Technology and Social Media

Arts and Media: Music, Video Games and Literature

Gender Issues

Sports and Athletics

Politics and the Legal System

Parenting and Childhood

Health and Nutrition

Personal Character and Morality Questions

Science

Other Questions
(Gonchar 2014)

I use Gonchar's list to show my students how to generate thinking that may lead to interesting arguments. Under "Technology and Social Media," for example, one of the links is entitled "Does Technology Make Us More Alone?" When a student clicks on that link, he or she will find a YouTube video entitled "I Forgot My Phone" that follows a young woman through her day as the world ignores her because people are too engrossed in their phones. Below the YouTube link, Gonchar posts a series of questions:

- Does technology make us more alone? Do you find yourself surrounded by people who are staring at their screens instead of having face-to-face conversations? Are you ever guilty of doing that, too?
- Is our obsession with documenting everything through photographs and videos preventing us from living in the moment?
- Do you ever try to put your phone down to be more present with the people in the room?
- Do you have rules for yourself or for your friends or family about when and how you use technology in social situations? If not, do you think you should?
- Do you think smartphones will continue to intrude more into our private and social spaces, or do you think society is beginning to push back? (2014)

At the bottom of the web page there is a comments section, where readers are invited to join the argument. It is not my intention that my students pick one of the questions from Gonchar's list to argue. It is my intention that they pick one of the questions on the site as a jumping-off point to begin reading a data stream that will eventually lead them to form their own arguments. This is where their inquiry starts—inquiry that will eventually lead them to arguments that are yet undiscovered.

To illustrate to my students how starting with one link can grow into wider thinking, I create a "data tree" (see Figure 4.9).

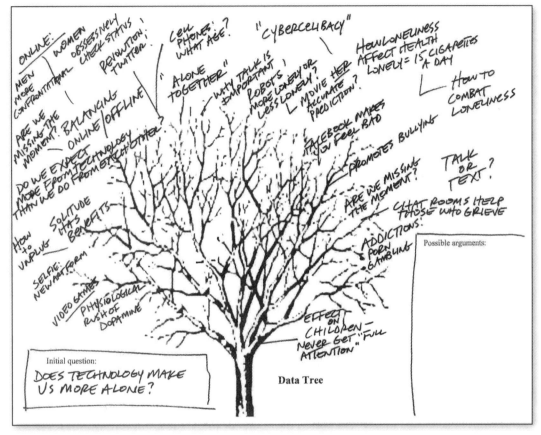

Figure 4.9 My data tree.

For the technology example, I start with the link "Does Technology Make Us More Alone?" and, starting from the article on that page, I begin to branch my searches for information outward from there. As I read through the data (in this case, a number of related articles), other ideas catch my eye, and I jot them on my data tree. Once the branches of my tree are full, I step back and consider where on the tree some arguments may emerge. For example, here are possible arguments generated by my data tree in Figure 4.9:

Technology is pulling our society apart.

Twitter is a powerful tool for democracy.

Talk is more valuable than texting.

Technology fuels addiction.

Cyberbullying deserves more attention.

It is time to unplug.

The movie *Her* is a warning we should heed.

Selfies are a new art form.

Being "alone together" is unhealthy.

Facebook contributes to narcissism.

Airlines should not allow phone calls during flight.

Solitude has its benefits.

Technology has weakened parenting skills.

Technology is creating serious health issues.

Shopping from home is not a good thing.

The robot age will be awesome.

Chat rooms have tremendous value (e.g., for people who are grieving).

I can now choose an argument that intrigues me ("Technology has weakened parenting skills"), presenting me with an area to explore in depth via further research. This process has led me to an argument I care about, which will in turn motivate me to take my writing task more seriously. Because I care, I am more likely to conduct deeper inquiry.

The key point here bears repeating: I have decided on an argument ("Technology has weakened parenting skills"), but *I didn't start with that argument in mind*. Instead, I started by reading lots of data under the umbrella of the unit of study, and it was through the reading of this data that my research question emerged. Don't have students start with a question and then go find the supporting data. Have them discover arguments through the inquiry process. In Figure 4.10, for example, you can see how Grace, an eighth-grade student, started with the question "Why do people idolize celebrities?" After swimming through data, she settles on her argument: "Celebrity worship is breaking what American culture is supposed to be about." Granted, her argument statement is a bit rough and needs revision (it is an initial draft), but Grace is now invested in doing research to support her argument.

Having students start with inquiry before they generate their arguments works in all content areas, not just in the ELA classroom. If I were a teacher of American history and my students were studying the Civil War, I would want them to read widely about the Civil War before generating their arguments. A student who, through inquiry, generates the argument that economic disparity played a more important role than slavery in causing the Civil War, and another student who, through inquiry, argues that the seeds of the Civil War can be found in the tension between states' versus federal rights, are going to write much better papers than a student who is simply assigned to respond to the following prompt: "Write an essay explaining the three causes of the Civil War."

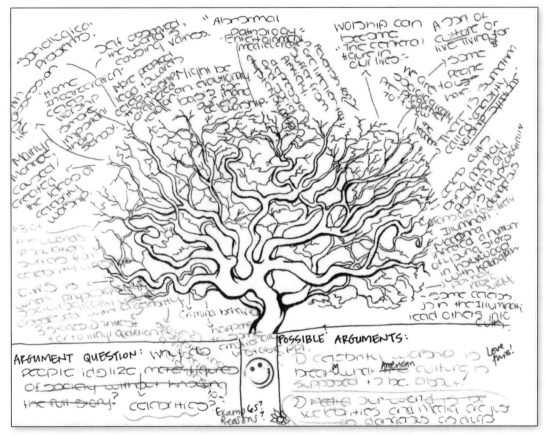

Figure 4.10 Grace's data tree

When students are taught to approach argument through inquiry, good things happen: they choose topics worthy of arguing, they gain ownership (through choice) of their writing, and their teacher is not stuck in *Groundhog Day* reading the same argument paper over and over.

Key Point 4: Effective arguments do not come packaged in five-paragraph essays.

Can you imagine living in a world where the five-paragraph essay really existed? In a five-paragraph essay world, you would turn on ESPN for some post-Super Bowl game analysis, and you would hear Chris Berman read the following off the teleprompter:

The Seattle Seahawks defeated the Denver Broncos in Super Bowl XLVIII tonight, and in this broadcast we will give you three reasons why.

The first reason the Seahawks won is because their defense shut down Payton Manning and the vaunted passing game of the Broncos. Let's look at a highlight that demonstrates this.

The second reason the Seahawks won is because they committed fewer turnovers. Let's look at a highlight that demonstrates this.

The third reason the Seahawks won is because their special teams units outplayed the special teams unit from the Broncos. Let's look at a highlight that demonstrates this.

As you can see, the Seahawks defeated the Broncos because their defense shut down Payton Manning, they committed fewer turnovers, and their special teams unit outplayed the special teams unit of the Broncos.

At this point, ESPN would cut to a Chevy truck ad. The voiceover would go as thus:

There are lots of trucks to choose from, but the Chevy Silverado is the right truck for you. In this commercial, we will tell you three reasons why.

The first reason you should buy a Chevy Silverado is that it has a new, more fuel-efficient engine. This is important because you will now get better gas mileage, which will save you some of your hard-earned cash.

The second reason you should buy a Chevy Silverado is that it has a quiet highway ride. After a hard day at work, you will want a peaceful ride home.

The third reason you should buy a Chevy Silverado is because it has generous passenger and cargo space. This truck gives you all you need to cart friends and/or cargo around.

The Chevy Silverado is the truck for you because it gets good gas mileage, it provides a quiet highway ride, and it has generous passenger and cargo space.

I hope my point is obvious by now, but in the small chance that it is not, repeat after me: *Arguments are not crafted this way!* An argument is much more than a claim followed by three reasons. Arguments that are shoehorned into five-paragraph structures are actually weakened by the artificiality of the structure itself. The lameness of the structure diverts the reader's attention from the argument itself.

As I argue in *Write Like This*, if students are going to write effective arguments, they need to see what effective arguments look like. They need models, like the following one from

Miami Herald columnist Leonard Pitts Jr. (2014). As you read it, notice the "moves" the writer makes that contribute to the effectiveness of his argument.

A few disclaimers on the 4th Amendment
By Leonard Pitts Jr.

Perhaps you've heard of the Fourth Amendment.

That's the one that guarantees freedom from unfettered government snooping, the one that says government needs probable cause and a warrant before it can search or seize your things.

That guarantee would seem to be ironclad, but we've been learning lately that it's not. Indeed, maybe we've reached the point where the Fourth ought to be marked with an asterisk and followed by disclaimers in the manner of the announcer who spends 30 seconds extolling the miracle drug and the next 30 speed-reading its dire side effects:

To wit: "Fourth Amendment not available to black and Hispanic men walking in New York, who may be stopped and frisked for no discernible reason. Fourth Amendment does not cover black or Hispanic men driving anywhere as they may be stopped on any pretext of traffic violation and searched for drugs. Fourth Amendment does not protect library patrons as the Patriot Act allows the FBI to search your library records without your knowledge. Fourth Amendment does not apply to anyone using a telephone, the Internet or email as these communications may be searched by the NSA at any time."

To those disclaimers, we now add a new one: "Fourth Amendment not effective at the U.S. border."

Just before New Year's, you see, federal Judge Edward Korman tossed out a suit stemming from something that happened to Pascal Abidor, a graduate student who holds dual French and U.S. citizenship. He was taken off an Amtrak train crossing into New York from Canada in May 2010, cuffed and detained for hours by U.S. Customs and Border Protection agents. They seized his laptop and kept it for 11 days.

It seems the computer contained photos of rallies by Hamas, the radical Islamist group, and his passport indicated travel in the Middle East. Abidor explained that he's a student of Islamic studies at McGill University and that he's researching his doctoral thesis. According to at least one news report, he's not even Muslim.

None of this moved the border agents—or the judge. He rejected the suit, brought by the ACLU, among others, on behalf of Abidor and the National Press Photographers Association, among others, on grounds the plaintiffs had no standing to bring suit because, he says, the searches are so rare there is little risk a traveler will be subjected to one.

More jarring, Korman found that even had the suit gone forward the plaintiffs would have lost on the merits.

It is permissible, he said, for border agents to seize your devices and copy your files, even without any suspicion of wrongdoing. He questioned whether people really need to carry devices containing personal or confidential material and said that dealing with a possible search of such a device is just one of the "inconveniences" a traveler faces.

As it happens, border-control officers already operate under a looser constitutional standard. They are allowed to conduct warrantless, suspicionless searches of our bodies and our bags.

But our laptops? Our iPads? These devices are repositories of financial records, health information, confidential news sources and diaries.

Are you required to surrender even the most intimate stuff of your life and work on the whim of a border agent because he or she doesn't like your looks?

Apparently, yes.

It is a sobering reminder—not simply that the law lags the innovations of the Information Age, not simply that the whole idea of privacy is shrinking like an ice cube in a tea kettle, but also that if you lard a right with too many "exceptions," that right becomes impotent.

So maybe instead of counting the places and situations where the Fourth Amendment no longer applies, we should start counting the ones where it still does.

It's getting so that might be a shorter list.

When I have students read arguments like this one, I have them do what I asked you to do—notice the moves employed by the writer to sharpen the argument being made. Here are a few moves they noticed Pitts made in this essay:

Uses intentionally short, one sentence paragraphs

Weaves in an anecdote to support the claim

Uses humor to connect with the reader

Asks rhetorical questions

Makes a claim that is implied, rather than directly stated

After we read the Pitts essay closely, I have my students read other argumentative models. Students need to know what the genre looks like before they can write in the genre (see Chapter 6 for more on the importance of modeling).

Key Point 5: Sometimes it is okay for students not to take a stand.

Once in a while, a kid will say to me, "I don't know which side of the argument to take. Both sides have good points." I am fine with that, as long as the student has demonstrated that he or she has thoughtfully read about and given careful consideration to the issue at hand. I am afraid I have been guilty in the past of forcing children to take positions on complex issues when they may not be intellectually or developmentally ready to do so. Sometimes, I have to remind myself, it is more important that a kid carefully consider both sides of an argument than take a definitive stand.

A Recap: The Common Core Anchor Writing Standards Bring Some Good News

Amid the controversy swirling around the CCSS, let's be mindful that when it comes to the teaching of writing, the anchor writing standards get the following right:

- The new Common Core standards, unlike many state standards in the NCLB era, recognize that reading and writing are interconnected. They encourage students to read like writers and to write like readers.
- Since exams of the Common Core standards value writing across the curriculum, they may drive more writing across the curriculum. This, in turn, may drive deeper thinking across the curriculum. More writing is always good for kids.
- The Common Core anchor writing standards will sharpen writing skills in the following discourses: narrative, inform and explain, and argument. These discourses all hold value long after graduation.

All of these bulleted items align nicely with our core values of teaching writing, and I hold out hope that the Common Core standards will induce more and better writing in our schools. But a careful examination of what the anchor writing standards get right illuminates the flip side as well—it raises awareness of what the new standards get wrong. And, unfortunately, when it comes to the teaching of writing, these new standards come with major shortcomings. For what they get wrong, and for how to ensure that our writing instruction stays true to our students' best interest, let's move to Chapter 5.

Where the Common Core Writing Standards Fall Short

I n Chapter 4 we focused on what the Common Core writing anchor standards get right. Let's now turn our attention to what they get wrong. Specifically, when it comes to the teaching of writing, the new standards have five key shortcomings.

Shortcoming 1: Though narrative writing is one of the genres required by the CCSS, it remains undervalued.

David Coleman, one of the authors of the CCSS, argued in his now infamous speech, that narrative writing should be deemphasized:

> Do you know the two most popular forms of writing in the American high school today? . . . It is either the exposition of a personal opinion or the presentation of a personal matter. The only problem, forgive me for saying this so bluntly, the only problem with these two forms of writing is as you grow up in this world you realize people don't really give a shit about what you feel or think. What they instead care about is can you make an argument with evidence, is there something verifiable behind what you're saying or what you think or feel that you can demonstrate to me. It is a rare working environment that someone says, "Johnson, I need a market analysis by Friday but before that I need a compelling account of your childhood." (Coleman 2011, 10)

And true to his word, Coleman and the other writers of the standards have gradually deemphasized narrative writing as students move through the K-12 system. This deemphasis emanates from the 2011 NAEP Writing Framework, which recommended that the breakdown of student writing be as follows (NGA/CCSSO 2010e, 5):

GRADE LEVEL	TO PERSUADE	TO EXPLAIN	**To Convey Experience**
4	30%	35%	**35%**
8	35%	35%	**30%**
12	40%	40%	**20%**

Consistent with these NAEP recommendations, the Common Core Standards for Language Arts now call for an "overwhelming focus of writing throughout high school to be on arguments and informative/explanatory texts" and that the distribution of writing purposes across grades "should adhere to those outlined by NAEP" (NGA/CCSSO 2010e, 5). This de-emphasis on narrative writing is a mistake. The best teachers, doctors, lawyers, salespersons, managers, nurses, CEOs, taxi drivers, scientists, football coaches, and politicians have one thing in common: the ability to connect with people through storytelling. Being able to tell a good story is not a school skill, it is a life skill, and as such, it should be given greater, not less, emphasis. If we want our students to be good storytellers, they need to read and write more narratives.

It turns out that reading and writing narrative texts is very good for you. Here are some reasons our students should be doing a lot more reading and writing of narrative texts.

Reading and Writing Narrative Texts Builds "Literary Thinking"

In Chapter 3 I discussed Judith Langer's notion that there is a unique kind of thinking that is developed when people read rich, literary works—a kind of thinking that is different than the thinking that is generated when one reads expository text. Langer (1995) argues that literary thinking is an important cognitive piece in the development of deeper thinkers. The CCSS's de-emphasis on narrative reading and writing (and, conversely, its increased emphasis on expository reading and writing) will move our students away from developing the unique thinking that is generated by reading rich literature and poetry.

Reading and Writing Narrative Texts Builds Empathy in Students

An area of psychology that has been given a lot of attention of late is the concept of "theory of mind," or ToM (Sapolsky 2013). This area of research examines a person's ability to understand the emotions, thoughts, beliefs, and intentions of others. Developmental psychologists, in trying to figure out when ToM is developed, might ask young children to consider the following story:

> Every day, Sally puts her beloved toy rabbit Stuffy on her pillow before going to preschool. One day, after Sally leaves for school, her father notices that Stuffy is quite dirty and puts him in the washing machine. He intends to then put him in the dryer, but forgets. When Sally returns from school that day, she wants to tell her friend Stuffy about her day. Where would she expect to find him? (Sapolsky 2013)

A child who "has not yet developed the skills of theory of mind will answer, 'In the washing machine.' The child knows where Stuffy is from having heard the story, and so assumes that Sally must know this too. Only when a child has developed the intuitive ability to put herself in another's shoes can she recognize that Sally would not know about the laundering, because it happened after she left for school, and so would look for Stuffy on her bed" (Sapolsky 2013).

Why are psychologists so interested in how children develop ToM? Because there is strong evidence that the development of ToM is a precursor for building empathy. The relevance of this for English teachers begins to emerge when you consider a series of experiments conducted by David Comer Kidd and Emanuele Castano (2013). Kidd and Castano began by looking at the effects that reading has in building one's empathy. More specifically, they were interested in whether different kinds of reading had equal effect on ToM, so they conducted experiments where participants were divided into groups and assigned to read in one of the following areas: literary fiction, popular fiction, or nonfiction reading. Their findings? Participants who read a lot of literary fiction performed significantly better on the ToM tests than did those assigned to read in the other experimental reading groups.

It should also be noted Kidd and Castano's studies found that it wasn't simply the reading of any fiction that fostered ToM; it was the reading of *literary* fiction. "Literary fiction" in this case is defined as recent National Book Award finalists or winners of the PEN/O'Henry awards. In other words, the participants who did the best on the ToM tests were those who were immersed in "heavy," high-quality literature. Not surprisingly, literary fiction was found to be more "writerly" and was "more likely to challenge the reader's expectations, to contain many voices and perspectives" (Sapolsky 2013). As Kidd and Castano note, "The worlds of literary fiction are replete with complicated individuals whose inner lives are rarely easily discerned but warrant exploration" (Perry 2013).

In addition, the readers of literary fiction did significantly better than participants who read popular fiction (selected from Amazon.com best sellers), and they also did significantly better than the participants who read nonfiction (works selected from *Smithsonian* magazine). Reading literary fiction, it turns out, "may be the equivalent of aerobic exercise for the parts of your brain most involved in the theory-of-mind skills" (Sapolsky 2013). This is good news for those of us who still believe in teaching the classics. Not only do our students gain cultural literacy when they read noteworthy books, but the evidence suggests that they are also building the capacity to have empathy for others.

Reading and Writing Narrative Texts Improves Students' Social Skills

Beyond developing ToM, reading narrative texts has another benefit: it can change a young reader's social skills. In his study "In the Minds of Others," Keith Oatley, professor emeritus of cognitive psychology at the University of Toronto, notes that recent research has found

> that far from being a means to escape the social world, reading stories can actually improve your social skills by helping you better understand other human beings. The process of entering imagined worlds of fiction builds empathy and improves your ability to take another person's point of view. It can even change your personality. The seemingly solitary act of holing up with a book, then, is actually an exercise in human interaction. It can hone your social brain, so that when you put your book down you may be better prepared for camaraderie, collaboration, even love. (2011, 1)

Oatley's studies dispel the stereotype that people who read a lot of fiction are isolated bookworms. In fact, he found the opposite: Readers of fiction were "less socially isolated and had more social support than people who were largely nonfiction readers" (Oatley 2011, 3). Oatley found that the reading of fiction facilitated the development of social skills because it provides the reader with the experience of thinking about other people. He notes that the "defining characteristic of fiction is not that it is made up but that it is about human, or humanlike, beings and their intentions and interactions. Reading fiction trains people in this domain, just as reading nonfiction books about, say, genetics or history builds expertise in those subject areas" (2011, 3).

In summary, Oatley (2011) found the following:

- The solitary act of holing up with a book is actually an exercise in human interaction (5).
- We internalize what a character experiences by mirroring those feelings and actions (5).
- Reading stories can fine-tune your social skills by helping you better understand other human beings (6).

- Entering imagined worlds builds empathy and improves your ability to take another person's point of view (6).
- Reading narrative may gradually alter your personality—in some cases, making you more open (6).
- Reading stories exposes readers to new experiences and helps them to become more socially aware (6).

Neil Gaiman, author of short fiction, novels, comic books, graphic novels, audio theater, and films, echoes this sentiment. When you read narrative, Gaiman argues, you recognize what happens to other people. Gaiman notes that prose fiction is "something you build up from 26 letters and a handful of punctuation marks, and you, and you alone, using your imagination, create a world and people it and look out through other eyes" (2013). When you read fiction, Gaiman adds, "You get to feel things, visit places and worlds you would never otherwise know. You learn that everyone else out there is a me, as well. You're being someone else, and when you return to your own world, you're going to be slightly changed" (2013). Both Oatley's and Gaiman's work bring me back to Judith Langer, who found that "stories provide us with ways not only to see ourselves, but also to re-create ourselves" (1995, 5).

The studies mentioned in this chapter—by Langer, by Kidd and Castano, and by Oatley—all illuminate the importance and value gained by *reading* narrative. So why am I sharing them in a chapter that argues students should be *writing* more narrative? Because to write narratives well, students first need to read and emulate strong narratives, and I can't help but believe that the mental processes that are fostered when students read narrative are in line with the mental processes students develop when they write narratives. As *Time* humorist Joel Stein writes,

> When I want my writing to improve, I read something that forces me to think about words differently: a novel, a poem, a George W. Bush speech. Sure, some nonfiction is beautifully written, and none of Jack London's novels are, but no nonfiction writer can teach you how to use language like William Faulkner or James Joyce can. Fiction also teaches you how to tell a story, which is how we express and remember nearly everything. If you can't tell a story, you will never, ever get people to wire you the funds you need to pay the fees to get your Nigerian inheritance out of the bank. (2012)

The Nigerian inheritance reference aside, it is helpful to remind ourselves that the CCSS define narrative as "real or imagined," and when students *write* their way into imaginary worlds, surely they benefit from giving careful consideration to the decisions, the relationships, and the actions of others.

When students are reading and writing narratives, they are in the process of re-creating themselves.

Shortcoming 2: The big three writing discourses are too limiting.

The good news is that the CCSS focus on three important writing genres: narrative, inform and explain, and argument. The bad news is that the CCSS focus on *only* three important writing genres. Beyond the walls of school—in the real world—other types of writing occur. Sometimes, for example, I might sit down to write a proper thank-you note to a friend. Or I might write to an apartment owner to inquire about a property. Or I might write to help me flesh out an inchoate thought. Or I might write as a means to process events that are happening in my life. And sometimes I have no defined purpose when I sit down to write, trusting that the act of writing itself will lead me to discover my purpose.

The kinds of writing we want our students to develop do not always fit neatly under the umbrella of the three big writing types pushed by the CCSS, and my concern is that teachers will become so laser-focused on teaching the "big three" types (since these will be the only three types tested) that the other types of writing—the types we utilize in the real world—will be ignored. Since the CCSS only value part of our writers' potential, I worry that only part of our students' writing potential will be developed.

Jamming young writers into these three narrowly defined writing boxes is limiting. We need to make sure our students get lots of practice through and beyond the Common Core anchor writing standards. You wouldn't limit an aspiring architect by asking her to strictly adhere to only three standardized building blueprints, would you?

Shortcoming 3: There is an artificial separation between writing discourses.

As I write this paragraph, I am a new resident of New York City, and when I moved to this neighborhood, I needed to find someone to cut my hair. To figure out where I might go, I surfed Yelp, where I came across reviews of a local hair salon, Salon Above. Here is what Linda O. thinks of this salon:

> I've been seeing Desi for more than 6 years now. She's been with me through thick and thin—literally! After losing quite a bit of weight, quite a bit of my hair fell out, but she kept me looking great through it all.
>
> The space is lovely—so tastefully decorated by the owner, Frank—and is always a calm retreat, located a floor above street level. I am always delighted to be offered a

drink when I arrive and a chocolate when I leave.

Desi is a gifted stylist who always helps me to look fabulous. She is supported by many other excellent hairstylists as well. But don't take my word for it—go in for a cut!

Reread this post and ask yourself: Which discourse does this piece of writing fall under? Is it narrative? Is it informative? Is it argument? The answer? Yes, yes, and yes. It has elements of narrative ("I've been seeing Desi for more than 6 years now . . . quite a bit of my hair fell out"). It has elements of inform and explain ("The space is lovely—so tastefully decorated by the owner, Frank—and is always a calm retreat, located a floor above street level"). And it has elements of argument ("But don't take my word for it—go in for a cut!"). This piece is not narrative. It is not informative. It is not an argument. It is all three.

In the real world, writing is not artificially separated into specific discourses. It is blended for effect. In teaching this idea to my students, I often start with the annual State of the Union address. In 2013, for example, President Obama was appealing to the nation to strengthen gun laws in the wake of the school shootings in Newtown, Connecticut. In making his point, the president shared the following story:

> Because in the two months since Newtown, more than a thousand birthdays, graduations, anniversaries have been stolen from our lives by a bullet from a gun—more than a thousand.
>
> One of those we lost was a young girl named Hadiya Pendleton. She was 15 years old. She loved Fig Newtons and lip gloss. She was a majorette. She was so good to her friends they all thought they were her best friend. Just three weeks ago, she was here, in Washington, with her classmates, performing for her country at my inauguration. And a week later, she was shot and killed in a Chicago park after school, just a mile away from my house.
>
> Hadiya's parents, Nate and Cleo, are in this chamber tonight, along with more than two dozen Americans whose lives have been torn apart by gun violence. They deserve a vote. They deserve a vote. Gabby Giffords deserves a vote. The families of Newtown deserve a vote. The families of Aurora deserve a vote. The families of Oak Creek and Tucson and Blacksburg, and the countless other communities ripped open by gun violence—they deserve a simple vote. They deserve a simple vote. (Obama 2013)

The president could have simply made an appeal to the American people to support his call to strengthen gun laws. He could have said something direct, something like, "We are becoming increasingly a violent society and it is the time to take a hard look at some of our gun laws." Instead, he chose to weave the Hadiya Pendleton story into his argument. Why? Because telling Hadiya's story makes the president's point real, and this realness connects to readers (or, in this case, listeners). It lends poignancy to his argument.

Using narrative to strengthen argument is not a strategy used exclusively by Democrats; it is a favorite technique used by both parties. Look at any president's State-of-the-Union address and you will find places where narrative has been woven into the president's argument. Why do both parties employ this strategy? Because it makes their arguments more effective.

One of the problems I encounter when I have students write argument papers is that they often begin writing without knowing much about the argument. Yes, they know a little bit about *their side* of the argument, but they rarely show evidence of deep consideration of the opposing argument. Without my guidance, they churn out shallow "X is bad and here are three reasons why" essays. To illustrate how I move my students beyond these types of papers, let me walk you through a unit where my students wrote various arguments under the umbrella topic of immigration. As you read, you will see how my students strengthened their arguments by blending narratives into them.

To prepare students, I had them read a lot about the current immigration debate. They read the president's proposal. They read the opposition's criticisms and counterproposals. They read arguments posted on both sides of the debate on ProCon.org (a good site for researching arguments). In short, they swam in the immigration debate, highlighting both sides of the argument. From this data swim, students then chose arguments that fit under the big umbrella of "immigration," and they wrote claims (in complete sentences) that captured their arguments. Here were some of their claims:

- The term "illegal aliens" is racist and should not be used.
- Military service should move someone here illegally to the front of the citizenship line.
- Building a fence along the border is a bad idea.
- Building a fence along the border is a good idea.
- Illegal immigrants take jobs away from American citizens.
- Our economy will suffer if all illegal immigrants are forced out of the country.
- If you are here illegally, you should pay to stay.
- Amnesty should be granted to illegals who have proven to be productive citizens.
- Granting amnesty rewards illegal immigration.
- Having civilian border patrols is a bad idea.
- Having civilian border patrols is a good idea.

After students created their claims, I asked them to find specific stories that supported their claims. If, for example, a student believed that military service should move an illegal immigrant to the front of the citizenship line, then she was asked to find a story about a specific immigrant that supported her assertion. The selected story could be about someone she knew personally (e.g., a relative or neighbor) or it could be someone she had never met but had found via research.

As we began to work our way through drafting and revising this paper, I adopted an "I go, then you go" approach. I wrote an argument paper alongside them, and in doing so, I modeled the steps required of them. I wanted them to outline their essays before they wrote, so I outlined my essay before I wrote. There was one problem with this approach: if I had modeled an essay about immigration, many of them would have copied my stance. To avoid this, I wrote my model essay under a different big topic. Though my topic was different, the features of my model had the same features I wanted students to emulate, especially the skill of weaving a narrative into an argument paper.

I started by picking a different topic, and I showed my students, through a graphic organizer, that I had read both sides of the issue (see Figure 5.1). I chose a controversial topic—gun policy—recognizing that a topic that invites strong opposition makes a good argumentative topic. I know some of my students (and some of you reading this) will strongly disagree with my claim that high-capacity ammunition magazines should be banned. I *want* this disagreement; that is why it is called an *argument*. Also, it should be noted that the example I am sharing with you in these pages was written with the Newtown school shootings in mind, and though I am not anti-gun ownership (my father was a police officer who often took me shooting on the range), I argue in my paper that there is really no place for private citizens to own guns that have high-capacity magazines. In my graphic organizer, I listed the main reasons behind my stance, I anticipated the counterarguments, and I thought through how I would respond to the counterarguments.

So far, this was a pretty standard way to set up an argumentative paper. The twist comes in to play at the bottom of the graphic organizer, where I consider a personal experience of someone whose story strengthens my argument. In this case, I chose the true story of Vicky Soto, a teacher who lost her life trying to protect her children during the Newtown shooting tragedy. (I recognize that writing about real victims of Newtown may be difficult for readers of this book, especially those with ties to that tragedy. I apologize for any pain this may cause, but after long and careful consideration I decided to use this anecdote in my classroom because the "realness" of the example deeply strengthens the argument—an argument also made by some of the families of the victims.)

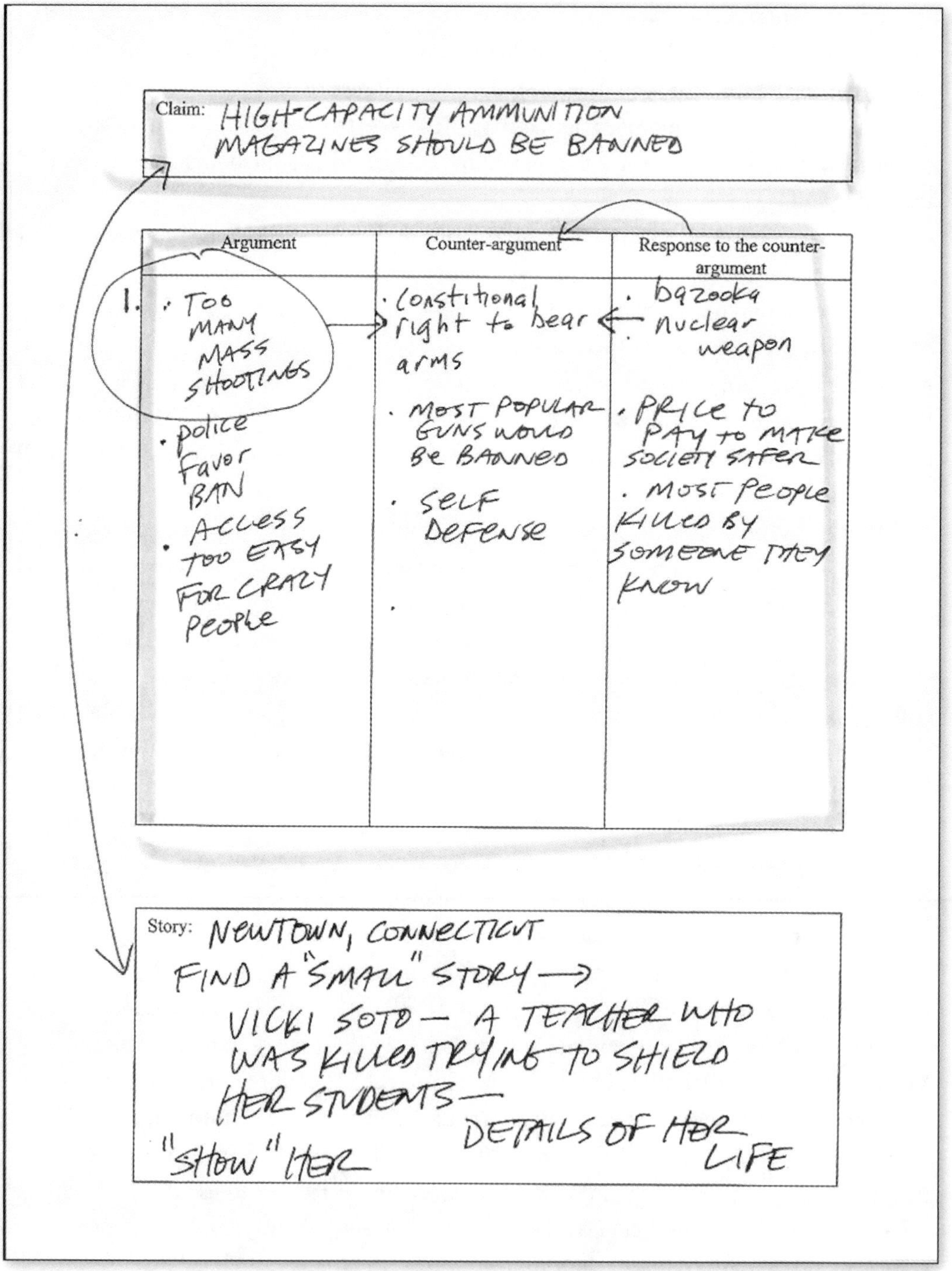

Claim: HIGH-CAPACITY AMMUNITION MAGAZINES SHOULD BE BANNED

Argument	Counter-argument	Response to the counter-argument
1. • TOO MANY MASS SHOOTINGS	• Constitional right to bear arms	• bazooka • nuclear weapon
• police favor BAN	• MOST POPULAR GUNS WOULD BE BANNED	• PRICE to PAY to MAKE SOCIETY SAFER
• Access too EASY FOR CRAZY PEOPLE	• SELF DEFENSE	• MOST PEOPLE KILLED BY SOMEONE THEY KNOW

Story: NEWTOWN, CONNECTICUT
FIND A "SMALL" STORY →
VICKI SOTO — A TEACHER WHO WAS KILLED TRYING TO SHIELD HER STUDENTS —
"SHOW" HER   DETAILS OF HER LIFE

Figure 5.1 Argument graphic organizer

After a little research, I jotted down notes of Soto's story—notes I would use to support my argument against the use of high-capacity gun magazines. My students then researched narratives that supported their claims. In Figure 5.2, you will see that Karina stated a claim—"If all immigrants were deported our economy would suffer"—and in addition to considering the points she would make and the counterarguments she would address, she chose to strengthen her argument with a story about her Uncle Miguel, who, as an undocumented worker, toils in a low-paying job.

Before we begin drafting, students will have done the following:

Made claims and gathered evidence to support their claims

Decided what the counterarguments would be and how they would respond to these counterarguments

Found narratives that strengthen their arguments

Then, and only then, is it time to draft.

To model the drafting process, I began by writing the argument section of the paper first, starting with reasons why high-capacity magazines should be banned. Here are my (rough draft) body paragraphs (counterarguments are in bold, which I explain following the draft):

High-capacity ammunition magazines should be banned for one simple reason: there have been far too many mass shootings in our country. Columbine High School. Virginia Tech University. A movie theater in Aurora. Sandy Hook Elementary School in Connecticut. **People who disagree with this ban will argue that the Constitution gives them the right to bear arms,** *but that document was written in the 1700s—long before modern weapons were made to be much more deadly. If one were to take their argument to the extreme, where does the right to bear arms end? Can we arm ourselves with bazookas? A drone? A nuclear weapon? Their argument simply does not make sense in the modern world. The level of violence in our society today was surely not anticipated by our Founding Fathers.*

Another problem with high-capacity magazines is that many people who are unbalanced can get access to these weapons at gun shows, where background checks are virtually nonexistent. **Pro-gun advocates often claim that guns are not the problem, that it's really a people problem.** *Exactly! It's crazy people who are the problem, and as such, we should not let everyone off the street to have instant access to purchasing guns. We need to build in a waiting period for all guns sold. The law needs to be toughened so that any crazy person can't walk in to a gun show and walk out with a gun (high capacity or not). No one should be able to purchase a gun without a thorough background check.*

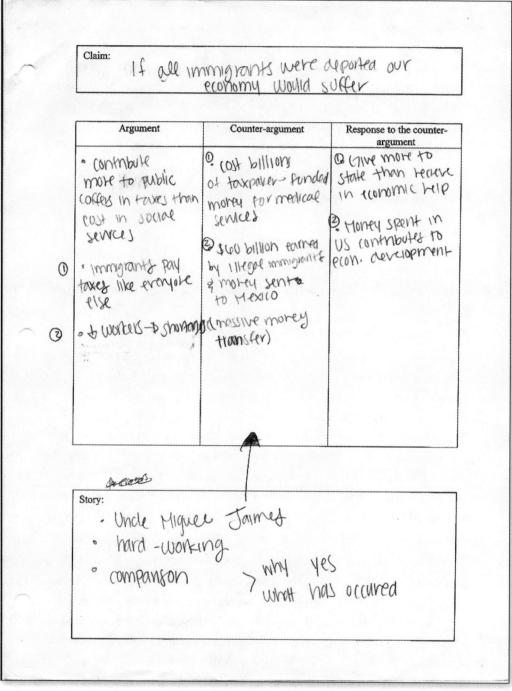

Claim: If all immigrants were deported our economy would suffer

Argument	Counter-argument	Response to the counter-argument
• contribute more to public coffers in taxes than cost in social services ① • immigrants pay taxes like everyone else ② • ↓ workers → shortage	① cost billions of taxpayer-funded money for medical services ② $60 billion earned by illegal immigrants & money sent to Mexico (massive money transfer)	① Give more to state than recieve in economic help ② Money spent in US contributes to econ. development

Story:
- Uncle Miguel Jaimes
- hard-working
- comparison   ⟩ why yes
what has occurred

Figure 5.2 Karina's argument graphic organizer

*Many prominent people support the banning of high-capacity magazines, as well. Numerous lawmakers—both democratic and republican—have come out in favor of the ban. Also supporting this movement are a large number of our nation's police chiefs, who are tired of being outgunned by criminals. Here in California, "An overwhelming 83 percent of voters support providing more money for efforts to take guns away from convicted felons; 75 percent support requiring anyone buying ammunition to first get a permit and undergo a background check, none of which is required now; and 61 percent support putting higher taxes on ammunition, with proceeds going to violence prevention programs" (Richman 2013). **Gun advocates will say that these measures are the beginning of a slippery slope, that taking some rights away from gun owners will lead to other rights being stripped.** But I agree with the voters of California, who now say it's more important to put new limited controls on gun ownership than it is to protect Americans' rights to own guns. Putting a limit on these types of high-volume weapons does not interfere with a person's right to bear arms; it's simply a sensible approach to trying to stop the next mass shooting from occurring.*

In modeling these paragraphs for my students, I wanted them to recognize that each paragraph has the following features:

- A central argument that supports my claim
- The recognition of a counterargument to my argument (which I have set in bold for my students to see)
- A response to the counterargument
- Some research to support my argument (I am not simply spouting off the top of my head)

My students then emulated this process by writing the argument sections of their papers. Elias, a sophomore, took his claim ("Deporting everyone who is here illegally is not the answer") and, after a bit of research, created a rough draft of his argument section (where you'll see that I asked him to place his counterarguments in bold):

Elias's Argument Section

*The reality of deporting illegal immigrants is an issue lawmakers must really consider. When thinking about deporting illegal immigrants, they must consider the issue of time. If the US were to deport, let's say, ten illegal immigrants a day, it would take at least three thousand years to deport every single illegal immigrant. **People might say the goal to deport all illegal immigrants can be possible if we***

deport them by the thousands a day. *This will only be possible if we deport around ten thousand immigrants each day, for a full three years. Let's say we did have the money and resources to do this, do you know how long it takes for one illegal immigrant to be deported back in a civilized way? According to the Department of Homeland Security, the process to deport a single illegal immigrant back to Mexico, can take up to eight years. Eight years! As opposed to maybe a few hours to cross the border back into the United States again.*

Another factor that we must consider with the reality of deporting illegal immigrants is that of money. According to an immigration and customs enforcement deputy, it costs the US around $12,500 to deport a single illegal immigrant. There are currently ten to eleven million illegal immigrants here; I'll let you do the math. **People might say this can be done by paying more money in taxes. But is this really a good idea?** *As of this year, the cost for deporting all of the United State's illegal immigrants would be $285,000,000,000. This money can go to more important issues such as money going towards schools, a big problem the US is facing. This money can even go to the deficit of the US which currently stands at 1.1 trillion.*

Businesses will also be affected if the deportation of all illegal immigrants were to occur. Illegal immigrants get any job that is willing to pay even the least amount of money. This makes businesses act and want to hire them. **Many people see this as a problem since they feel it takes away job opportunities and money from legal citizens.** *Many legitimate businesses have now made it almost impossible for illegal immigrants to get these jobs for a long time now making them get open to anyone who is legal. The only jobs available are going to be the ones that no one really wants to get, and illegal immigrants will still get them. All this just means legal citizens come first at job opportunities, leaving the unemployed with an excuse.*

Once the argument section of the paper was drafted, it was time to draft the narrative chosen to strengthen the argument. I went first, and it was my goal to connect my argument ("high-capacity magazines should be banned") to a victim of a high-capacity shooting spree—in this case, Vicki Soto, the teacher who heroically lost her life trying to shield her students in Newtown. After some research, I began drafting the narrative section of the essay:

Vicki Soto loved books, the Yankees, flamingos, and Roxie, her big black Labrador retriever. She also loved kids, which is why as a first-grade teacher she often spoke of her students with "such fondness and caring" (Pearce 2012).

Vicki was murdered in the Newtown massacre.

She was killed at Sandy Hook Elementary School when a deranged gunman, Adam Lanza, opened fire on students and staff with his Bushmaster AR-15 assault-type weapon, the latest in a long line of mass shootings in the United States. Vicki, who was only 27 years old, was shot and killed after hiding some of her students in a closet. According to her mother, she loved her students "more than life" (Pearce 2012).

Vicki was buried on Wednesday, as were twenty innocent children and five other adult educators—all victims of yet another madman who had easy access to a high-capacity magazine weapon.

My students then began drafting narratives that supported their arguments. To support his claim ("Deporting everyone who is here illegally is not the answer"), Elias chose to begin his essay by writing about his own family:

I have always feared the day when I.C.E (Immigration and Customs Enforcement) would show up on my doorstep looking for my family. Some days I even ran and hid under my bed when I looked outside my home window and saw what appeared to be a policeman.

I am currently fifteen and have been here in the U.S. for almost thirteen years now. I am currently illegal, but not for long. My sister and brother both have gone through the process to becoming legal here in the US. My sister has already gotten her California ID card and my brother is just waiting on his. I am actually just a few steps away from also becoming a resident of California. My mother is going to the school to get some documents she needs to send off to get back more documents to make me legal. I consider myself very lucky now of no longer having that fear of being taken away from everything and everyone I have come to know.

At this point, I had written a draft of an argument and a draft of a narrative (as had Elias and the other students). This raised a question about the essay's construction: How could the narrative be blended into the paper in a way that increased the effectiveness of the argument? There is no "correct" answer of course, so I wrestled with this decision in front of my students. Should I start with my Vicki Soto narrative as a way of leading into my gun control argument? Or should I first make my gun control argument and follow it with the Vicki Soto narrative? Which approach would be more effective? I thought aloud in front of my students, trying various combinations. Did I like it in this order? Or did I like it in that order? After trying a number of approaches, I decided to mix it up: I started with the Soto narrative, transitioned into my gun control argument, and then finished by circling back to the Newtown tragedy (see Figure 5.3 for my rough draft). Elias decided to start by writing about his family before transitioning into his immigration argument (see Figure 5.4 for Elias's rough draft). Though we took slightly different approaches, blending narrative into the mix strengthened both of our arguments.

Vicki Soto loved books, the Yankees, flamingos, and Roxie, her big black Labrador retriever. She also loved kids, which is why as a first-grade teacher she often spoke of her students with "such fondness and caring." Vicki Soto was murdered last week.

She was killed at Sandy Hook Elementary School when a deranged gunman, Adam Lanza, opened fire on students and staff with his Bushmaster AR-15 assault-type weapon, the latest in a long line of mass shootings in the United States. Vicki Soto was shot and killed after hiding some of her students in a closet.

Vicki, who was only 27 years old. According to her mother, she loved her students "more than life."

Vicki Soto was buried on Wednesday, as were twenty innocent children and five other adult educators—all victims of a crazy person with a high-capacity magazine weapon.

High capacity ammunition magazines should be banned for one simple reason: there have been far too many mass shootings in our country. Columbine High School. Virginia Tech University. A movie theater in Aurora. And the latest, Sandy Hook Elementary School in Connecticut. **People who disagree with this ban will argue that the Constitution gives them the right to bear arms,** but that document was written in the 1700s—long before modern weapons were made to be much more deadly. If one were to take their argument to the extreme, where does the right to bear arms end? Can we arm ourselves with bazookas? A drone? A nuclear weapon? Their argument simply does not make sense in the modern world. The level of violence in our society today was surely not anticipated by our Founding Fathers.

Another problem with high capacity magazines is that many people who are unbalanced can get access to these weapons at gun shows, where background checks are virtually non-existent. **Pro-gun advocates often claim that guns are not the problem, that it's really a people problem.** Exactly! It's really crazy people who are the problem, and as such, we should not let anyone off the street to have instant access to purchasing a gun. We need to build in a waiting period for all guns sold. The law needs to be toughened so that any crazy person can't walk in to a gun show and walk out with a gun (high capacity or not). No one should be able to purchase a gun without a thorough background check.

The banning of high capacity magazines is supported by many prominent people, as well. Numerous lawmakers—both democratic and republican—have come out in favor of the ban. Also supporting this movement are a large number of our nation's police chiefs, who are tired of being outgunned by criminals. Here in California, "An overwhelming 83 percent of voters support providing more money for efforts to take guns away from convicted felons; 75 percent support requiring anyone buying ammunition to first get a permit and undergo

Figure 5.3 The rough draft of my argument essay on gun control, with narrative woven in

a background check, none of which is required now; and 61 percent support putting higher taxes on ammunition, with proceeds going to violence prevention programs" (Smith). **Gun advocates will say that these measures are the beginning of a slippery slop—that taking some rights away from gun owners will lead to other rights being stripped**. But I agree with the voters of California, who now say it's more important to put new controls on gun ownership than it is to protect Americans' rights to own guns. Putting a limit on these types of high-volume weapons does not interfere with a person's right to bear arms; it's simply a sensible approach to limiting mass shooting.

Still not convinced that these weapons should be banned? Here are twenty more reasons:

> Charlotte Bacon, 6
>
> Daniel Barden, 7
>
> Olivia Engel, 6
>
> Josephine Gay, 7
>
> Dylan Hockley, 6
>
> Madeleine Hsu, 6
>
> Catherine Hubbard, 6
>
> Chase Kowalski, 7
>
> Jesse Lewis, 6
>
> Ana Marquez-Greene, 6
>
> James Mattioli, 6
>
> Grace McDonnell, 7
>
> Emilie Parker, 6
>
> Jack Pinto, 6
>
> Noah Pozner, 6
>
> Caroline Previdi, 6
>
> Jessica Rekos, 6
>
> Avielle Richman, 6
>
> Benjamin Wheeler, 6
>
> Allison Wyatt, 6

These are the names and ages of the children in Newtown who were mowed down by a high capacity weapon. Perhaps if the ban were in place, they would still be with us. And perhaps their teacher, Victoria Soto, would still be teaching.

Figure 5.3 (continued) The rough draft of my argument essay on gun control, with narrative woven in

Deportation

I have always feared the day when I.C.E would show up on my doorstep and looking for my family. Some days I even ran and hid under my bed when I looked outside my home window and saw what appeared to be a policeman uniform.

I am currently fifteen and have been here in the US for almost thirteen years now. I am currently illegal, but not for long. I am currently illegal, but not for long. My sister and brother both have gone through the process to becoming legal here in the US. My sister has already gotten her California ID card and my brother is just waiting on his. I am actually just a few steps away from also becoming a resident of California. My mother is going to the school to get some documents she needs to send off to get back more documents to make me legal. I consider myself very lucky now of no longer having that fear of being taken away from everything and everyone I have come to know.

tells a story

The reality of deporting illegal immigrants is an issue lawmakers must really consider. When thinking about deporting illegal immigrants, they must consider the issue of time. If the US were to deport, let's say, ten illegal immigrants a day, it would take at least three thousand years to deport every single illegal immigrant. People might say the goal to deport all illegal immigrants can be possible if we deport them by the thousands a day. This will only be possible if we deport around ten thousand immigrants each day, for a full three years. Let's say we did have the money and resources to do this, do you know how long it takes for one illegal immigrant to be deported back in a civilized way? According to the Department of Homeland Security the process to deport a single illegal immigrant back to Mexico, can take up to eight years. Eight years! As opposed to maybe a few hours to cross the border back into the United States again.

Another factor that we must consider with the reality of deporting illegal immigrants is that of money. According to an immigration and customs enforcement deputy, it costs the US around $12,500 to deport a single illegal immigrant. There are currently ten to eleven million illegal immigrants here; I'll let you do the math. People might say this can be done by paying more money in taxes. But is this really a good idea? As of this year, the cost for deporting all of the United State's illegal immigrants

makes an argument

Figure 5.4 The rough draft of Elias's argument essay on deportation, with personal narrative woven in

In the real world we do not artificially separate discourses; we blend them. I want my students to understand how the power of narrative can be used to strengthen an argument.

Shortcoming 4: The Common Core anchor writing standards endanger student choice.

With the adoption of the CCSS, I am concerned that the testing pressures around the big three writing types—narrative, inform and explain, and argument—will create classrooms in which the teacher, as a way to ensure students gain proficiency across the tested discourses, prescribes exactly what the students write. I am afraid that given the testing pressures, student choice will be endangered. This concern might come across as a bit hypocritical, given the fact that the previous example in this chapter illustrated a unit in which I chose the topic for my students. (The topic was immigration—though even when I choose a big topic like immigration, my students have lots of fertile ground in which to develop a variety of arguments. There is not one argument to be made under the umbrella of "immigration";

there are several possible choices.) But beyond assignments like the immigration argument paper, I am careful to make sure my students have plenty of other opportunities to self-select the topics they want to explore via writing (more on this soon).

As much as possible, I am trying to create agency in my young writers. Students who have acquired agency don't need the teacher to assign them a prompt; they are young writers who are able to independently generate writing from self-initiated ideas. They revel in choice—the very choice I am afraid will disappear in classrooms operating under the testing pressures generated by the Common Core writing standards.

One way I generate agency in my students is through the formation of writing groups, a weekly structure where students share self-generated writing. Let's take a closer look at how these groups help to develop agency in young writers.

Writing Groups as a Vehicle to Develop Agency in Young Writers

Every Thursday my students meet in their writing groups. Each group consists of five students of mixed gender and ability. All written pieces brought to the writing groups are self-generated by the students, and for each writing group meeting, students are asked to bring either a new draft or an old piece they have significantly revised. They are also asked to bring copies of their pieces for each of the other members of their groups. This means that if a student is in a group of five, she brings five copies of her piece to the discussion.

Once in the groups, each student takes a turn sharing his or her piece with the other members of the writing group. When it is a student's turn to share, he or she distributes copies of it to the other group members and, before reading it aloud to the other group members, indicates the level of response he or she would like from peers. The student asks the group to provide one of the following three levels of response (these originated years ago somewhere in the National Writing Project):

> *Bless:* When a student requests "bless," he asks for his peers to note only the things they like about the paper. Elements students might bless include diction, sentence structure, the introduction and/or the conclusion, sequencing, realistic use of dialogue, or a favorite segment of the paper. When the writer requests "bless," no criticism of the paper is allowed. All comments are positive. Hakuna matata only.

> *Address:* When a student requests "address," she is asking for peers to look at a very specific element of the paper. For example, a student might ask the others in the group to pay close attention to a particular section of the paper she is having trouble with and to offer some thinking on how to work through the difficulty. When a student asks for "address," she dictates exactly where in the paper she

would like her fellow group members to focus their feedback.

> *Press:* When a student requests "press," he is indicating to his partners that all comments are welcome. Partners can offer constructive criticism, praise, and/or suggestions. Anything goes—provided the feedback helps the writer to make the paper better.

Let's say it is Robert's turn to share his piece with his writing group. Robert distributes copies to the others in his group, and because he is a reluctant writer, he asks his partners to "bless" his paper. Once the copies are distributed, Robert reads his paper aloud to his group, who are following the reading with pencils in hand and quickly marking areas they may "bless." When Robert finishes reading, he sits silently for a couple of minutes while his partners revisit the paper, highlighting areas of strength in the paper. This is all done silently. His partners then grab precut quarter sheets of paper and write comments to Robert (based on the markings they made while Robert read the paper to them).

When each group member has had a chance to write his or her comments on individual quarter sheets of paper, the conversation phase begins. The writer remains silent while each group member—one at a time—shares his or her thinking aloud with the group. Once every member has shared thinking about the piece, Robert is then invited to talk. He can respond to one or more of the comments that came his way, or he can send the conversation in a new direction. At this point, the conversation is open—anyone can share his or her thinking. When the conversation has run its course, the partners pass their comment sheets to Robert, who then collects and staples them to his paper. If Robert wants to revisit the paper later in the year, he will have these written notes attached to his draft to jog his memory.

The group then turns its attention to the next person in the group. She distributes her paper, indicates whether she wants her paper blessed, addressed, or pressed, and the process is repeated.

When the groups meet again the following week, students bring copies of new drafts (or heavily revised) previous drafts, and the bless, address, press process begins anew.

If you are interested in setting up similar writing groups in your classroom, here are some suggestions:

- *Model how the groups work.* I cannot simply give my kids a handout that explains the process; students need to *see* the process. Last year, all senior classes participated in writing groups, so on the day the three senior English teachers introduced the idea, we gathered all of our seniors into the school's theater where we modeled the process. This means we each wrote a separate piece. We were careful to mix up genres—I wrote a poem, one of my colleagues wrote a personal narrative, and my other colleague wrote an argument. We had the students watch us as we modeled the process (one of us asked for "bless," one of us asked for "address," and one of us asked for "press"). We had the students take notes on the drafts as well, and we had them fill out quarter-sheet comments. When it came time to discuss the papers, we invited all the students in the theater to participate. This fishbowl demonstration was crucial in getting our students to understand the process.

- *Do not begin the writing groups too early in the year.* I want to make sure I get to know my students pretty well before groups are formed. I also want the writing culture of the classroom to develop before asking kids to share their writing with one another. My writing groups are usually formed around the beginning of the second quarter of the school year.

- *The teacher should select the writing groups, taking into careful consideration the makeup of each group.* I mix gender, because boys and girls often think differently. I mix ability levels as well, making sure that students have access to at least one strong writer in each group. I try to place reluctant writers with students who will be nurturing.

- *Writing groups should stay together for the remainder of the year.* Many groups start off a bit shy, but one of the beauties of writing groups is the bond that grows within them over time. At first, most students are a bit freaked out about sharing their writing with their new group members. Initially, most ask for "bless" only. But as time passes and they begin to trust one another, they start to open up. Last year, some of my groups celebrated each week by bringing small snacks for their fellow group members. By the end of the year, the groups really know one another well and are often sad to "break up."

Here are some problems I have encountered in setting up and running writing groups, and how I addressed them:

WRITING GROUP PROBLEM	HOW I ADDRESS THE PROBLEM
A group has trouble generating conversation for an entire class period.	I sit in with the group and participate alongside them. When the conversation lags, I interject a comment or question to restart the conversation. If a group finishes with a few minutes remaining, its members can take out their writer's notebooks and begin quietly drafting a new piece for the next week's meeting.
A student shows up unprepared for the group discussion.	I adopt a "three strikes, you're out" policy. For a first or second offense, I allow students to participate without bringing a piece to share (I believe they benefit from seeing others' writing, and I want the peer pressure of being part of the group to kick in). If it becomes habitual, I remove the student from the group and have him or her sit off to the side of the class where he or she will draft quietly. Usually, this is enough to get the student back on track.

WRITING GROUP PROBLEM	HOW I ADDRESS THE PROBLEM
A student is absent on writing group day.	If a student misses the writing group day but shows up the next day with a draft, I give half credit (even if the absence is excused). A student cannot receive full credit unless she participates in the group discussion, since that's where much of the value lies. This is explained to my students ahead of time.
A student keeps writing the exact same type of paper each week (for example, a student shows up with a poem every week and doesn't stretch himself into other writing discourses).	Though students can freely choose topics and discourses, they are encouraged to do so with the end-of-the-year portfolio in mind (more on the portfolio requirements later in this chapter). A student who writes a poem every week will be unprepared when it comes time to select portfolio pieces. Students are reminded of the portfolio requirements every few weeks and told that by the end of the year they should have written broadly.
A student writes way too much for the group to respond to in a short time.	Last year, I had a student, Eric, who decided that he would use writing group as a way to get feedback on the novel he was writing over the course of the year. Every time his group met, he handed each of them twenty pages to read. To streamline the discussion, I had Eric select a two-page excerpt from his weekly work for the group to bless/address/press.
A student shows up with his writing piece but doesn't have copies for his partners to track while he shares.	I teach in a low-income school, so many of my students do not have printers (or ink) at home. They can print in our media center for ten cents a page, or they can come in to my classroom before school and print for free. Yes, I run through a lot of ink and paper, but I have secured funding from various school sources to keep the printers printing.

One last question that always arises regarding writing groups: How do you score all those papers? The short answer: I don't! My goal is to get my students to write independently—to see themselves as writers who write regularly. This is much more likely to happen if I don't grade everything. Grading doesn't make my students better writers. Lots of practice coupled with meaningful feedback makes my students better writers. On writing group day I quickly move between the groups, stamping their drafts with the date. Later I give them points for every stamp they accumulate. Many of their writing group papers will never be graded. Others will be selected for and assessed in the end-of-the-year portfolio.

As stated earlier, I am afraid that the adoption of the Common Core writing standards will drive many teachers to micromanage writing topics. This is the beauty of writing groups. Kids choose their own topics.

The End-of-the-Year Portfolio Requirements

How do I ensure that my students get a good mix of writing experiences, from wide-open, student-generated to topics generated from the teacher? I start with my end-of-the-year portfolio requirements and work backward. Here, for example, are the pieces I require my students to include in their portfolios (along with brief explanations):

1. *Baseline Essay:* During the first week of school I have my students write an essay without any help from me. The purpose is to gather a writing sample that establishes a baseline of where they started the year as writers. The baseline essay is not revised in the portfolio. Students are asked to revisit the baseline essay at the end of the year to remind themselves where they were as writers at the beginning of the school year. This enables them to reflect on their growth.

2. *Myself, the Writer, Reflective Letter:* This is the most important portfolio piece. Students are asked to read through their body of work and to reflect on their year as writers. Some questions I have them consider before they draft their letters:

   - In what areas—specifically—did you grow as a writer? Can you point to these areas in this portfolio?
   - What are your favorite discourses? Least favorite? Why might that be?
   - Reflect on a struggle you faced as a writer this year. What did you learn from the struggle?
   - Discuss specific writing strategies you've used with references to specific pieces you've written.
   - Where does your writing still need improvement? How will you improve?
   - Reflect on your experiences in your writing group. What worked? What did not work? How could writing groups be improved?
   - What are your immediate and long-range goals as a writer?
   - Have you developed agency as a writer? Do you write without being asked to? Why? Why not?

3. *Best On-Demand Writing:* Over the course of the year, my students are asked to do one timed-writing per month. Students are asked to select their best on-demand writing performance. This essay is not revised for the portfolio.

4. *Best Narrative Piece:* Each student is asked to include a narrative (real or imagined). Students are encouraged to blend other discourses into their narrative

pieces. The selected piece should be revised at least one more time.

5. *Best Inform and Explain Piece:* Each student is asked to include an informative and/or an explanatory piece. Students are encouraged to blend other discourses into their inform and explain pieces. The selected piece should be revised at least one more time.

6. *Best Argument Piece:* Each student is asked to include an argument piece. Students are encouraged to blend other discourses into their argument pieces. The selected piece should be revised at least one more time.

7. *Best Poetry:* Students are asked to include samples of their best poetry.

8. *Best Article of the Week Reflection:* My students are given an article to read each week, and as part of that assignment, they write one-page weekly reflections. I have students select their best reflections, which should be revised before entering the portfolio.

9. *Best Writing from Another Class:* Each student selects a writing sample from another class and revises it before placing it in the portfolio. He or she includes a brief note explaining the context of the writing assignment and why he or she likes this piece of writing.

10. *Best One-Page Evidence of Revision:* Each student is asked to include one page where the ability to deeply revise is evident. This page should be heavily marked up—very messy—and is accompanied by a note that explains what the writer did to make this paper better.

11. *Wild Card:* Students are asked to select something they wrote inside or outside of class. Maybe it is something they wrote in their writer's notebooks but never turned in. Or it can be something more unconventional (an e-mail or tweet). It can be secretive (a poem written without anyone's knowledge). It can be anything. This is also the place where a student might submit a piece that does not fit neatly under the big three CCSS writing genres.

12. *Sentence of the Week Checklist:* If I do a mini-lesson on the proper use of semicolons, then I want to see that my students are incorporating semicolons into their writing. I provide students with a list of all the mini-lessons we did that year, and I ask them to indicate on which pages of the portfolio I will be able to find the infused skills. This list is the final piece placed inside the portfolio.

13. *Best Single Line You Wrote This Year:* Each student selects the one favorite line he or she wrote that year and places it on the back cover (facing out). It is not accompanied by anything else. It just stands there, alone, out of context.

My students spend the last two weeks of the school year working on their portfolios. I do not, however, wait until the end of the year to share the portfolio requirements with them. These requirements are given to them at the beginning of the school year, and they frequently revisit them as they write their way through the year. To help keep them on track, I give them a "Track Your Writing" chart and every time they finish a draft, they add it to the chart (see Appendix A or go to http://www.kellygallagher.org [click on "Resources" and select the "Track Your Writing" chart from the drop-down menu]). If a student is writing nothing but narratives, for example, the empty spaces in his chart tells him that that he needs to start to venture into other writing discourses.

It is also important to note that even though I am prescribing the categories to be placed in the portfolios, there is a lot of student choice built in. For example, a student might fulfill the narrative requirement of the portfolio by selecting a self-generated piece that was written for her writing group.

Shortcoming 5: The CCSS exam may actually lower the writing bar.

Because the standardized tests that assess Common Core standards use "one and done" writing activities, they may not value the deeper kind of writing we want to nurture in our students. To illustrate this concern, let's look at a sample middle school argumentative writing task as prepared by the Smarter Balanced Assessment Consortium:

Read the text and complete the task that follows it.

Cell Phones in School—Yes or No?

Cell phones are convenient and fun to have. However, there are arguments about whether or not they belong in schools. Parents, students, and teachers all have different points of view. Some say that to forbid them completely is to ignore some of the educational advantages of having cell phones in the classroom. On the other hand, cell phones can interrupt classroom activities and some uses are definitely unacceptable. Parents, students, and teachers need to think carefully about the effects of having cell phones in school.

Some of the reasons to support cell phones in school are as follows:

- Students can take pictures of class projects to e-mail or show to parents.
- Students can text-message missed assignments to friends that are absent.
- Many cell phones have calculators or Internet access that could be used for assignments.

- If students are slow to copy notes from the board, they can take pictures of the missed notes and view them later.
- During study halls, students can listen to music through cell phones.
- Parents can get in touch with their children and know where they are at all times.
- Students can contact parents in case of emergencies.

Some of the reasons to forbid cell phones in school are as follows:

- Students might send test answers to friends or use the Internet to cheat during an exam.
- Students might record teachers or other students without their knowledge. No one wants to be recorded without giving consent.
- Cell phones can interrupt classroom activities.
- Cell phones can be used to text during class as a way of passing notes and wasting time.

Based on what you read in the text, do you think cell phones should be allowed in schools? Using the lists provided in the text, write a paragraph arguing why your position is more reasonable than the opposing position. (Smarter Balanced Assessment Consortium 2014b)

Looking at this sample question, I am struck by how many factors get in the way of students actually producing good writing: (1) It is on-demand. (2) Students are handed the "argument" to be made. (3) There is no inquiry involved. (4) The reasons supporting a student's thesis are already provided. (5) Students are not required to think.

Students who answer this prompt are not being asked to craft an argument; they are being asked to spit back information that has already been spoon-fed to them. This prompt almost invites students to write in the five-paragraph format I warned against in Chapter 4. However, if we teach students how to write deeper arguments like those outlined in these chapters, they will do fine on the state tests. On the other hand, if we only teach students to write to the level of the test, they will never master the skill of argumentative writing. (The same holds true when it comes to the teaching of narrative and informational writing.) We should aim our writing instruction far above the bar posited by the exams thus far created to assess Common Core skills.

Recap: Our Core Values in the Teaching of Writing

Let's briefly revisit the strengths and weaknesses of the Common Core anchor writing standards:

COMMON CORE ANCHOR WRITING STANDARDS	
THE STRENGTHS	THE SHORTCOMINGS
1. Reading and writing are connected. 2. The new Common Core writing standards may drive more writing across the curriculum. 3. Process writing is valued. 4. Writing skills are sharpened in the following discourses: narrative, inform/explain, and argument.	1. Though narrative writing is one of the genres required by the CCSS, it remains undervalued. 2. The big three writing discourses are too limiting. 3. There is an artificial separation between writing discourses. 4. The Common Core writing standards endanger student choice. 5. The CCSS exam may actually lower the writing bar.

Teachers who adhere blindly to the new Common Core writing standards without considering their shortcomings will not be serving their students well. Let's take the best of what the new anchor writing standards have to offer while remaining mindful of their shortcomings. Most importantly, when it comes to the teaching of writing, let's make sure our core values (rather than the current standards movement) continue to drive us to do what is in the best interest of our students.

CHAPTER 6

Using Models to Elevate Our Students' Reading and Writing Abilities

I n the 1964 World Series between the New York Yankees and the St. Louis Cardinals, some of the Cardinals players noticed that Yankee outfielder Tom Tresh had a slight limp as he ran out to his position in left field.

"Does he have a bum knee?" someone asked.

"No," replied third baseman Ken Boyer. "He runs like that because that's the way (Mickey) Mantle runs" (Halberstam 1994, 323). This form of emulation amongst ballplayers is not uncommon, notes Tim McCarver, Cardinal catcher and Hall of Famer. McCarver often noticed that "young players, consciously or unconsciously, tended to take on the mannerisms of the best players of their teams" (Halberstam 1994, 323). There is no mystery as to why they did this: Aspiring young players study the superstars in hope of discovering the magic ingredients that fuel their amazing feats—from how they carry themselves to the way they swing the bat. After all, there's no better model for success than those who are successful.

It's not my job to teach my students how to play baseball, but if it were, I'd want them to run (and hit) like Mickey Mantle, too. Instead, my job is to build young readers and writers, which is why I want them to consciously and unconsciously emulate the mannerisms of the Mickey Mantles of adolescent literacy—the John Greens, the Laurie Halse Andersons, the Chris Crutchers. Providing models for emulative purposes is critical to deepening my students' ability to read and write.

Models Matter in the Teaching of Writing

To show my students the importance of models, I begin by distributing a blank sheet of paper to everyone in the class. I tell them that I am going to name an item and that I want them to draw it to the best of their abilities. When they are ready, I write "Kakapo" on the board and tell them to begin. Without fail, they ask, "What is a Kakapo?" I tell them that if they don't know what it is, they should guess what it might be and to begin drawing what they think it might look like.

Students come up with some unique creations. After some sharing (and some laughter), I show them a photograph of an actual Kakapo, which is a flightless member of the parrot family with a greenish-yellow underbelly, a broad head, a large bill, and an owl-like circular facial disk (BirdLife International 2014). Of course, their original drawings are inaccurate, so after they have looked at the photograph for a few seconds, I remove it and then give them two minutes to revise their drawings. Immediately, their drawings improve. The point of the lesson? To draw a Kakapo, one must know what a Kakapo looks like. This lesson helps them to internalize the importance of having a model at their sides.

I am not charged with teaching my students how to draw birds, but I am charged with teaching them how to read and write better. Instead of photos of Kakapos, they need lots of models of exemplary writing. If we want our students to write compelling arguments, or interesting explanatory pieces, or engaging narratives, we need to have our students read, analyze, and emulate compelling arguments, interesting explanatory pieces, and engaging narratives. Before they begin writing, they need to know what the writing task at hand looks like.

Models Help Young Writers

When it comes to the teaching of writing, effective modeling entails much more than handing students a mentor text and asking them to emulate it. It is not a "one and done" process. Rather, students benefit when they pay close attention to models before they begin drafting, they benefit when they pay close attention to models while they are drafting, and they benefit when they pay close attention to models as they begin moving their drafts into revision. Mentor texts achieve maximum effectiveness when students frequently revisit them *throughout* the writing process. Let's explore the value of modeling in each of these stages.

Modeling in the Prewriting Stage

If we want our students to write in a particular discourse, such as poetry, then we should begin by providing them with lots of poems to read. As students are swimming in poems, we must move beyond simply asking them to retell what the poems say; to maximize the effectiveness of the models, students need to be taught how to read like writers—how to notice the techniques, the moves, and the choices the poets make. Students are accustomed to being asked *what* is written, but asking them to recognize *how* the text is written is a different kind of reading than many of them are accustomed to. This shift—from *what* something says to *how* it is said—is seen in three of the ten Common Core anchor reading standards:

Craft and Structure

CCSS.ELA-Literacy.CCRA.R.4 Interpret words and phrases as they are used in a text, including determining technical, connotative, and figurative meanings, and analyze how specific word choices shape meaning or tone.

CCSS.ELA-Literacy.CCRA.R.5 Analyze the structure of texts, including how specific sentences, paragraphs, and larger portions of the text (e.g., a section, chapter, scene, or stanza) relate to each other and the whole.

CCSS.ELA-Literacy.CCRA.R.6 Assess how point of view or purpose shapes the content and style of a text.

All three of these standards ask readers to answer the same basic question: What did the writer do? To get my students to begin thinking in these terms, I start them with "Four Skinny Trees," a vignette from Sandra Cisneros's *The House on Mango Street*:

> They are the only ones who understand me. I am the only one who understands them. Four skinny trees with skinny necks and pointy elbows like mine. Four who do not belong here but are here. Four raggedy excuses planted by the city. From our room we can hear them, but Nenny just sleeps and doesn't appreciate these things.
>
> Their strength is secret. They send ferocious roots beneath the ground. They grow up and they grow down and grab the earth between their hairy toes and bite the sky with violent teeth and never quit their anger. This is how they keep.
>
> Let one forget his reason for being, they'd all droop like tulips in a glass, each with their arms around the other. Keep, keep, keep, trees say when I sleep. They teach.
>
> When I am too sad and too skinny to keep keeping, when I am a tiny thing against so many bricks, then it is I look at trees. When there is nothing left to look at on this street. Four who grew despite concrete. Four who reach and do not forget to reach. Four whose only reason is to be and be. (1991, 74)

After reading this passage, students are asked to identify the techniques employed by Cisneros. For example, I want them to recognize how she employs personification ("Four skinny trees with skinny necks and pointy elbows like mine"), how she uses similes ("they'd all droop like tulips in a glass"), how she uses intentional repetition ("Four who . . . Four who . . . Four whose . . ."), and how she stacks the end of the passage with a series of intentional fragments. I also want them to understand that she uses four skinny trees as a central metaphor for the struggle of growing up in poverty.

Having students recognize these techniques *before they begin writing* helps students adopt these techniques when they get to the drafting stage.

Modeling in the Drafting Stage

When George Lucas was making *Star Wars*, his special effects team was at a loss on how to realistically film the aerial dogfight scenes. They storyboarded them, but they found that simply drawing the scenes on paper did not help them to understand the pacing and the rhythm of the fights. Needing additional inspiration, they spliced together footage of real dogfights from World War II documentaries and copied them. Many of the dogfight scenes shown in *Star Wars* are frame-by-frame replicas of actual war footage.

This *Star Wars* anecdote reminds me of the first time I was asked to write a grant proposal. I was feeling very unsure of myself, understandable given the fact that my bosses were counting on me to write something I didn't know how to write. Can you guess what I did next? (Anyone who has written a grant proposal knows where I am going with this anecdote.) I found a previously successful grant proposal and studied it, paying close attention to its structure, syntax, and tone. Like the *Star Wars* special effects team, I found a strong model and I emulated it.

Today, when my students sit down to write, they also benefit greatly when they have exemplary models to read, analyze, and emulate—models to guide them *as they are drafting*. These models should not come solely from professional writers; students also benefit greatly from studying models produced from the best writer in the classroom—the teacher. I am not suggesting that we should make students sit still while the teacher drafts an entire essay in front of the class; I am suggesting that the teacher write in short five- to seven-minutes blasts in front of students, thinking out loud while composing, and that this kind of modeling be done frequently. For those who are reluctant to write in front of their students for fear that they may be revealed as mortal, remember that students benefit greatly by seeing the teacher struggle. It reinforces a central lesson: that for all writers, even for the teacher, struggle is a central part of the writing process. It's what writers do.

Mentor Sentences

While my students are in the drafting process, I conduct a number of mini-lessons designed to get them to emulate at the sentence level. I give them a group of sentences that all have something in common, and I ask them what they notice. For example, I might give them the following mentor sentences:

"I want to go," she said, "but I don't have any money."

"If you think I am happy," John yelled, "you are wrong!"

"I bought tickets for the game," he said, "for I am a huge fan."

There are a number of things I want my students to notice about these sentences:

- They all contain quotations.
- They all have middle attribution.
- When a quotation is interrupted by middle attribution, it has to be closed before the attribution, and it has to be reopened after the attribution.
- Because the quotation is not completed, the first word after the attribution is not capitalized. (There is an exception to this rule when the first word after the attribution is a proper noun.)
- End marks go inside any closing quotation mark.
- When you have an exclamation point (or a question mark) as an end mark, it takes the place of a period. You do not need both.

I don't give this list to my students. I have them generate it from paying close attention to the mentor sentences. When students notice the construction behind good sentences, they construct good sentences. So how do I choose the mentor sentences that I want them to emulate? I read their papers and look for patterns of weaknesses. For example, if I notice an overabundance of simple sentences, I will have them study mentor sentences that infuse dependent clauses. Sometimes I select sentences for them to study because they need to learn a specific punctuation rule (e.g., they misplace the commas when using middle attribution quotations). Other times I select sentences to try to amp up the craft of their papers, as I did when I brought them this whopper of a sentence from Donna Tartt's *The Goldfinch*, where the author describes the frenzy of living in the New York City rat race:

> People gambled and golfed and planted gardens and traded stocks and had sex and bought new cars and practiced yoga and worked and prayed and redecorated their homes and got worked up over the news and fussed over their children and gossiped about their neighbors and pored over restaurant reviews and supported political candidates and attended the U.S. Open and dined and traveled and distracted themselves with all kinds of gadgets and devices, flooding themselves incessantly with information and texts and communication and entertainment from every direction to try to make themselves forget it: where we were, what we were. (2013, 477)

My students examine the construction of this sentence, discussing how the intentional run-on reinforces the pressures of daily living. They then imitate the sentence as they write about the pressures of school. Here is Shaniah's sentence:

> Students press their alarm clocks and roll out of bed and get ready for school and wait a long time for the train and arrive to school late and get lectured by the attendance lady for their tardiness and read lots of long novels and study SAT vocab and wrestle with chemistry formulas and tackle pre-calculus problems and annotate primary source Civil War documents and work their way through a 6.5 hour day and meet with teachers and have mountains of homework and get report cards and get yelled at by parents and go to study halls and take numerous tests and stress over their grades and sacrifice sleep just to get to this finish line we call graduation.

Language traditionalists may be shocked that I am using a run-on sentence for emulation purposes, but I believe it is okay to break the rules if there is intentional thinking behind breaking the rules (an argument put forth in Edgar Schuster's [2003] *Breaking the Rules*). Shaniah's intent here, of course, is to illustrate the rat race of high school, and breaking the rules adds power to her intent. As Shaniah's sentence shows, having students emulate mentor sentences is the first step in elevating their writing.

Beyond the Mentor Sentence

From the mentor sentence level, I first move students to chunks of writing before moving into more developed pieces. I start by having them write 100-word stories, an idea taken from the website www.100wordstory.org. As the title of the website indicates, the stories are exactly 100 words. I write mine first in front of the students, sharing my thinking, adding a bit here and subtracting a bit there to shape it into exactly 100 words:

> Sitting on the uptown 3 on my way to school. Different walks of life on the train: Mr. Yankees fan quietly lamenting his team's elimination from the playoffs. A mom herding her three sleepy kids to school. The homeless man bundled and huddled in the corner. A young couple lost in each other. A teenager, with ear buds in place, singing loudly. A woman lost in playing Candy Crush. A war vet walking through asking the passengers for money. An angry man is glaring at me from across the car. Twenty-three strangers in my subway car. Some coming, some going.

My students then follow. Here is Jocelyn's draft:

> Look in front of you and what do you see? A crush? A dream? What about what you don't see? The valuable things that are staring back at you, but you don't notice. The best friend who wants something more. The sister who has always been

beside you. The mother who left, but will always love you. We keep our eyes ahead and don't realize who is standing next to us. In that way, we are all farsighted. We constantly stick our hands out for more but don't take the time to realize what we already hold in our hands.

From 100-word passages, you might move your students into drafting 100-word poems. I use Neil Gaiman's "A Hundred Words to Talk of Death" as a mentor text:

A Hundred Words to Talk of Death

By Neil Gaiman

A hundred words to talk of death?
At once too much and not enough.
My plans beyond that final breath
are currently a little rough.

The dying thing comes on so slow:
reluctance to get out of bed
is magnified each day and so
transmuted into dead.

I dream of dying all alone,
nobody there to watch me pass
nothing remains for me to own,
no breath remains to fog the glass.

And when I do put down my pen
My memories will fly like birds.
When I am done, when I am dead,
and finished with my hundred words. (2009)

From practicing 100-word stories and 100-word poems, we transition to emulating other mentor passages, like this one culled from *Of Mice and Men*, where John Steinbeck describes the men's living quarters:

The bunk house was a long, rectangular building inside, the walls whitewashed and the floor unpainted. In three walls there were small, square windows, and in the fourth, a solid door with a wooden latch. Against the walls were eight bunks, five of them made up with blankets and the other three showing their burlap ticking. Over each bunk there was nailed an apple box with the opening forward so that it made two shelves for the personal belongings of the occupant of the bunk. And these shelves were loaded with little articles, soap and talcum powder, razors, and those Western magazines ranch men love to read and scoff at and secretly believe. And there were medicines on the shelves, and little vials, combs; and from nails on the box sides, a few neckties. Near one wall there was a black cast-iron stove, its stovepipe going straight up through the ceiling. In the middle of the room stood a big square table littered with playing cards, and around it were grouped boxes for the players to sit on. (1993, 17)

My students then imitate the passage. Here is Eduardo's description of the subway train he takes to school every morning:

The #6 trains are rectangular cars linked together, making a silver metal sausage, with the decal number 6 on the side rectangular windows of the cars. Inside, the baby blue seats line both sides of the car, above a black and white speckled floor. People sit opposite each other, sleeping, gazing off into space, or silently wondering about the lives and problems of their fellow passengers. Metal poles are strategically placed through the middle of the car, giving standing passengers a place to grab. Above the seats hang advertisements for sleazy lawyers or television shows, many of which are inappropriate for the youngsters on the train. After repeated stops, the car fills, becoming so crowded that the floors and windows are no longer visible.

As the year progresses, I move students into more challenging writing tasks. For the last ten years, for example, my seniors have written historical investigations into the events of September 11. Some of these students have never written a three-page paper, but last year the papers averaged twenty-five pages in length. How did I move my young writers into writing such in-depth pieces? I employed numerous strategies, but perhaps the most effective was allowing them to study exemplary papers from previous years. Holding models in their hands helped them to discover the appropriate voice. It taught them how to properly imbed research. It showed them what a works cited page looks like. Seeing how previous examples were structured was invaluable in enabling them to take on such an arduous writing task. Before they could do it, they had to know what it looked like, and as they were writing, they benefitted greatly from studying models placed at their sides.

Mentor texts help elevate inexperienced writers, of course, but they are also effective in improving the writing of our best young writers. Consider, for example, how you might prepare your students to answer this advanced placement prompt:

A bildungsroman, or coming-of-age novel, recounts the psychological or moral development of its protagonist from youth to maturity, when this character recognizes his or her place in the world. Select a single pivotal moment in the psychological or moral development of the protagonist of a bildungsroman. Then write a well-organized essay that analyzes how that single moment shapes the meaning of the work as a whole. (College Board 2013, 4)

The best AP teachers I know prepare their students for rigorous questions like these by having them analyze previously scored essays. The College Board, who creates these prompts and scores the responses, also understands the importance of models, which is why they post examples of high, middle, and low student essays on their website for teachers and students to study. The College Board knows that even our best writers benefit when they stand next to exemplary writing and analyze what makes it good.

While I have argued in this chapter that modeling plays a key role in deepening our students' ability to write, teachers need to keep in mind two caveats:

Caveat 1: Do not over-model. Too much of anything can be a bad thing; this is true with modeling as well. If I write for too long in front of my students, they will turn off. I have found five to seven minutes to be about the right amount of time before their interest begins to wane. Other times I will simply cut to the chase by handing them a model I have written (as opposed to creating it in front of them). If they are examining someone else's writing—a mentor text—we can go a bit longer (perhaps twelve to fifteen minutes). When modeling, too much can be counterproductive. There is a tipping point.

Caveat 2: Recognize the balance between the benefits of modeling and the danger of developing dependency. Sometimes I do not provide my students with a model because I want them to wrestle with creating drafts on their own. Other times I will wait until after they have written first drafts before presenting them with a model (which is often the case after they have completed an on-demand writing). The model then helps to drive meaningful revision of an existing draft. Though I believe strongly in the value of models, sometimes I want my students to experience the blank page. I want to avoid building young writers who get to a place where they always wait for me to hand them a model before they can get started. I am constantly searching for the right balance between using models to help them get started and asking them to develop independence by writing from scratch.

Modeling in the Revision Stage

One of my favorite strategies to spur meaningful revision is to have my students compare two different drafts and then ask them which of the two is better. Following are two drafts

I wrote about the day I learned my father had died. I gave both drafts to a group of eighth-grade students and asked them to determine which draft is better. I now invite you to do the same. Which one is better, Draft A or Draft B?

DRAFT A	DRAFT B
The day that changed my life was the day my father died.	A tiny blinking red light changed my life.
My father, Big Jim, and his wife, Sylvia, were home that fateful Saturday, preparing to meet some friends for dinner. Before leaving the house, however, my dad decided he needed to water a couple of plants in his greenhouse. He told Sylvia he would be right back. When he did not return, she grew worried and stepped outside to check on him.	It had sat there blinking for a couple of hours before being noticed. Flashing. Daring someone to pay attention to it. Daring someone to push it.
She found him slumped over in the greenhouse. She hurriedly ran and called 911. When the paramedics arrived, they told her there was nothing to be done. He had passed away. In a panic, she called my house, but I wasn't home. She got my voicemail and that is where she left the message that my father had died (she was in shock and doesn't remember leaving the message).	While it sat there flashing, I went on as if life was normal. I swept the leaves off the back patio. I threw the ball to my dog, Scout. I relaxed, reading my *New Yorker* in the backyard, continuing my "normal" Saturday, oblivious to the little red light flashing a few feet away from me.
I came home shortly after she left the message. Unfortunately, I did not see the red light flashing on the answering machine. I went on with my day like it was any other day. A couple of hours went by before my daughter noticed the blinking red light. She was the one who pushed the button. She was the one who first heard the terrible news. She then yelled for me to come into the house.	As it turns out, I would not be the one to discover the little red flashing light. My daughter, who was home visiting for the day, saw it first. It was my daughter who pushed "play" on the telephone answering machine, and it was she who was the first to hear the fateful words: "Kelly, I have terrible news. We lost your father today . . ." It was my daughter's horrific screams that brought me rushing into the house.
That happened fifteen months ago. Since then, I have changed a lot. I've always . . .	My father, Big Jim, had died.
	He and his wife, Sylvia, had been getting ready to meet some friends for dinner, but before leaving he stepped out to tend to his greenhouse. "I'll be just a minute," he told her. "I need to water some plants." His last words.
	When he did not return as expected, Sylvia ventured out to the greenhouse to check on him, finding him slumped over his workbench. She rushed to the phone and dialed 911. Hanging up in a panic, she then called my house, only to find my voicemail. In her shock, she left the horrible news on the answering machine where it sat undetected for a couple of hours. A bomb waiting to be detonated.
	Fifteen months have passed since that fateful day, and looking back I recognize a change that has come over me. I . . .

Which one did you pick? Most of my students chose Draft B as the better draft. In Draft A, I wrote the narrative much like a typical student, straightforward, in sequence, and devoid of many of the craft moves we'd want our students to make. (Note the typical student-written introduction: "The day that changed my life was the day my father died.") In Draft B I revised, infusing many of the craft moves we want students to adopt. (Note how the introduction in Draft B teases the reader: "A tiny blinking red light changed my life.")

I ask my students which draft they like better, and once they have chosen, I ask them to return to the chosen draft and identify what makes it better. They do this by physically circling the parts that make it a better piece of writing. Once they've circled these moves made by the writer, I have students label them. In Figure 6.1, you will see what Grace identified as the parts she felt were better. One (of many) move Grace noted is that the sequence in Draft B was different. As Grace writes at the bottom of her notes, Draft B is "kind of like 'Criminal Minds' (TV show.) You reveal the moment and then flashback . . ." Recognizing this move, Grace immediately went back to her first draft and started experimenting with rearranging its sequence. Other students suggested that the dialogue found in Draft B made it a better piece of writing; many of these same students then returned to their drafts and added dialogue.

The effectiveness of the "Which Draft Is Better?" strategy is not limited to narrative writing. I use it in other contexts, as I did recently when working with students in an eighth-grade history class. They were studying post-Civil War Reconstruction, and the students were given a number of primary source documents outlining the emergence of the Ku Klux Klan. Each student was asked to read through the various documents, to make a claim about the KKK, and to support his or her claim.

Students turned in woefully underdeveloped drafts. Here, for example, is what Lassan wrote (unedited) in his first draft:

> *The Ku Klux Klan were a group of people who hated Negroes. They lynched, bombed, and burned many blacks. Abram Colby is a perfect example. He was beat for 3 hours in the woods and left for dead. This clearly shows how much the Ku Klux Klan hated blacks.*

This is not the introduction to Lassan's first draft; this is his *entire* first draft. To help him improve his first draft, I had him undergo the "Which Draft Is Better?" exercise with the following passages (written by me):

Which draft is better?

A	B
The day that changed my life was the day my father died. My father, Big Jim, and his wife, Sylvia, were home that fateful Saturday, preparing to meet some friends for dinner. Before leaving the house, however, my dad decided he needed to water a couple of plants in his greenhouse. He told Sylvia he would be right back. When he did not return, she grew worried and stepped outside to check on him. She found him slumped over in the greenhouse. She hurriedly ran and called 911. When the paramedics arrived, they told her there was nothing to be done. He had passed away. In a panic, she called my house, but I wasn't home. She got my voicemail and that is where she left the message that my father had died (she was in shock and doesn't remember leaving the message). I came home shortly after she left the message. Unfortunately, I did not see the red light flashing on the answering machine. I went on with my day like it was any other day. A couple of hours went by before my daughter noticed the blinking red light. She was the one who pushed the button. She was the one who first heard the terrible news. She then yelled for me to come into the house. That happened fifteen months ago. Since then, I have changed a lot. I've always…	A tiny blinking red light changed my life. It had sat there blinking for a couple of hours before being noticed. Flashing. Daring someone to pay attention to it. Daring someone to push it. While it sat there flashing, I went on as if life was normal. I swept the leaves off the back patio. I threw the ball to my dog, Scout. I relaxed, reading my *New Yorker* in the backyard, continuing my "normal" Saturday, oblivious to the little red light flashing a few feet away from me. As it turns out, I would not be the one to discover the little red flashing light. My daughter, who was home visiting for the day, saw it first. It was my daughter who pushed "play" on the telephone answering machine, and it was she who was the first to hear the fateful words: "Kelly, I have terrible news. We lost your father today…" It was my daughter's horrific screams that brought me rushing into the house. My father, Big Jim, had died. He and his wife, Sylvia, had been getting ready to meet some friends for dinner, but before leaving he stepped out to tend to his greenhouse. "I'll be just a minute," he told her. "I need to water some plants." His last words. When he did not return as expected, Sylvia ventured out to the greenhouse to check on him, finding him slumped over his workbench. She rushed to the phone and dialed 911. Hanging up in a panic, she then called my house, only to find my voicemail. In her shock, she left the horrible news on the answering machine where it sat undetected for a couple of hours. A bomb waiting to be detonated. Fifteen months have passed since that fateful day, and looking back I recognize a change that has come over me. I…

[Handwritten annotations on draft B:] Builds suspense — Flashing. Daring — Intentional repetition. Fragmenting. Not normal (Irony). Use of dialogue gives it more impact. Create focus. Dialogue use. Organized better.

[Handwritten annotations on draft A:] More vivid. Fragment. Better wording.

*Kind of like 'Criminal Minds' (Tv show.) you reveal the moment and then flashback · ex. reverse.

Figure 6.1 Grace's "Which Draft Is Better?" chart

DRAFT A	DRAFT B
The Ku Klux Klan were a group of ex-slave owners who did not believe in change or at least free African Americans. They went around burning free African Americans' houses. In the Abram Colby case, members of the Ku Klux Klan dragged Colby out of his house (in front of his wife and daughter) into the woods and beat him for more than three hours.	In the Reconstruction Era, the Ku Klux Klan was allowed to gather too much power.

Draft B (continued):

One needs to look no farther than the case of Abram Colby to see this abuse of power. Colby, a former slave and member of the Georgia legislature, was beaten savagely in 1869 in an attempt to scare him away from politics. Colby recalls the horrors of the day the Klan came to get him:

"The Klansmen broke my door open, took me out of bed, took me to the woods and whipped me three hours or more and left me for dead . . . they set in and whipped me a thousand licks more, with sticks and straps that had buckles on the end of them."

It is a myth that the Klan was made up of a small group of renegades. How, then, was the Klan able to gather too much power? According to Eric Fomer, "Most of the leaders of the Klan were respectable members of their communities, business leaders, farmers, ministers . . . it became very clear that they were respectable people, so to speak. And all that comes out in the hearings and trials. It really puts a face on Klan activity, and you see the victimization and the terrible injustice that have been suffered."

And this explains why the Klan was able to gain and keep so much power. Many Klan members were made up of "Southern white aristocrats who had owned slaves for generations." These leaders believed that black people could not be equal to whites, and since they had the power, they ensured that this injustice continued. African Americans often couldn't turn to their town leaders for help because often it was their town leaders who were in the Klan.

The story of Abram Colby, and others like him, raises some troubling questions: How could the nation stand by and allow the Klan to gain so much power? Why did it take the federal government so long to fight the Klan? Whatever the answers may be, one thing is clear: the KKK was allowed to gain too much power, and they were allowed to keep it too long.

Lassan read the two drafts, determined that Draft B was better, and identified the moves that I made as a writer. Amongst the moves he noticed, for example, is that Draft B started with a direct claim and that later in the draft a number of primary sources were cited.

Of course there is a danger in modeling the same piece I want the students to do, for they will be inclined to simply copy what I have done. To prevent this, I collected my "Which Draft Is Better?" model from Lassan and his classmates (after they recognized the craft moves), and replaced it with a different model. The new model made many of the same craft moves as the KKK draft, but focused on an entirely different historical event (the events of 9/11):

DRAFT A	DRAFT B
On September 11, 2001, nineteen terrorists hijacked four airplanes and flew them into American targets. Two crashed into the World Trade Center in New York, one crashed into the Pentagon in Virginia, and one crashed into a field in Pennsylvania. When it was all said and done, 2,996 Americans lost their lives on that tragic day.	The events of 9/11 could have been avoided, if only our government had paid more attention to the warning signs. Everyone knows the basics of the day: nineteen terrorists hijacked four airplanes and flew them into American targets. Two crashed into the World Trade Center in New York, one crashed into the Pentagon in Virginia, and one crashed into a field in Pennsylvania. When it was all said and done, 2,996 Americans lost their lives on that tragic day. "The day was avoidable," says Joe Smith. "The FBI had been warned by one of their agents that a number of suspicious men were taking flight training classes in Florida. He even wrote a report warning his superiors of the plot, but somehow that report was not acted on. The FBI dropped the ball on this one" (Smith 112). It is a myth that . . .

It should be noted that Draft B is not historically accurate (I made up the quotation for demonstrative purposes, and I informed my students as such). I simply wanted the students to note that the model started with a straight claim and that citing a primary source supported the claim. Once students recognized these moves, I had them revise the first drafts of their KKK pieces. With the 9/11 example in his hand, note the difference Lassan made between his two drafts:

LASSAN'S DRAFT *BEFORE* THE MODELING	LASSAN'S DRAFT *AFTER* THE MODELING
The Ku Klux Klan were a group of people who hated Negroes. They lynched, bombed, and burned many blacks. Abram Colby is a perfect example. He was beat for 3 hours in the woods and left for dead. This clearly shows how much the Ku Klux Klan hated blacks.	During the Reconstruction Era, the Ku Klux Klan wanted power. Violence became the way they gained this power.
	The Ku Klux Klan, also known as the Klan or the "Hooded Order," was a group who directed hatred towards blacks. They often beat blacks to show their power. This terrorist organization in the United States tried to get white supremacy and hatred towards blacks legalized. Abram Colby, a famous victim, is a perfect example of pain the Klan caused:
	"On the 29th of October, 1869," Colby stated, "they broke my door open, took me out of the bed and whipped me for three hours . . . they said to me, 'Do you think you will ever vote for another damned Radical Ticket?'"
	It is crazy that the Klan could almost kill another human being because of who he voted for. The KKK were clearly heartless attackers who would do whatever it took to maintain their power and to keep blacks down. They tried to control the vote by beating people who would not vote in their favor.
	Some people argued back then that the KKK did not have bad intentions. If that is true, why did they base their entire organization on public violence against blacks as intimidation? How do you explain former confederate Brigadier General George Gordon, who developed a dogma that said the world should be based off the white man's beliefs? He believed the world should follow a "white man's government."
	KKK members during Reconstruction were often rich men from the South. They had no real reason to hate the blacks, unless there was a personal issue. So, why the hatred toward blacks? Why did they burn black churches and schools without a legitimate reason? Why did our government stand by when this was happening, why didn't it get more involved? Will this organization gain power again and start another era of hatred towards blacks?
	Anything may occur, but one thing is known: the KKK used violence to gain power in the Reconstruction Era.

Lassan's second draft is certainly not polished—it still needs a lot of work—but his revised version starts with a much clearer claim, it has much more detail, it is supported by two primary sources, it has a recognizable conclusion, and it contains other craft moves taken from the 9/11 model (for example, he uses a series of rhetorical questions).

In both of these examples—the writing of a narrative in an English class and the writing of an analysis about the emergence of the KKK in a history class—the students' writing was elevated through their ability to *read* closely.

The ability to read like a writer also proved beneficial to Yolanda, an inexperienced seventh-grade writer, who in her English class was drafting a narrative about being stood up by a boy at a dance. After comparing two mentor drafts, she changed her introduction:

YOLANDA'S FIRST-DRAFT INTRODUCTION	YOLANDA'S SECOND-DRAFT INTRODUCTION
I was in summer camp and there was a dance that was happening tomorrow night. I decided to ask my first crush, who was Australian. His name was Vincent and we were friends since the second day of camp.	Where is Vincent? Did he forget? Did he change his mind? Standing alone in a ravishing dress, I am shocked, feeling a heat wave come across my face. Where is that boy?

When I conferred with Yolanda, I told her that I really liked her line, "Where is that boy?" She responded with a confession. She said, "I stole it from a book called *That Boy* by Jillian Dodd (2012). I read it in a scene where two people were trying to find each other in a crowded restaurant. I liked it."

The work of the students shared in this chapter reminds us that the act of reading well leads to the act of writing well.

The Importance of Modeling in the Teaching of Reading

Thus far I have described the importance of modeling in building young writers. Let's now turn our attention to the value modeling holds when building young readers. The modeling I provide in hopes of making my students better readers springs from one simple question: What do I want my students to be able to do as readers? In short, I want my students to do these things:

Read for enjoyment

Read widely

Know what readers do when they are confused

Track their thinking over the course of a book

Be able to read between the lines—to infer

Be able to meaningfully discuss their reading

Think about their reading via writing

Develop agency as readers, thus reducing their dependence on the teacher

Consider their reading in the context of their worlds

Let's look at each of these goals, taking a moment to consider how modeling helps students achieve them.

I want students to read for enjoyment.

Since the Common Core anchor reading standards virtually ignore recreational reading, I am concerned that students will lose opportunities to read for enjoyment. And students who are not given a chance to read for enjoyment are much more likely to become adults who do not read for enjoyment. Don Holdoway, the respected New Zealand educator and father of shared reading, once noted in a talk at a conference that there is a lot of "criminal print starvation" going on in our schools. Holdoway's comment reminds us that Priority 1 is to make sure our students have ample opportunities to read good books, and to ensure that this happens, I strongly suggest beginning with three steps:

1. Build an extensive classroom library.
2. Build an extensive classroom library.
3. Build an extensive classroom library.

I can't model that reading is fun unless my students are surrounded by books that are fun to read. I want most of the reading my students do this year to be self-selected and high interest in nature (more about this in Chapter 8), and access to lots of good books is where achieving this goal starts.

I want students to read widely.

You have to know stuff to read stuff. To demonstrate this to my students, I bring in covers from the *New Yorker* and ask them if they can explain the covers to me. Most cannot do so. Take the cover shown in Figure 6.2, for example. To understand this cover, a reader would have to know all of the following:

- The winter Olympic games were held in Russia.
- Vladimir Putin is the president of Russia.

- The government of Russia is homophobic.
- Russia's homophobia stirred a lot of controversy.
- Male figure skaters are often stereotypically associated with being gay.

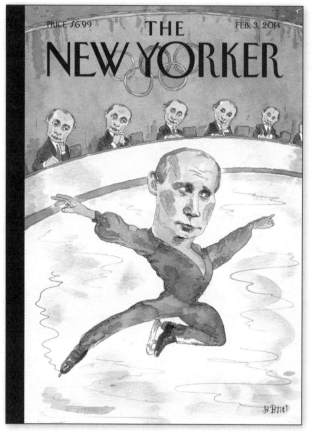

Figure 6.2 The *New Yorker's* satirical take on the Sochi Olympics

That is a lot to bring to the page before the reader can reach understanding (and this is *before the magazine is even opened*). If the reader comes to this cover not knowing who Putin is, or not knowing that Russia had passed antigay laws, it doesn't matter what reading strategies he or she possesses. The game is already over. Rereading, or visualizing, or slowing the reading pace will not help. Reading is more than simply having the right reading tools on the reader's tool belt. Readers have to know stuff to read stuff.

Which brings me back to a seventh-grade reading class I was working in last year, where I was struck by the barrenness of the students' background knowledge. While conferring with a student, for example, I was asked if China was part of the United States. In the very next conference, a different student asked me if I knew the name of the president of Utah. (These questions came from *middle school* students, mind you.) Recognizing that these students needed to immediately broaden their reading, we set aside a day each week for students to read *Upfront* magazine, a weekly current events magazine jointly published by Scholastic and the *New York Times*. *Upfront* is an excellent tool to help students broaden their knowledge of the world. It helps students learn about what is happening in the world, which, in turn, deepens their ability to read widely. If we don't build prior knowledge, deeper reading will not occur. (Information about *Upfront* can be found at http://www.upfront.scholastic.com.)

Beyond *Upfront*, I model to my students that wide reading is important by reading widely myself and by consistently sharing what I am reading with my classes. Every day, I begin each class period by reading something to my students—a poem, a newspaper article, a blog, a passage from a novel or a work of nonfiction—something to show my students the value and the fun that comes from reading widely. I also build in time so that my students can share what they are reading with one another.

I want students to know what readers do when they are confused.

When reading gets hard, experienced readers become active. The first thing they do is monitor exactly where the confusion arises (you can't fix your comprehension unless you are aware of the exact spot where it falters). Once they identify the confusion, readers apply strategies in an attempt to make meaning. (For an extensive list of what readers do to make sense of confusion, see pages 104–105 of *Readicide* [Gallagher 2009]). I want my students to adopt these moves, but for that to happen, I—the teacher—have to model them.

I also want my students to know that applying tools to their confusion doesn't always remedy the problem. There are times as readers in which we have to live with ambiguity. When experienced readers get confused—especially early in a novel—they recognize that the confusion is normal and that, often, one has to embrace and hold on to that confusion until it begins to clear. Anyone who has ever watched a Terrence Malick film understands this point.

The best way, of course, to teach my students how to handle the confusion encountered while reading is to model how I handle confusion when I read. To achieve this, I do a lot of read-aloud/think-alouds in front of my students, sharing with them what I do to make sense of the hard parts.

I want students to track their thinking over the course of a book.

Sometimes we focus so intently on getting students to demonstrate that they can read a passage closely that we forget the bigger picture of teaching students how to track their thinking over the course of a book. Not only do I want my students to be able to track their thinking throughout a book, but also I want them to note how their thinking may shift over time. What you think in the beginning of the book may be different from what you think in the middle of the book, and what you think in the middle of the book may be different from what you think at the end of the book. (For example, the view my students have of Prince Hamlet at the end of the play is often very different from the impression they originally formed of him in act 1.) As my colleague Donna Santman (personal communication) notes, at the beginning of a novel students' thinking will be grounded in a lot of exposition—Who is who? Where are we? What is happening? By the middle of the book, Santman suggests, the students, thinking shifts toward the conflicts that arise—Who is doing what to whom? Why is that character acting that way? Why is this happening? At the end of the book the thinking shifts again toward resolution and big ideas—Why did the book end this way? What is the author trying to say? What big ideas are hiding in this book?

To help students think about their thinking while they read, Santman has developed the following sentence stems:

- I started by thinking _____ and as I read I added/learned

  _____.

- I used to think _____, but now I think _____.

- Some people think _____, but I think _____.

These sentence starters prompt students to track their thinking as they read across chapters. To help students capture their thinking, I give them composition books with unlined paper. I give them unlined paper to send the message that there are a number of ways they can capture their thinking: they can write, draw, make T-charts, create graphs, post sticky notes and then comment on them—anything that demonstrates that they are actively thinking as they read. I do not tell them how much they need to write or how many entries they must produce. I let them decide. I do tell them that if they overannotate they will kill the book, and that if they underannotate they will not get to levels of deeper reading.

I don't ask my students simply to track their thinking over the course of reading their books; I ask them to do so *with the intention of discovering one of the author's big ideas.* There are two important points to consider here: (1) I am careful not to establish *the* big idea for my students to consider; I want them to determine the possibilities. (2) I want them to recognize that in any rich book there are numerous big ideas to consider, and that no book is driven by one theme. It could be argued, for example, that the big idea in *To Kill a Mockingbird* is "It takes courage to stand up to racism." But it could also be argued that one of the following is the big idea:

Because you can't win doesn't mean you shouldn't fight.

You never really understand a person until you stand in his or her shoes.

One person can make a difference.

Heroism is often quiet.

Schools often get in the way of a good education.

Parenting is the most important job in the world.

Some people can be judged at first sight; others can't.

Education provides the ladder out of poverty.

Because something is legal doesn't make it moral.

Coming of age involves innocence being lost.

Or there might be other big ideas that I have yet to consider. Because there are many big ideas in a given book, it is counterproductive for the teacher to establish *the* big idea. Doing so denies students the opportunity to hone their own thinking.

There is another benefit to having students find their own big ideas: It drives more meaningful annotation while they read. When students annotate with the purpose of discovering a big idea in the book, it drives a richer reading of the text. It encourages them to consider how they came to their big idea, and it prompts them to pay attention to what the author did to establish the theme. Instead of isolated or "one and done" annotation (e.g., "This reminds me of my grandmother . . ."), tracing an idea across a book requires a deeper level of reflection. This kind of annotation is very different than blind, unattached "drive by" annotation, where students are asked to generically annotate whatever comes to mind without any thought to the larger picture.

So I hear the question resonating in many of your minds at this moment: How do I grade my students' thinking? For accountability purposes, I confer with each student three times— once at the one-third point in the book, once at the two-thirds point in the book, and once at the end of the book. We sit down together each of these times to consider the level of thinking the student is doing. I score each student's thinking in two ways: through the work found in the notebook and through the discussion that occurs while we confer. I don't have a rubric. I don't have a checklist. We simply talk and look through the notebook together, and then I make a professional judgment. If the student disagrees, I ask for a defense of the disagreement. Sometimes negotiation occurs. And, as always, when I find excellent work, I bring it up for the entire class to see. It is the sharing of excellent student work that provides my students with the rich models needed to understand how to meaningfully track thinking across a book.

I want students to be able to read between the lines—to infer.

In *Deeper Reading*, I argue that our students' ability to infer is sharpened when we teach them to consider what is *not* said in the text (Gallagher 2004). Here are a few more inference activities I have brought to my classroom since the writing of that book.

Infer from a Photo

Every January, *National Geographic* publishes the most memorable photographs of the previous year. Figure 6.3 shows one taken by Sue Ogrocki. I start by showing students the photo and asking them to read the photograph carefully and consider what might have happened. Most of them correctly infer that some sort of natural disaster (tornado? earthquake?) has occurred. Others guess that it depicts a war zone. (The natural disaster inference is correct—this photo was taken near the collapsed Plaza Towers Elementary School in Moore, Oklahoma, after a massive tornado struck the Oklahoma City suburbs in 2013.) After I tell the students what the photo actually shows, I ask them what else the photograph suggests. In other words, what does the photograph imply? Here are some of their responses:

- There may not have been an adequate warning system.
- Maybe it happened in the morning while people were sleeping.
- There are no emergency responders in the photo. Maybe the devastation is so widespread that these people were left on their own.
- Some victims may have survived and might have needed to be rescued.
- The dead will have to be recovered.
- The survivors will need a place to sleep.
- They will need food and water.
- The children who survived will have to attend a different school.

Figure 6.3 Inferring from photographs: Moore, Oklahoma, May 20, 2013

Infer from a Painting

After we work with photographs, I have students apply the same inference skills while reading paintings. I start with Ralph Fasanella's *Lawrence 1912—The Bread and Roses Strike* (see Figure 6.4). I do not share the title of the painting with my students beforehand because I do not want to influence their "reading" of it. Students are asked to infer what might be happening in the scene. This painting depicts a massive strike of textile workers in Lawrence, Massachusetts, which at the time was one of the most important textile manufacturing towns in the United States. The strike led to violence (notice the striker in the painting being trampled by the horse) before eventually being settled a year later. Though I certainly do not expect my students to possess specific background knowledge regarding the Bread and Roses Strike, it is always interesting to see how much they can infer from the painting.

Figure 6.4 Ralph Fasanella's *Lawrence 1912–The Bread and Roses Strike*

Infer from a Comic Book

Take a page from a comic book and white out the bubbles where the characters' speech is written. Have the students fill in the dialogue, predicting what is said based only on the graphics. Once they make their predictions, show them the original dialogue. I choose a student whose created dialogue comes very close to the original, and I have this student share his or her inferential thinking with the class.

Infer from a Cartoon

The last page of each issue of the *New Yorker* includes a cartoon caption contest. The magazine editors select a cartoon and publish it without the caption. Readers then write in and supply possible captions. Figure 6.5 shows a recent example without the caption.

Students write their own humorous captions, which are then compared to the three finalists (following) chosen by the magazine editors.

Figure 6.5 Creating cartoon captions from the *New Yorker*

1. "Let's flip this house."
2. "I told you to tip the movers."
3. "We're not really utilizing our wall space."

Infer from a One-Minute Mystery

Wrestling with Sandy Silverthorne and John Warner's *One Minute Mysteries* (http://www. oneminutemysteries.com) also develops my students' inference skills. Here is one example, titled "Lunch Time":

> Robbie goes into a restaurant and orders a deli sandwich and a cola for lunch. Afterward, he pays his bill, tips his waitress, and goes outside. He slowly takes in his surroundings. The sky is black and the city streets are deserted. What happened? (2007, 12)

Using inference skills, the students have to come up with a plausible answer. (In this example, the man worked the night shift and took his lunch break in the middle of the night.) Having students wrestle with one-minute mysteries helps to sharpen their inference skills.

Infer from a Passage in a Novel

I want my students to apply inference skills to the novels they are reading. I might start with a passage like this one, which appears on the first page of Laurie Halse Anderson's *Chains*:

> Pastor Weeks sat at the front of the squeaky wagon with Old Ben next to him, the mules' reins loose in his hands. The pine coffin that held Miss Mary Finch—wearing her best dress, with her hair washed clean and combed—bounced in the back when the wagon wheels hit a rut. My sister, Ruth, sat next to the coffin. Ruth was too big to carry, plus the pastor knew about her peculiar manner of being, so it was the wagon for her and the road for me. (2008, 3)

After a close read, my students came up with the following inferences:

- This takes place in a rural area.
- This story takes place in the "old days."
- Old Ben is a dog.
- Mary Finch died young.
- Ruth might have special needs.
- The narrator might be related to Miss Mary Finch—maybe a sister?

The beginning of a novel—where it pays to notice how characters are introduced—is an excellent place to practice inferential skills. I often have students infer from a book's opening paragraph.

Once students move past the exposition, I sharpen their inference skills by having them predict what might happen next. Anyone can make a prediction, but I have my students cite textual evidence that lends credence to their predictions. What have you inferred, I ask, that leads you to that prediction? Later, I might have them return to their predictions and reflect where their inferences were strong and where they were weak.

⊢——————⊣

In every one of these examples—how to infer from a photo, a painting, a comic book, a cartoon, a one-minute mystery, a novel—I always begin by modeling my thinking. For example, if I want my students to make inferences from reading Painting A, I model the kind of thinking I am looking for by sharing my inferential thinking about Painting B. When teaching inference, I go, and then they go.

More Modeling

Thus far I have discussed how I want my readers to do these things:

> Read for enjoyment
>
> Read widely
>
> Know what readers do when they are confused
>
> Track their thinking over the course of a book
>
> Be able to read between the lines—to infer

But as I stated earlier in the chapter, I also want them to be able to do these things:

> Be able to meaningfully discuss their reading
>
> Think about their reading via writing
>
> Develop agency as readers, thus reducing their dependence on the teacher
>
> Consider their reading in the context of their worlds

Let's look at how I work on each of these in the classroom.

I want students to be able to meaningfully discuss their reading.

When meaningful talk happens around books, everyone gets smarter. The key word here, of course, is "meaningful." Because talk is central to deepening my students' thinking, I build a lot of opportunity for students to talk into every day's lesson. My students frequently interact verbally through partner talks, group discussions, and whole-class discussions (ranging from wide-open exchanges to Socratic seminars), and I work hard to make sure that through these discussions it is my students who are generating the thinking.

This is the opposite approach to what I found in a classroom I visited last year—a seventh-grade classroom where the students were reading Lois Lowry's *The Giver*. To sharpen the students' reading, the teacher had determined that the theme of the novel centered on the idea of the dangers of oppression. The students were told this before the reading commenced and all their annotation of the novel centered on finding evidence of oppression. Every time the students met in groups to discuss the novel, their discussions centered on how Lowry developed the notion of oppression. When they finished the novel, they were given an essay question asking how oppression played a role as the central theme, which they were able to answer dutifully (since they had read the entire book and taken notes through this lens).

The problem with this approach is that much of the thinking was done for the students, and it was done for them before they even read the first page of the novel. By determining the central theme to be studied, the teacher denied students the chance to make their own meaning. Who is to say, for example, that the theme chosen by the teacher is the definitive theme? Someone else might argue that Lowry's book is really about the importance of individuality. Or that the book is a commentary on the value of our memories. All rich books have several themes. When a teacher predetermines "the" theme, the teacher also predetermines the students' thinking.

So what do I mean when I say I want students to generate their own thinking? Let's return to *The Giver*, for example. Before reading the novel, I would have told my students that there were several large ideas imbedded in the text and that their job as they read would be to identify one or more of them and to track the development of the ideas. After reading a few chapters, I would schedule a day for the class to revisit their reading. Instead of assigning a theme to track, I might put them in small groups and ask them, "What's worth talking about in this chapter? What big ideas are beginning to emerge?" After they had a chance to explore *their* thinking, I would then open up the discussion for the entire class to participate. This approach is a different approach than the one often taken in a traditional classroom, where the teacher has prepared a list of questions for the students to answer—a list of questions designed to lead the students to adopt *the teacher's interpretation* of the novel. This is not to say, of course, that I, as the teacher, do not have anything valuable to contribute to the conversation. But I am careful to have the discussion *start with what the students are thinking*. If, over the course of their discussion, I think they have missed a big idea, I can throw a question into the mix to get them to begin thinking in that direction. But the point here is that the conversation starts with what the students are thinking, and it is my students— through lots of talking—who determine which big ideas are worth tracking and discussing.

Student-centered talk is crucial. If the teacher is the only one talking in the room, the students will never get to the deepest level of thinking. In Chapter 7, I explore additional strategies for strengthening our students' speaking and listening skills.

I want students to think about their reading via writing.

As I demonstrated earlier in this chapter in the discussion about using mentor sentences, one of the best ways to develop young writers is to have them carefully emulate the craft of established writers. This emulation occurs through careful *reading* of excellent writing. Reading makes us better writers. Conversely, let us not forget that the opposite is also true: Writing makes us better readers. The act of writing deepens our comprehension.

To illustrate this, let's return to the teaching of *The Giver*. Let's say students have read the first few chapters, and I am getting ready to ask them the following: "What's worth talking about in this chapter? What big ideas are beginning to emerge?" Before I allow students to discuss this, I have them explore their thinking by writing for five minutes. At the end of the quick-write, I place them in small groups and have them silently pass their papers to the next person. Each person in the group reads someone else's thinking, and then responds silently in writing. The students continue to pass the papers every five minutes, until every student has read and responded to multiple perspectives. This written silent conversation always generates new thinking for my students, and it primes the pump for the ensuing small-group and/or whole-class discussion.

I use this strategy often, mixing in different questions to spur the thinking. Last year, for example, students came to class having just read the section in *Of Mice and Men* where Steinbeck introduces the character of Crooks. I put students into groups and asked the following: "Why do you think Steinbeck introduced the character of Crooks? What is his purpose for doing so?" Students wrote silently and then passed their papers several times. This writing led them to a rich discussion—a discussion that deepened their comprehension of the novel and motivated them to continue to read. For more on how to deepen students' reading comprehension through writing, I recommend Harvey and Elaine Daniels's *The Best Kept Teaching Secret: How Written Conversations Engage Kids, Activate Learning, and Grow Fluent Writers, K–12* (2013).

I want students to develop agency as readers, thus reducing their dependence on the teacher.

The goal in every ELA classroom should be to help students develop agency as readers—students who take ownership of their reading without being constantly prodded by the teacher. To accomplish this, our classrooms must move away from the all-or-nothing reading approach adopted in many schools—classrooms where books are either subject to hyperattentiveness (and thus killed) or books that are simply assigned with little or no attention to the readers' journeys. Instead, to develop agency, our students would be better served if we created what Judy Wallis, a veteran teacher in Houston, refers to as a "three-text" classroom: a place where students encounter texts we all read, where students encounter texts that some of us read, and where students encounter texts that they read independently. Our students need a blended reading experience, and in Chapter 8 I discuss a model for developing this kind of a classroom.

I want students to consider their reading in the context of their worlds.

I want my students to take the wisdom they encounter in the books they are reading and apply that wisdom to the world they will soon inherit. I want them to move beyond the ability to recognize theme or foreshadowing, and to consider how reading books makes them wiser as they approach adulthood. I am much less interested in their ability to answer a question like, "How does the author use personification?" than I am in their ability to answer a question like, "What lessons does *The Great Gatsby* teach the modern reader?" If we don't use the books as springboards to help our students think about the world today, then our students are simply reading stories. And though they may be great stories, they have much more to offer young readers than sharpening their ability to recognize literary elements. Students need to stretch their thinking beyond the four corners of the text.

If we want our students to make connections between the books they are reading and the modern world, we need to design lessons that ask students to make those connections. Students who have read *1984*, for example, should be prompted to think about when and where our world remains Orwellian. Of course, I might begin the unit by modeling some of these connections to my students (for example, I might bring in editorials or political cartoons that refer to Big Brother), but eventually I want my students to be able to go out in the world and find connections on their own. If a book is worthy of whole-class instruction, it should enable students to make deep connections to today's world.

Standing Next to Worthy Models

Like the up-and-coming baseball players who mimic the mannerisms and techniques of their idols, developing readers and writers benefit from being able to see, analyze, and emulate the strategies and approaches of great readers and writers. With this in mind, let's make sure we provide our students with plenty of opportunities to stand next to worthy models of reading and writing. Doing so will help them—consciously and unconsciously—deepen their reading and writing abilities. Amongst all the noise currently surrounding the new standards and testing, let's not forget that building better readers and writers often begins with finding good models for our students to emulate.

CHAPTER 7

Sharpening Our Students' Listening and Speaking Skills

How important are listening and speaking skills? One recent study found that adults spend an average of 70 percent of their time engaged in some sort of communication. Of the time spent communicating, an average of 45 percent is spent listening, 30 percent is spent speaking, 16 percent is spent reading, and 9 percent is spent writing (Adler, Rosenfeld, and Proctor 2012). In other words, *75 percent of all communication in adulthood directly involves listening and/or speaking skills.*

Unfortunately, many of our students will soon leave school inadequately prepared to be active listeners and effective speakers (largely because these skills have not been tested). Many of our students come from classrooms where there seems to be "an implicit belief that the subtle skills of active listening and reasoned speaking will develop simply through children's involvement in whole class and small group dialogues" (ITE English 2014). And while it is true that children will develop their language skills through the traditional "turn-and-talk" kinds of practices found in schools, it is also true that students need much deeper practice before they will become listeners and speakers who will thrive in an ever more complex world.

Talk Matters

Because one of the aims of the CCSS is to address career readiness, it makes sense to start thinking about teaching speaking skills by looking at the annual survey by the National Association of Colleges and Employers. In the survey, employers are asked what skills and qualities they look for when hiring students out of college. In order of importance, here are the skills and qualities they value most:

THE SKILLS AND QUALITIES EMPLOYERS WANT IN THEIR CLASS OF 2013 RECRUITS

SKILL/QUALITY	WEIGHTED AVERAGE RATING*
Ability to verbally communicate with persons inside and outside the organization	4.63
Ability to work in a team structure	4.60
Ability to make decisions and solve problems	4.51
Ability to plan, organize, and prioritize work	4.46
Ability to obtain and process information	4.43
Ability to analyze quantitative data	4.30
Technical knowledge related to the job	3.99
Proficiency with computer software programs	3.95
Ability to create and/or edit written reports	3.56
Ability to sell or influence others	3.55

* 5-point scale, where 1=Not at all important; 2=Not very important; 3=Somewhat important; 4=Very important; and 5=Extremely important. See more at: http://www.naceweb.org/s10242012/skills-abilities-qualities-new-hires/#sthash.bD472ZFL.dpuf.

Source: National Association of Colleges and Employers (2012)

Potential employers list the "ability to verbally communicate with persons inside and outside the organization" as their highest priority skill, which is ironic given the fact that speaking and listening skills receive much less attention in our schools than do reading and writing skills. Our students probably will be doing a lot more talking in the real world than they will be reading and writing, yet you wouldn't be able to tell this from the over 500 workshops offered at the 2013 National Council of Teachers of English Conference in Boston, where exactly *one* workshop was offered to help our students improve their speaking skills. One workshop out of 500. For those interested in the math, think about it in these terms: .002 percent of the workshops offered at NCTE in 2013 addressed the skill most valued by employers.

Sadly, it is not hard to figure out the source of the neglect when it comes to the teaching of speaking and listening skills. In the previous educational era (NCLB), speaking and listening skills weren't tested, and as we know by now, skills that are not tested quickly fall out of favor in the classroom. Speaking and listening skills were no less important in actuality, of course, but without test emphasis on these skills, they withered on the vine. This is yet another argument why our core values should always supersede any current educational testing movement. Speaking and listening skills are important whether they are tested or not, and our job is to teach competency in all four of the language arts (reading, writing, speaking, and listening). This, again, is why hitching instruction only to what is being tested can be harmful to the overall development of our students.

The good news is that the Common Core standards value speaking and listening skills, even if the current exams do not. To be honest, my goal in teaching my students to speak and listen better is not to get them ready for the next wave of exams. Nor is it to prepare them for a successful career at a Fortune 500 company. I am placing more emphasis on speaking and listening skills in my classroom because these skills are foundational to becoming literate human beings. First and foremost, they are important elements of the language arts. If this renewed emphasis on speaking and listening skills also helps my students to score higher on the state exams or helps to position them to secure good jobs, even better.

Before getting into specific speaking and listening strategies, let's take a look at the Common Core speaking and listening standards, which, at each grade level from kindergarten to grade 12, are divided into two sections: "Comprehension and Collaboration" and "Presentation of Knowledge and Ideas." As students progress through the grade levels, these standards increase in sophistication. Here, for example, are the speaking and listening standards for grades 9 and 10.

CCSS Speaking and Listening Standards, Grades 9–10
Comprehension and Collaboration

> CCSS.ELA-Literacy.SL.9-10.1 Initiate and participate effectively in a range of collaborative discussions (one-on-one, in groups, and teacher-led) with diverse partners on grades 9–10 topics, texts, and issues, building on others' ideas and expressing their own clearly and persuasively.

> CCSS.ELA-Literacy.SL.9-10.1A Come to discussions prepared, having read and researched material under study; explicitly draw on that preparation by referring to evidence from texts and other research on the topic or issue to stimulate a thoughtful, well-reasoned exchange of ideas.

CCSS.ELA-Literacy.SL.9-10.1B Work with peers to set rules for collegial discussions and decision-making (e.g., informal consensus, taking votes on key issues, presentation of alternate views), clear goals and deadlines, and individual roles as needed.

CCSS.ELA-Literacy.SL.9-10.1C Propel conversations by posing and responding to questions that relate the current discussion to broader themes or larger ideas; actively incorporate others into the discussion; and clarify, verify, or challenge ideas and conclusions.

CCSS.ELA-Literacy.SL.9-10.1D Respond thoughtfully to diverse perspectives, summarize points of agreement and disagreement, and, when warranted, qualify or justify their own views and understanding and make new connections in light of the evidence and reasoning presented.

CCSS.ELA-Literacy.SL.9-10.2 Integrate multiple sources of information presented in diverse media or formats (e.g., visually, quantitatively, orally) evaluating the credibility and accuracy of each source.

CCSS.ELA-Literacy.SL.9-10.3 Evaluate a speaker's point of view, reasoning, and use of evidence and rhetoric, identifying any fallacious reasoning or exaggerated or distorted evidence.

Presentation of Knowledge and Ideas

CCSS.ELA-Literacy.SL.9-10.4 Present information, findings, and supporting evidence clearly, concisely, and logically such that listeners can follow the line of reasoning and the organization, development, substance, and style are appropriate to purpose, audience, and task.

CCSS.ELA-Literacy.SL.9-10.5 Make strategic use of digital media (e.g., textual, graphical, audio, visual, and interactive elements) in presentations to enhance understanding of findings, reasoning, and evidence and to add interest.

CCSS.ELA-Literacy.SL.9-10.6 Adapt speech to a variety of contexts and tasks, demonstrating command of formal English when indicated or appropriate. (See grades 9–10 Language standards 1 and 3 here for specific expectations.) (NGA/CCSSO 2010f)

The remainder of this chapter explores ways to sharpen our students' speaking and listening skills with specific exercises I have found helpful.

How Should It Be Read?

I start by showing students a short clip from a local television newscast and ask them to pay close attention to how a reporter in the field reads the copy. I ask them to note the vocal "moves" the reporter makes: Does he or she pause for effect? When, where, and why does the reporter speed up (or slow down)? When, where, and why does the reporter raise (or lower) his or her voice?

On a second viewing, I have students note the mannerisms employed to make the speech more effective: How are the hands positioned and used? How does the reporter change the angle of his or her head? Are facial expressions used? How is eye contact utilized for effect? Does the reporter stand still, or does the reporter move? Are there graphics or background visuals used to support the speech?

After some practice watching television news, I take excerpts from newspaper stories and I ask my students, "If you were a television reporter in the field, how would you read this copy on the air?" Here is the first line from a recent newspaper article I used in my classroom:

> Listen up loners: A new study says having friends can make you smarter, at least if you're a baby cow. (Netburn 2014)

It is interesting to hear how many ways this line can be read aloud. Pretend you are a reporter in the field and try it. Where do you raise your voice? Do you pause anywhere for effect? What pace "fits" the copy? Do you use your hands? I have students stand up and give their various interpretations of the line, and then I have them practice with more from the same excerpt:

> Researchers from the University of British Columbia found that young calves that live alone performed worse on tests of cognitive skill than calves that live with a buddy.
>
> On most dairy farms, calves are removed from their mothers soon after they are born and put in a pen or a hutch where they live alone for eight to 10 weeks while they wean. The practice developed to keep disease from spreading among susceptible baby cows.
>
> But a few years ago, researchers at UBC's Animal Welfare Program were observing two sets of calves on a farm run by the school. One set of calves had been raised in a group environment—the other set had been raised individually. (Netburn 2014)

To introduce my students to the elements of an effective speech, I use Erik Palmer's acronym "PVLEGS" found in his excellent book, *Well Spoken*:

Poise
- Appear calm and confident
- Avoid distracting behaviors

Voice
- Speak every word clearly
- Use a "just right" volume

Life
- Express passion and emotions in your voice

Eye Contact
- Connect visually with the audience
- Look at each audience member

Gestures
- Use hand movements
- Move your body
- Have an expressive face

Speed
- Talk with appropriate speed
- Use pauses for effect and emphasis (2011, 57)

To help familiarize my students with Palmer's PVLEGS, I play a number of TED Talks for them and have students score the speeches through the PVLEGS lens. We begin by viewing and scoring one together through a whole-class discussion, and from there, students practice scoring a few more in small-group settings before eventually scoring speeches on their own. I use PVLEGS as a scoring guide when the time comes to evaluate my students' speeches.

Poker Chip Discussion

Another strategy recommended by Erik Palmer, this time in his book *Teaching the Core Skills of Listening and Speaking,* is the Poker Chip Discussion (2013). Prior to whole-class discussion, each student is handed a poker chip. Students "spend" their chips by talking, and all students are asked to spend their chips before the end of the discussion (depending on the situation, the teacher might start each student off with two or three chips instead of just one). This strategy encourages all students to participate, instead of the usual five or six students who typically carry the conversation. It is a low-stress way to make sure all voices are heard.

Interrupted Book Report

Students in my class often read self-selected books (more on this in Chapter 8). The Interrupted Book Report is an accountability measure for self-selected reading, but it also strengthens students' speaking skills. I pick a student randomly and have her stand up and tell the class about the book she is reading. At some point while the student is talking, I interrupt by calling out, "Stop." Sometimes I let the speaker talk for a minute or two; sometimes I cut her off (often mid-sentence) after a few seconds. I then call on another student and he stands and starts sharing a summary of his book. The Interrupted Book Report is fun, because students don't know when the "stop" will come. They have to keep talking until they hear it. The other benefit, of course, is that students get to hear what others in the class are reading. Interrupted Book Reports often serve as commercials for what students might read next.

If the class is reading a whole-class novel, the Interrupted Book Report is a good review strategy. A student begins by retelling what happened from the beginning of the book (or from the beginning of the chapter) and when she is stopped, another student is chosen to pick up the summary exactly where the first student stopped. This second student continues the summary until he is interrupted, and a third student is then called to pick up from where the latest interruption occurred. And so forth. Because students are picked randomly to continue the summary wherever it may be interrupted, this sharpens listening skills as well.

Context-Free Sentence from the Writer's Notebook

Esquire magazine prints letters from its readers in every issue, but what is really funny is that the magazine always features one line out of context from a letter they have decided not to publish. Here are some recently published, context-free sentences from various issues:

> "Did you know that she went to Space Camp three times?"

> "I woke up at 6:00 a.m. just to brush my teeth."

> "The next day, I'd apply a tincture of benzoin to the blister, pop in a plastic tooth guard, and go at it again."

After introducing the concept of the context-free sentence, students are asked to revisit their writer's notebooks and to choose one line out of context to read to the rest of the class.

But I don't want them to simply read their lines; I want them to read their lines *dramatically*. Even though it's only one line, I want each student to consider PVLEGS when deciding how to deliver it. I model this by choosing one line I have written and performing it with the elements of PVLEGS in mind.

When we begin sharing the lines out loud, I do not indicate any order of speakers. I require every student to stand and deliver one context-free line, and I set a time limit of five minutes for everyone to have shared. Who goes first and who goes next is up to the students (this creates a funnier chain of context-free lines). If a student asks, "How will I know it's my turn?" I reply with, "It is your turn when no one else is talking."

Oral Newspaper Leads

In a novel, the reader has to read many chapters before finding out the resolution. In *Of Mice and Men*, for example, the reader does not find out Lenny's fate until very late in the novel. Newspaper articles, on the other hand, are often written in the exact opposite fashion. They adopt the "inverted pyramid format," in which the "ending" is revealed in the lead paragraph. An example:

> **Los Angeles (CNN)** — A magnitude-5.1 earthquake struck the Los Angeles area Friday night, jolting nearby communities and breaking water mains in some neighborhoods. Its epicenter was in Orange County, one mile east of La Habra and four miles north of Fullerton, the U.S. Geological Survey said. (Karimi and Sutton 2014)

In inverted pyramid writing, the reader is told what happened immediately, and he or she can choose whether to read deeper into the article for further details.

Once students understand how newspaper leads are written, I model how a newspaper lead for a novel might be written. The lead for *Of Mice and Men*, for example, might read as follows:

> *Weed, CA — In what some are calling an act of mercy, George Milton, an intelligent but uneducated man, shot and killed his friend, Lennie Small, after it was found that Small had accidentally broken the neck of Curley's wife. Milton allegedly acted to prevent Small from facing a painful death from the lynch mob that was closing in on him.*

When students finish a whole-class book study, I often have them write one-paragraph leads recapping the books. I ask them to stand up and share them in front of the class.

There are two benefits to this activity: (1) it strengthens summary skills and (2) it presents students with a low-pressure way to get up in front of the class and practice their oral skills. Writing one-paragraph leads can also be assigned after reading specific chapters.

2 X 2 Speech

When students draft a speech they have to know their purpose and their audience, because knowing purpose and audience not only determines how the speech will be written but also determines how the speech will be delivered. If, for example, you are giving a speech about the intricacies of basketball, your speech to a group of college basketball coaches is going to sound very different from your speech to a class of third graders. *Who* receives the speech determines *how* it should be written and delivered.

For the 2 x 2 Speech assignment, students are asked to take one topic and write to two different audiences: two 2-minute speeches. Sam, for example, first wrote a two-minute speech explaining how to excel at playing *Call of Duty* with a high school audience in mind. He then rewrote the speech so that it would be understandable to his grandmother. The 2 x 2 Speech assignment teaches students to pay close attention to purpose and audience. Students can then be asked to give one—or both—of their speeches.

Favorite 5

Favorite 5 is a writing assignment, but it easily can be turned into a short speech. I begin by modeling my Favorite 5s in a number of areas:

Favorite 5 Baseball Players of All Time

Hank Aaron

Willie Mays

Pete Rose

Greg Maddox

Mike Trout

Favorite 5 Bill Murray Films

Lost in Translation

Groundhog Day

Kingpin

Caddyshack

Rushmore

Favorite 5 Candy Bars

Snickers

Butterfinger

Three Musketeers

Heath Bar

Chick-O-Stick

Favorite 5 Television Characters

Phil Dunphy (*Modern Family*)

Frank Underwood (*House of Cards*)

"Matt LeBlanc" (*Episodes*)

Walter White (*Breaking Bad*)

John Luther (*Luther*)

Once students have generated a number of Favorite 5 lists, they choose one list and write a defense of it. They then stand up and orally defend their lists.

Yes/No Argument

Another written assignment that lends itself to having students speak in front of the class is the Yes/No Argument, which I have modeled after a column featured in *Upfront* magazine. This column features a debatable question (e.g., "Does the U.S. Need Illegal Immigrants?" [Jacoby and Tancredo 2012]) and runs opposing arguments (see Jacoby's and Tancredo's responses in Figure 7.1). Students are then asked to generate argumentative questions they care about and to write both sides of the argument. See Figure 7.2 for Jesuson's arguments on whether schools should offer cash bonuses for good test scores.

DEBATE

Does the U.S. Need Illegal Immigrants?

There are 11 million illegal immigrants in the United States and intense disagreement over whether they help or hurt the U.S. economy

YES Somewhere between 7 and 8 million of the 11 million illegal immigrants in the U.S. are working, doing jobs we need done, and contributing to the economy.

With the unemployment rate above 8 percent, couldn't those jobs be filled by U.S. workers? Actually, no: Even the unemployed make choices about which jobs they're willing to take, and not enough of them want to work in the fields or wash dishes or work on an assembly line in a meatpacking plant to keep American agriculture, restaurants, hotels, and food processing alive.

There are historical reasons for this. Americans have become more educated over time. In 1960, half of the native-born men in the labor force were high school dropouts eager to do unskilled, physically demanding work. Today, it's less than 10 percent. But we still need unskilled workers, and there is only so much employers can pay them before the prices they charge for their products increase so much that no one will buy them.

In fact, most unskilled immigrants support and sustain jobs for more highly skilled American workers. Think about your favorite restaurant. If the owner had to close for lack of busboys or dishwashers, that would put a lot of Americans out of work: the chef, the waiters, and the manager. It would also mean less work for other workers up- and downstream in the local economy: farmers, food processors, truckers, insurance agents—the list goes on and on.

Of course, employers should try to hire Americans first, and the law should require that. But there is no question: Whether they're legal or illegal, America needs these immigrant workers—and we will need them even more as the economy recovers and adds more jobs. •

—**TAMAR JACOBY**
Immigrationworks USA

Tomato pickers in Florida

NO The United States does *not* need illegal immigrants. In fact, the 11 million illegal immigrants currently in the U.S. are an enormous burden to our country at a time when our ability to provide services for Americans is already strained.

The official unemployment rate is above 8 percent, and it's closer to 15 percent if you count those who can't find full-time work and those who are so discouraged that they've stopped looking. The federal government is struggling to deal with a $15 trillion national debt. And the U.S. already accepts more than 1 million legal immigrants each year.

Most illegal immigrants have no health insurance and end up seeking medical care in hospital emergency rooms. Our hospitals are already providing care to millions of uninsured Americans who can't afford to pay. That cost is passed along to American taxpayers.

According to the Federation for American Immigration Reform, illegal immigration costs U.S. taxpayers $113 billion a year. The biggest expense—nearly $52 billion a year—is educating the children of illegal immigrants, a cost borne mostly by state and local governments.

It's often claimed that our economy needs these low-skilled workers "to do jobs Americans will not do." But what are those jobs? In every type of field you can name, Americans and legal immigrants perform the majority of those jobs. In only one area, seasonal agricultural jobs, is there a case that we need more temporary workers, and we already have a federal program to fill those jobs legally.

Illegal immigration is not only unneeded, it imposes great costs on our country and cheapens the value of legal immigration. •

—**TOM TANCREDO**
Former Republican Congressman from Colorado

Figure 7.1 *Upfront's* Yes/No Argument

Should Schools Offer Cash Bonuses for Good Test Scores?

Yes

Money, these days, can get you nearly anything. Clothes for the next generation to video games that kids could play; all can be utilized. But- what if we put that same control of wealth in the hands of kids? Should we perform this act if they earned it: by doing a great job on their test? Kids deserve money for their good test scores, because it shows a symbol of accomplishment. Since souvenirs are "actually related to remember," (dictionary reference.com) it will be good for kids to recall to the day that they got rewarded for their success.

Yes, money can be a memento for success in tests, but the average U.S. student would want to buy something (e.g. a bag of chips from a bodega) before they show the proof to their parents. When this happens, the student's parents will disagree towards their "claim" of passing their test (especially if their parents see them a liar because of previous moments). Like most problems, there is a solution. The student who "claims" to be successful might ask the teacher that administered the test, and from their experience, they will tell the truth about this student's achievement.

Of course, students can spend their money memento and make their parents become convinced of it. However, if failing and dishonest students are in the same room where the money is given to the student who does a good job on their test, they can steal it if the rewarded student isn't self-aware. The paid student will be gravely upset if they find out that the money they earned rightfully has vanished. To make this student feel safer after getting his/her money bonus, the teacher that promised to give the money should not tell the class that they will be rewarded for a good test score. Therefore, the teacher can take the student with a good test score out of a class, and reward them without anyone recognizing.

In favor of many additions to be added for tests that are considered to be exemplar, they trigger a sign of confidence in one's self. Mementos like these show the day when this student knew he could conquer every obstacle in his way opposing him. Then this moment goes through a chain of episodes. This student starts to do well because of their confidence that they will succeed in the next test they have. This student may find the interest of studying, which may be surprising for parents that think their kids are not succeeding academically. Finally; this student will cooperate in class more often to receive the educational skills he/she needs.

It's become common on whom to put the blame on why kids don't perform well in schools. Why are kids having Fs on their report cards? Why do kids tell different stories to their parents? Who is to blame for the weak performance of most kids in schools? We should all point our judgmental, huge index fingers on the students themselves. But- if schools allow kids to earn wealth bonuses for their academic success, students' rate of good grades will raise, allowing kids to not put stress on their bodies because of late projects to do on their frail, unexperienced bodies.

No

What would you choose? Money or friends? If you chose money, you're most likely to be an excellent student in school, but don't socialize often with other students. In other words, you don't have that many friends. This is the effect of cash being the reward of achievement. And if you're not the kid who obtains these rewards, you almost certainly feel like targeting the rewarded student negatively. Schools offering cash bonuses for good test scores are not the best way to reward students for their success. It influences other kids to make their objective to make the rewarded student unable to find their money.

Yes, money may cause students to target kids negatively, however, what if the teachers don't tell the students about getting cash rewards? The students that want to threaten the content student cannot steal it. They can't threaten them if they don't know what they possess. But-actually, it can be stolen. "Each day an estimated 400,000 pick pocket incidents occur around the world" (irishexaminer.com). One of these robberies can include the student who did well on their examination. And kids wouldn't want to experience the miserable moment that their money that was rightfully earned is nowhere in sight.

Of course, the student might not have it taken away, but - even if it wasn't stolen, students could still target the rewarded student. In addition, the rewarded student could tell an 'trustworthy' friend that may gossip it to other students that would want to target that rewarded student.

Having money bonuses for worthy test scores doesn't help students to get the best grade they potentially can on the test. "At least two dozen studies have shown that people expecting to receive a reward for completing a task... simply do not perform as well as those who expect nothing" (Kohn, 1933). This means if the proctors that are administering tests tell the students (who are going to do their examination) that they will be paid for their excellence on their test; they will perform more poorly than people who are not told about this.

Money can manipulate people into doing things we never thought we could, as humans. We create conflict over money. And we never share money, especially if you're greedy to most people. Kids nowadays would do anything to get money, either for fame, popularity or being rich. This is why kids shouldn't own the power of wealth. We should be more careful of using our money the right way. As for kids, it may be hard for them for the reason that they still need to grow up to see what money can do to them. Maybe that's what they still need to learn. Giving them money right away for good test scores is not helping.

Figure 7.2 Jesuson's Yes/No Argument

Once students have written both sides of the issue, I randomly select them to stand up and read one or both sides of their arguments.

4 x 4 Debate

I use the 4 x 4 Debate after students have diligently researched a given issue. Begin by placing four chairs in a row in the center of the classroom (I clear out all the other furniture to the periphery). Have the students who support a "yes" position stand in a group behind these chairs. Take another four chairs, and place them in a row facing the first set of four chairs. Have the students who support a "no" position stand in a group behind these chairs. Tell the students that you, the teacher, will randomly choose debate team members to fill the chairs and that all students will have five minutes to put their heads together to help the chosen four consider the following: their main argument points, the counterarguments they will soon hear, and how they will respond to these counterarguments. If it is helpful, they can scribble bullet notes.

Though there are eight total chairs (four on each side facing each other), when it comes time to start the debate, I choose six students to participate, three on each side. This leaves an open chair on each side of the debate—sort of a "wild card" seat that can be filled at any time by any outlying student who wants in on the action. If all four seats are filled and another student wants to join the debate in progress, he or she simply walks behind a seated debater and taps that student on the shoulder. That student must then exit the debate, and the person who tapped the shoulder then slides into the chair.

To encourage reasoned debate (instead of having the exercise devolve into a shouting match), each side can speak only when it is their turn. The turns are set up as follows.

Three minutes	Side A chooses a spokesperson to give an opening statement. Side B listens.
Three minutes	Side B chooses a spokesperson to give an opening statement. Side A listens.
Two minutes	Side A has the floor, and anyone on that team may speak. They can continue to deepen the arguments they introduced in their opening statement, or they can begin to refute what the other side said in their opening statement. Or they can do both. Side B listens.

Two minutes	Side B has the floor, and anyone on that team may speak. They can continue to deepen the arguments they introduced in their opening statement, or they can begin to refute anything the other side has said to this point. Or they can do both. Side A listens.
4 minutes	Both sides leave the debate and return to their groups away from the four chairs to strategize where their argument(s) should go next. After four minutes, each side returns to its four chairs. They can choose to return the same four students, or they may elect to replace them with new representatives.
Two minutes	Side A has the floor and the debate continues. Side B listens.
Two minutes	Side B has the floor and the debate continues. Side A listens.
Two minutes+	This two-minute back-and-forth rhythm is repeated until the debate has run its course. Create other group breaks if necessary.

When the debate concludes, all students (whether they actively participated or not) are asked to write reflections. Here are some questions they might consider:

- Who "won" the debate? Why do you think so? Be specific.
- What grade would you give your team for its performance in the debate? Explain.
- Did the debate change your mind on this issue in any way? Explain.
- Reflect on something you learned in the debate.
- What was not said in the debate that should have been said? What was left out? Had it been said, how might that have changed the course of the debate?

Students are then chosen randomly to stand up and to share their reflections.

A variation to the 4 x 4 Debate: If you want to throw your students a curveball before the debate starts, force the teams to switch sides at the last minute. Those who believe "A" are now required to argue in favor of "B"; those who believe "B" are now required to argue in favor of "A."

Say Something

I like to use this strategy after students are assigned a large chunk of text to read. I place them in a circle, and I begin with a very simple direction: "Say something." One student says something to get the conversation started, and then a second student can either add to what has already been said or can take the conversation in a new direction. The order of speakers can be predetermined by simply going in a clockwise direction, or the conversation can be wide open, so that it jumps randomly around the circle. If I choose the latter, I trace the conversation (see below).

Trace the Conversation

I often use the Trace the Conversation activity when my students are gathering to discuss a book they are reading. In Socratic Seminar fashion, desks are placed in a rectangular seating arrangement so that students are facing one another when discussing the topic at hand. Before the conversation begins, students are told that I will trace the trajectory of the conversation and that I will score their participation on three levels: speaking, evidence, and leadership. To help assess the quality of the conversation, my colleague Justin Boyd created symbols to help keep track of the talk:

Speaking

C = Clear and convincing

U = Unclear/trails off

↑ = Too loud/disruptive

↓ = Too quiet/hard to hear

Evidence

A = Sophisticated, original, convincing argument

DR = Uses direct textual reference

DNQ = Alludes to text but doesn't quote it

O = Uses relevant outside evidence

EC = Evidence does not connect

Leadership

BLD = Refers to or builds on another student's comments

CQ = Asks a clarifying question of another student

Q = Poses a question to the class

S = Offers a summary/synthesis

L = Links one student's ideas to another's

— = Comment is disconnected to topic/listening?

* = Obvious leader of discussion

There is no particular order given to the conversation, and when it begins, I trace the trajectory of it on my seating chart. If, for example, Josiah starts the conversation and Alan speaks next, I draw a line from Josiah to Alan on the chart to show the direction of the conversation. If Stanley then speaks after Alan, I draw the line from Alan to Stanley. And so forth. Each time someone speaks, I quickly add one or more of the symbols next to his or her name so that later I will remember what he or she added to the conversation. By the end of the discussion, I have a visual that shows the history of who spoke (and how many times), who did not speak, and what each person contributed to the discussion. In Figure 7.3, you will see an example that my colleague, Martin Palamore, created to track a small-group conversation in his middle school history class. See Appendix B for a blank copy of the conversation chart, or download a copy of the chart at kellygallagher.org (click on "Resources" and select the "Track the Conversation" chart).

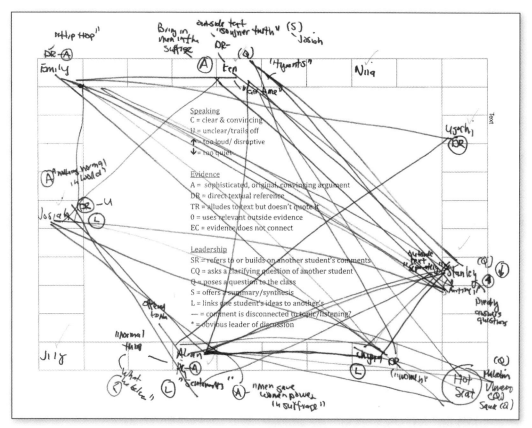

Figure 7.3 Tracing a conversation in a middle school history class

Teach Us Something

The Teach Us Something assignment is a simple way to get students up and talking in front of the class. The title is self-explanatory: Each student is given four minutes to teach the class something we didn't already know. Students are encouraged to support their teaching lesson with visual aids. The students and I enjoy this assignment because no two speeches are alike and we all learn.

Circle Chain

I want students to know there is a difference between hearing and *listening*. Listening moves deeper than simply hearing. It requires a level of focus. To work on developing my students' listening skills, I place them in a circle (they can be whole-class circles or small-group circles) and hand each one of them a playing card. A random topic is thrown out (e.g., "names of candy bars," "characters in *To Kill a Mockingbird*," "words that start with *Th*") and one student is selected to share an answer. If the topic is "fast food restaurants," for example, the student chosen to speak first says, "McDonald's," and then the conversation moves clockwise to the next person in the chain. The second person calls out a different answer ("Burger King"), and then it moves to the third person in the chain. Students remain in the chain if they can come up with an answer that has not yet been said (this is where the listening skills come into play). If a student cannot think of an answer, or if the student repeats an answer that has already been said, he or she drops out of the chain (which is demonstrated by dropping the playing card onto the floor). The last person holding a playing card wins. To raise the pressure a bit, I often impose a five-second response time.

Declamations

Regrettably, memorization has become a lost art in our schools. This is unfortunate, as Tom Newkirk reminds us in *The Art of Slow Reading*, because having students memorize meaningful historical passages is not simply an exercise in rote learning, "it is claiming a heritage. It is the act of owning a language, making it literally a part of our bodies, to be called upon decades later when it fits a situation" (2011, 77). Memorization, Newkirk argues, "allows language to be written on the mind" (2011, 76).

At the Harlem Village Academies High School (where I taught one year), it is standard practice that students conduct declamations, which are defined "as a recitation of a speech from memory with studied gestures and intonation as an exercise in elocution or rhetoric" (Vocabulary.com 2014). For example, students in history classes are asked to memorize and perform passages from iconic speeches (to see Sheck's performance of Napoleon

Bonaparte's proclamation to his soldiers, search "SM Declamation" on YouTube). In my English classes, I traditionally have students memorize twenty lines of Shakespeare (to see Felipe perform the famous advice scene in *Hamlet*, search http://www.kellygallagher.org/instructional-videos/).

Tell a Joke

Newkirk advocates another way to get students to practice their memorization skills in front of the class: Assign them to tell a joke. He cites the third-grade classroom of Tomasen Carey, who prepared her students "by first telling a joke herself, stressing the way a joke builds often through repetition, often of three instances (like so many fairy tales). She discussed the use of voices and pacing, creating anticipation for the punch line" (2011, 86). When we did this assignment one year, I had students consider the elements of PVLEGS as they practiced their deliveries. Before you ask students to stand in front of the class to deliver their jokes, introduce two major ground rules: (1) the selected jokes have to be appropriate for the classroom and (2) students have to practice the joke numerous times in different small groups where they receive suggestions from their peers on how best to deliver them (Newkirk 2011).

Book Soundtrack

This is a written assignment that I have students turn into a speech. The assignment is simple: Students create a soundtrack to accompany a book or play. I have the students pick scenes from the books they are reading and match them to appropriate songs. I model this with a song that I have selected for the masquerade scene in *Romeo and Juliet*:

SCENE	SONG	ARTIST	SAMPLE LYRICS
Romeo crashes the masquerade party and is struck by Juliet's beauty. He and Juliet share a kiss. At the end of the party, he has to go because he has been identified as a Montague. Juliet doesn't want him to leave and sends the nurse to seek his identity.	"Stay"	Rihanna	"Not really sure how to feel about it. Something in the way you move makes me feel like I can't live without you. It takes me all the way. I want you to stay."

Here are songs Dyamond selected for scenes in *Catching Fire* by Suzanne Collins (2009):

SCENE	SONG	ARTIST	SAMPLE LYRICS
Katniss leaves her boyfriend to go to the Hunger Games.	"One and Only"	Adele	"I don't know why I am scared, I've been here before, Every feeling, every word, I've imagined it all."
Katniss finds her way out of the dome by using the lightning	"Can't Hold Us"	Macklemore and Ryan Lewis	"So we put our hands up like the ceiling can't hold us."
Katniss shows off her dress. She didn't want to do it, but she powers through it.	"Girl on Fire"	Alicia Keys	"Looks like a girl, but she's a flame so bright, she can burn your eyes, better look the other way."
Katniss and the other players are on their podiums as the annual Hunger Games are about to begin.	"The Phoenix"	Fall Out Boy	"Put on your war paint. You are a brick tied to me that's dragging me down. Strike a match and I'll burn you down to the ground."

Once the students have chosen their songs, they give three-minute speeches explaining and defending their selections. Many students weave the music into their talks.

Spoken Poetry

My friend Penny Kittle turned me on to the power of spoken poetry in the classroom, a good way to get students up and speaking in front of the class.

I begin by sharing a number of spoken poems with my students (for a list of high-interest spoken poems, go to kellygallagher.org and search "Kelly's Lists" under "Resources"). When we read a poem for the first time, students put their pens or pencils down and simply enjoy and absorb it. Many of the poems are on YouTube, so we watch and listen to them being read by the poets. In the second-draft reading, we reread the poem, this time marking the "hot spots"—words, phrases, or lines that jump out at us. Once the hot spots are identified, we each choose one and begin writing. Some choose to write poems, others create prose. I do this first, projecting my draft on the screen for students to see as I think out loud while writing. After five minutes or so, I ask my students to begin writing as well, and we begin writing concurrently.

Getting a rough-draft poem down on paper is jusst a start. After we have written a number of them, we pick one poem to take into revision. In Figures 7.4a and 7.4b, you will see how

Draft 1

Nothing is forever.
When I got the news, I was sitting in an airport McDonald's.
Staring in disbelief at my Egg McMuffin.
A word I'll never forget: "glioblastoma."
"What's that?" I asked my wife, who was crying.
"Brain cancer."
Then two more words were uttered that I'll never forget: "It's fatal."
The floor spun underneath me.
Gasping for air. Dizzy. Shocked. Numb.
You watch the sun set too often, it just becomes 6 p.m.
You hang with your friends today you expect you'll hang with them tomorrow.
You forget that nothing is forever.

Flash forward three months: wedding day.
Brad is still standing.
When he walks his daughter down the aisle
there is not a dry eye . .
He stands proudly throughout the ceremony.

Later, I side up to him.
A photographer walks by.
He turns the camera on us,
And just before he takes the shot,
Brad turns and—as a joke—and kisses me on the cheek.
A moment frozen in time.
The scar from his surgery clearly visible.
Looking at the picture now,
I am acutely aware that it is not 6 p.m. anymore.
More like 11:59.
Tomorrow, when you watch the sun set,
Appreciate it in all its beauty.

Figure 7.4a My first poetry draft derived from Phil Kaye's "Repetition"

much my poem changed over the course of ten revisions, all of which were done—five minutes at a time—in front of my students. I began with a line from Phil Kaye's (2011) "Repetition" ("If you watch the sun set too often, it just becomes 6 p.m."), and it is interesting to note that even though that was the line that sparked me to begin drafting, it is a line that did not make it into the final draft of the poem. My last draft ended up far from my first draft.

Draft 2

The Kiss

The call came between flights.
"Glioblastoma," she said.
Words I'll never forget.
Then two more: "It's fatal."
The floor spun underneath me.
Numbly, I found myself quietly
crying in an airport McDonald's

Three months later: wedding day.
Still standing strong,
he walks his daughter down the aisle
Not a dry eye in the house.

Later, I side up to him.
A photographer walks by
turns the camera on us,
And just before his finger clicks the shot,
He turns, kisses me on the cheek.
The surgery scar visible on his head.

Two lives began anew that day.
While one life was slipping away.
This cruel irony
Forever captured
by a kiss frozen in time.

Figure 7.4b My second poetry draft derived from Phil Kaye's "Repetition"

Once we have taken our poems through a number of revisions, it is time to share them with the rest of the class. I pass out a sign-up sheet, and when the scheduled day arrives, students get up and perform their poems to the class.

Listen Closely

To develop my students' listening skills, I use a number of website resources. Here are three of my favorites:

- "Top 100 Speeches": I have students listen to some of the "Top 100 Speeches" found on the American Rhetoric (2014) website (americanrhetoric.com/top100speeches). Most of these speeches come with both audio recordings and transcripts, but in order to sharpen my students' listening abilities, I have them listen and take notes without the texts of the speeches in front of them. Not only do these speeches help my students improve their listening skills, they also shore up their lack of historical knowledge.
- "Left, Right, and Center": Los Angeles public radio station KCRW's free weekly podcast "Left, Right, and Center" provides a "civilized yet provocative antidote to the screaming talking heads that dominate political debate" (KCRW 2014). On this show, a panelist from the political left, a panelist from the political right, and a panelist from the political center civilly argue the week's events. Students are asked to take notes on the arguments made on both sides of the issues, and once the podcast is over, I often ask students to share their thinking in writing. Like the "Top 100 Speeches" assignment, this activity has proved invaluable in broadening my students' knowledge of the world.
- Old Time Radio: Another website that is excellent for building listening skills is RadioLovers.com, where access to classic radio shows is one click away. Teachers can choose from dramas, comedies, mysteries, westerns, science fiction, superheroes, or musicals.

For these listening exercises, students might be asked to apply what are traditionally considered to be reading and writing strategies. As they listen to old time radio programs, for example, I might have students chart literary elements (e.g., theme, foreshadowing) or the structure of the plot (e.g., rising action, conflict). While listening to political speeches or debate, I might have them chart both what was said and what was *not* said.

Student Podcasts

Students can develop their oral literacies by creating podcasts. A good place to start is with the Smithsonian American Art Museum (2014), which provides guidelines on how students can build podcasts around one or more of the pieces of artwork in the Smithsonian American Art Museum's collections (see http://americanart.si.edu/education/resources/ guides/podcast.cfm). Students choose an artwork, research it, and then write scripts aimed at hooking the listeners. The Smithsonian website offers teachers support materials—from how to technically set up the podcasts to providing student models.

Distracted Telephone

Play a modified version of the childhood game "telephone" to build listening skills. A message is whispered to one child, who then whispers into the ear of another child, who then, in turn, whispers it to the next child. The message is passed from child to child until it passes through the entire class. The goal is simple: to keep the message as close to the original as possible. I have older students play telephone as well, but I up the ante a bit. Not only do I start the game with a message to the first student but also I give a second message to the last student, thus creating a game where different messages are heading in opposite directions. To make it harder, I sometimes play annoying music in the background while the game is in progress, or I talk over the students as the messages are being passed.

Make a School Announcement

Almost all schools have morning announcements. Administrators at the Durham Academy in Durham, North Carolina, decided to have some fun when they announced via video that there would be no school due to a snow day: http://www.g105.com/onair/brooke-50858/ the-coolest-snow-day-announcement-you-will-ever-see-12062707/.

Have students create and film their own short morning announcement clips. Here are some topic possibilities for the school announcements:

- Results of a recent game or academic competition
- Student-of-the-month announcement
- Announcement of an upcoming event (game, dance, club meeting)
- A "shout out" for students or staff who deserve recognition
- College acceptance announcements
- Announcement of results on a test, essay, or project
- Preview of an upcoming assembly (or recap of an assembly)
- Infomercial for a given day or time period (e.g., Veteran's Day, Black History Month)

Add 1

National Geographic posts thousands of interesting short videos on its website (http://www. nationalgeographic.com). The topics range from animals to geography to weather disasters. For example, I may have students watch a clip on the violence exhibited by humpback whales (*National Geographic* 2014; to see the video "Wild Hawaii: Violence in the Deep," go to http://channel.nationalgeographic.com/wild/wild-hawaii/videos/violence-in-the-deep/?videoDetect=t%252Cf). As students watch, they are asked to take notes, writing down as many factoids as they can as they listen to the narration.

After showing the video, I place students in a circle. I start with the student to my left and ask him or her to share one factoid. The conversation then moves clockwise, and each student is asked to "add 1"—to share one factoid that has yet to be shared. If a student cannot add 1, or if a student repeats a factoid that has already been shared, he or she is out of the competition. The last student to present a fresh fact is the winner.

When students are first learning this activity, I allow them to consult their notes during the competition, but if I want to up the ante a bit, occasionally I will have them compete without their notes after giving them a moment or two to review them.

Adapting Other Assignments to Strengthen Speaking and Listening Skills

Many of the reading activities described in Chapter 2 and many of the writing activities described in Chapter 4 can also be adapted into short speech activities. For example, a student who has written a 17-word summary could be asked to stand up and share his or her response orally. Here is a list of strategies mentioned in Chapters 2 and 4 that easily could be turned into opportunities for our students to speak and to listen:

What I am advocating in this chapter flies in the face of what is currently favored by the latest rounds of testing of Common Core standards—at least on the speaking side of things. Yes, students might be asked to listen to a speech as part of a state test and be required to respond to it—and this is a step in the right direction—but it remains highly unlikely that students will be tested on their ability to speak effectively. If history is any indicator, what is not tested will fall out of favor in our nation's classrooms, which means teaching students how to speak effectively will be placed on the back burner. This is yet another example where teaching blindly to the latest round of tests is not in the best interest of our students. The development of our students' speaking and listening skills should remain a priority regardless of what is valued by this year's exam.

ACTIVITIES THAT CAN BE ADAPTED INTO SPEAKING AND LISTENING OPPORTUNITIES	
CHAPTER 2	CHAPTER 4
<ul><li>17-Word Summaries</li><li>Write a Headline</li><li>Window Quotes</li><li>Digital Text Summaries</li><li>Summary Plus</li><li>What Is Left Out?</li><li>Fiction/Nonfiction Weave</li></ul>	<ul><li>Moments That Matter</li><li>Stranded</li><li>When the Weather Mattered</li><li>A Change</li><li>First Attempt</li><li>Unprepared</li><li>Near Misses</li><li>Choosing Sides</li><li>You Are a Teacher</li><li>From A to B</li><li>Reverse Bucket List</li><li>Six Things You Should Know About . . .</li><li>Your Birthday in History</li><li>Photographs That Mattered</li><li>Who Made That?</li><li>36 Hours In . . .</li></ul>

CHAPTER 8

Shift Happens

Today, in most schools, the "effectiveness" of teachers is measured by their students' performance on annual state tests. Because of the importance placed on these test results, teachers walk into their classrooms every day focused on preparing their students for the standardized exams that will arrive in the spring (one school I visited this year had a "Countdown to Test Day" poster hung in the entranceway to the school—"34 More Days Until We Dominate on the State Tests!"). Unfortunately, when we focus on preparing students for distant standardized tests, three key problems ensue: (1) Preparing students for a standardized reading test is fruitless, because there is no such thing as a standardized reading test; (2) Standardized testing leads to a narrowing of the curriculum; and (3) Standardized testing leads to the creation of standardized students.

Let's take a closer look at these three issues.

Preparing students for a standardized reading test is fruitless, because there is no such thing as a standardized reading test.

Hirsch and Pondiscio (2010–2011) argue that there is no such thing as a standardized reading test, because the tests we give our students to measure their ability to read are really not testing their ability to read. Instead, these tests really measure the depth (or lack of depth) of our students' background knowledge. Here's an example:

> If a baseball fan reads "A-Rod hit into a 6-4-3 double play to end the game," he needs not another word to understand that the New York Yankees lost when Alex Rodriguez came up to bat with a man on first base and one out and then hit a ground ball to the shortstop, who threw to the second baseman, who relayed to first in time to catch Rodriguez for the final out. If you've never heard of A-Rod or a 6-4-3 double play and cannot reconstruct the game situation in your mind's eye, you are not a poor reader. You merely lack the domain-specific vocabulary and

knowledge of baseball needed to fill in the gaps. Even simple texts, like those on reading tests, are riddled with gaps—domain knowledge and vocabulary that the writer assumes the reader knows. (2010–2011, 50)

Students who know baseball would score well in responding to the A-Rod sentence; students who do not know baseball at all would struggle with it. Because there are thirty-five very diverse students sitting in my third-period class, there is no single test devised that accurately assesses their reading abilities without putting some of them at a distinct disadvantage. Any given test will value the background knowledge of some students while disregarding the background knowledge of others. Our children's reading ability is tested without regard to whether they possess the requisite background knowledge.

Standardized testing leads to a narrowing of the curriculum.

To get a sense of how national tests drive the bus, let's look back at what happened in our schools when NCLB was the flavor du jour. The following findings are cited in Yong Zhao's *World Class Learners*:

- Five years after the implementation of NCLB, "over 60% of school districts reported they had increased instructional time for math and English language arts, while 44% reported they had reduced time for other subjects or activities such as social science, science, art and music, physical education, and lunch and/or recess" (Zhao 2012, 38). This amounted to a 32% decrease in the teaching of these subjects. This decrease, of course, had an adverse effect on young readers, as they have to know stuff to read stuff. The less a student knows about history, science, art, and music, the narrower his or her prior knowledge will be.
- A second level of curriculum narrowing occurred within the math and English language arts classes, where most districts narrowed the curricula to what was covered on the state tests (Zhao 2012).
- "Instructional quality and opportunities to access a diverse curriculum deteriorated. Cognitively complex teaching became more basic-skill orientated and students became ultimately less cognitively nimble." (Zhao 2012, 40)

Clearly, the testing that coincided with NCLB narrowed the curriculum, and in doing so, it also narrowed our students' thinking. And now a new round of tests have arrived—those designed to measure implementation of the CCSS and of other standards newly adopted by outlier states—and once again it is troubling to consider how these exams are influencing our classrooms. As I write this, for example, I am teaching in New York and our students recently participated in the inaugural administration of CCSS-aligned high-stakes state exams. The students were given reading passages over three days—passages that leaned heavily toward nonfiction, with very little poetry mixed in. Close reading was heavily emphasized.

Because their "effectiveness" is measured by their students' performance on these exams, it is not hard to predict how the new exams will change how teachers teach. Nonfiction will be disproportionately ramped up, fiction and poetry will be deemphasized, and students will be given a lot of choppy, unconnected close reading practice. As a result, the new tests will narrow the reading curriculum and instruction in a way that is not in the best interest of our children.

Standardized testing leads to the creation of standardized students.

Another problem inherent in herding all students toward the same standardized test is that we end up leveling our students to the (often rather low) bar set by the tests. Do we really want to create a generation of "standardized" students? As Tom Newkirk notes in *Holding On to Good Ideas in a Time of Bad Ones*:

> A rationalized, consistent, centralized, uniform system of instruction is incredibly attractive. These systems allow administrators to speak with confidence about the education process and its product. *Standardization* and *standards* seem so linguistically close that one shades into another. It may be that there is something aesthetically pleasing in uniform action—the pleasure of watching a drill team, for example. Yet, standardization only leads to sameness, not necessarily quality, and rarely to excellence. (2009, 8–9)

Newkirk is right: Standardization rarely leads to excellence. When the curriculum is narrowed into a sameness, when we adopt a "one size fits all" approach, creativity suffers and students whose talents are not valued by the tests risk being marginalized. At a time of globalization—when it is crucial that we nurture creativity and intellectual risk taking in our students—this latest round of tests is having the opposite effect by standardizing our students. Instead of "racing to the top," our students are travelling in herds.

A Better Way

When I first proposed the idea for this book, I half-jokingly suggested *Calm Down* as the working title (actually, I had added a couple more words in this proposed title, but we'll keep it clean here). I had suggested this as a title because of the level of stress teachers are under. When you consider how daunting it is to teach thirty-six anchor language arts standards (ten reading standards, ten writing standards, six listening and speaking standards, and six standards in language conventions) to a classroom of adolescents, is it any wonder that in some schools the teacher dropout rate is actually higher than the student dropout rate (Kain 2011)? I can't think of another time in my thirty years in the classroom where teaching was as stressful as it is now.

It doesn't have to be this hard. Allow me to suggest a much simpler approach to measuring a teacher's effectiveness. Imagine teaching in a school where all this overtesting has been thrown out the window—a place where a teacher's effectiveness is instead evaluated on four simple criteria:

1. What percentage of your students can walk into a bookstore (or visit Goodreads.com) and know where to find books that interest them?
2. What percentage of your students write without being asked to do so by a teacher?
3. What percentage of your students can stand and speak effectively and confidently in front of a group of people?
4. What percentage of your students can actively listen to others—can carefully consider both what is said and what is not said?

Imagine these four questions forming the rubric that is used to measure a teacher's effectiveness, and thus, to determine a teacher's salary. The rubric might look like this:

	HIGH SALARY – – – – – LOW SALARY				
	100%-80%	79%-60%	59%-40%	39%-20%	19%-0%
1. What percentage of your students can walk into a bookstore (or visit Goodreads.com) and know where to find books that interest them?					
2. What percentage of your students write without being asked to do so by a teacher?					
3. What percentage of your students can stand and speak effectively and confidently in front of a group of people?					
4. What percentage of your students can actively listen to others—can carefully consider both what is said and what is not said?					

Ridiculous, right? Perhaps. But let's pause for a moment and think about how the teaching would change if this rubric were a reality. Let's look at just one of these questions—*What percentage of your students can walk into a bookstore (or visit Goodreads.com) and know where to find books that interest them?*—and let's explore how a question as simple as this would change how reading is taught.

What percentage of your students can walk into a bookstore (or visit Goodreads.com) and know where to find books that interest them?

If a teacher's salary was dependent on the percentage of students who could find interesting books on their own, my bet is that the teacher's approach would immediately change. How, specifically, would things change? Extensive libraries would be immediately built in every classroom, and as a result, students would have access to a lot more high-interest books. There would be a lot more choice when it came to what students read, and students would be given say in planning and mapping out their reading journeys through the school year. Book talks and book sharing would become a central tenet in all ELA classrooms, and students would discover authors they would have otherwise never encountered. Book club reading would gain higher prominence, and students who were exposed to books they liked would abandon the fake reading practices they have become so expert in. Students would be placed on the pathway to being lifelong readers.

It is also worth noting what would be *removed* from our classrooms should this question become the criteria for judging a teacher's effectiveness. Gone would be the worksheets. Gone would be the test prep. Gone would be the ten-week unit where students overanalyze a book to the point of readicide. Gone would be the bubbling in of multiple-choice quizzes and exams. Gone would be the boredom that is generated when all of these numbing teaching practices converge on fragile, reluctant readers.

I can hear the questions being directed to me as you read this: Is this a call for the abandonment of whole-class novels? Will teachers no longer be able to decide what students should read? Will I no longer be able to teach *To Kill a Mockingbird*? To answer these questions—and more—it might be helpful for us to revisit a proposal I made in *Readicide*; doing so will better explain the new shift that I am about to advocate in this chapter.

A Time of Shifts

We are living in a time of shifts in education. A focus on NCLB requirements has shifted to the CCSS (or other standards). Classrooms with less diversity are shifting into becoming classrooms with more diversity. Whole-class, blanket instruction is shifting to differentiated instruction. Professional development is shifting from traditional workshops to virtual learning and to social media. Traditional books are being replaced by e-readers. In the face of all this shifting, it is only natural to wonder: How much shift is occurring in the teaching of reading in the middle and high school?

To get a sense of this, let's return to the shift I advocated in *Readicide*—the 50/50 Approach—which called for half the reading done in school to be recreational in nature (Gallagher 2009, 117). In the chart that follows, you will find the ten recommendations made in the 50/50 Approach. Next to these recommendations is a scorecard indicating whether these shifts have indeed occurred in our schools.

RECOMMENDATION MADE IN *READICIDE*	IS THIS HAPPENING IN OUR SCHOOLS?	SCORECARD: HAS THE SHIFT OCCURRED?
Never lose sight that our highest priority is to raise students who become *lifelong* readers. What our students read in school is important; what they read the rest of their lives is *more* important.	Though there are certainly exceptions, I see very little evidence that schools are valuing the idea of developing lifelong readers.	**No**
Recognize that massive test preparation is not a justification for killing readers.	In most schools, test preparation remains the central focus.	**No**
Always keep the 50/50 Approach in mind. Do not allow recreational reading to be drowned in a tsunami of academic reading. Maintain a balance between the kinds of reading your students do. Place a higher value on fun reading.	Generally, especially in secondary schools, almost all the reading being done is academic in nature. In many schools, no recreational reading is occurring. Almost all reading is "hard." And when no recreational reading is occurring in school, often this means little or no recreational occurs at home.	**No**
Provide adequate time in school to read so that students have an opportunity to develop recreational reading habits.	Most schools have abandoned sustained silent reading because they see it as a "soft" use of time. It is increasingly rare to find a secondary school that sets time aside for students to read recreationally.	**No**
Make sure students have access to a book flood, a place on campus where they are surrounded by high-interest reading materials.	I ask this question wherever I go: "How many of you work at a school where the entire faculty has recently set aside time to talk in depth about whether our students have enough interesting things to read?" Very few teachers and/or administrators raise their hands. Student access to interesting books remains a huge problem in many schools.	**No**

RECOMMENDATION MADE IN *READICIDE*	IS THIS HAPPENING IN OUR SCHOOLS?	SCORECARD: HAS THE SHIFT OCCURRED?
Model the importance of reading to students by being a reader.	I have met a number of teachers who try to do this daily, but I also have met a number of teachers who do not read.	**In some places**
Encourage students to recognize, to seek, and to maintain reading flow.	Flow will not happen if kids do not have interesting books and time to read them. See previous comments about access to interesting books.	**No**
Stop chopping up recreational books with worksheets and quizzes.	First, recreational reading is hard to find in our schools. Where it is found, I still find lots of evidence that many teachers are building the wrong kinds of accountability measures.	**In some places**
Stop grading recreational reading. Teachers should give kids credit for recreational reading, but stop grading it.	See box above.	**In some places**
Understand that recreational reading actually is test preparation. When students read books recreationally they are building valuable knowledge capital that will help them in future reading.	If people in schools understood that recreational reading is actually an important component of test preparation, it would not be so hard to find recreational reading programs in secondary schools.	**No**

Of these ten recommendations, seven of them are generally not happening; three of them are spotty at best. In other words, in an age of great shifts in education, very little has shifted when it comes to the teaching of adolescent readers. The teaching of reading remains stuck in a paradigm that doesn't work, and when students are stuck in a paradigm that doesn't work, there are dire consequences:

- Here are SAT reading scores since 2002, the year No Child Left Behind was implemented:

2002	504	2008	501
2003	507	2009	501
2004	508	2010	501
2005	508	2011	497
2006	503	2012	496
2007	502	2013	496

Source: National Center for Education Statistics 2013a

- The 2012 and the 2013 SAT reading scores are the lowest scores in thirty years.

- Many of our college-bound students are not ready for postsecondary studies, even those heading to our most selective universities (see Figure 8.1). At the community college level, as many as 60 percent of students are not prepared for the academic demands that await them.

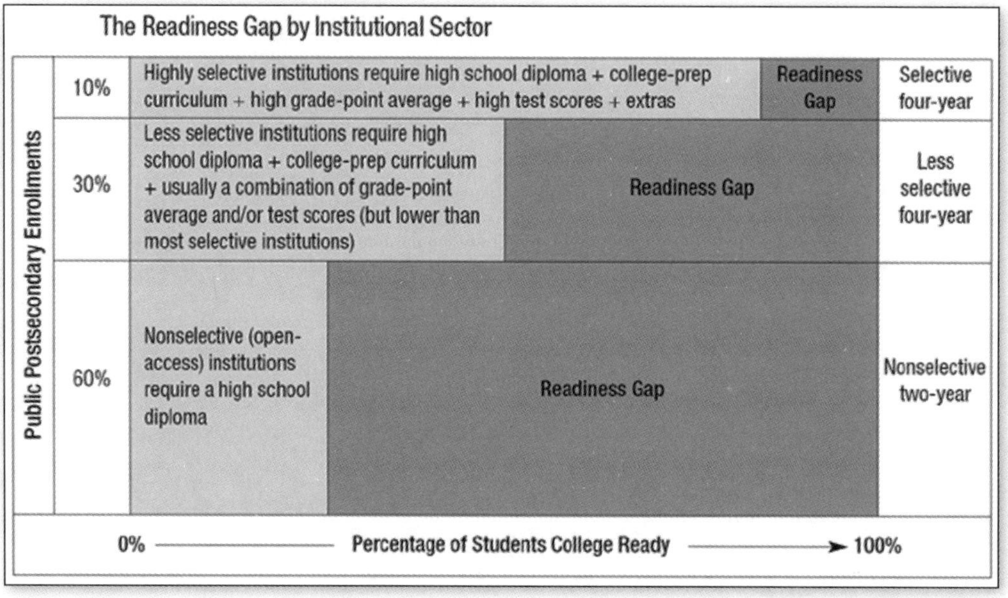

The Readiness Gap by Institutional Sector

	Public Postsecondary Enrollments			
10%	Highly selective institutions require high school diploma + college-prep curriculum + high grade-point average + high test scores + extras	Readiness Gap		Selective four-year
30%	Less selective institutions require high school diploma + college-prep curriculum + usually a combination of grade-point average and/or test scores (but lower than most selective institutions)	Readiness Gap		Less selective four-year
60%	Nonselective (open-access) institutions require a high school diploma	Readiness Gap		Nonselective two-year

0% ———— Percentage of Students College Ready ————▶ 100%

Figure 8.1 The readiness gap (National Center for Public Policy and Higher Education/SREB 2010)

- One study I cited in *Readicide* found that there is a "calamitous, universal falling off of reading that occurs around the age of 13" (112). Now, seven years after that study was published, little appears to have changed. According to new statistics released by the Labor Department, teenagers between the ages of fifteen and nineteen are down to reading *only four minutes a day* (Kurtzleben 2014). This year I have fewer dedicated book readers amongst my students than I have ever had in my thirty-year teaching career. Figure 8.2 shows that, generally speaking, the younger one is, the less likely that he or she is reading very much.

Let's recap: We are seeing the worst SAT scores in thirty years. A large percentage of students now enter college unprepared for the reading (and other) demands placed upon them. We are seeing fewer dedicated book readers and a continued fall in the amount of time spent reading. And a new set of reading standards that continue to narrow our students' reading experiences have been thrust upon us.

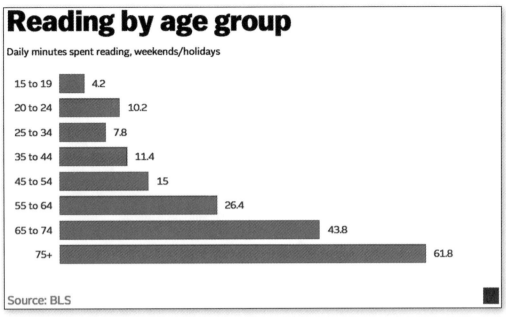

Figure 8.2 Reading by age group (Kurtzleben 2014)

All of this adds up to the need for us to shift our thinking once again.

A Middle Ground Between Too Easy and Too Hard

In considering where schools have gone wrong in building lifelong readers—and how this may help us to rethink our approach to teaching reading—we should start by looking at what kids are being asked to read in our classrooms. In most secondary schools I have visited, there is only one kind of reading going on: hard reading. Students spend a number of weeks dissecting *Hamlet* before moving on to wrestle with *Beowulf* before grappling with whatever core work is lined up next. When students finish "wrestling" with one hard text, another is thrust in front of them. I put "wrestling" in quotation marks because, in reality, many of the students are not actually reading. They are skimming and listening carefully in class. Very little wrestling of difficult text is actually occurring. Worse, many students—including those in our honors classes—are proud that they don't actually need to read the books. The "one hard book after another" approach, which, again, is predominant, is fertile ground for creating students who fake-read. It is a recipe for killing readers.

Paradoxically, I see another kind of reading going on in schools: reading that is too easy. On my campus, for example, we have a daily, twenty-four-minute, campus-wide reading block during which students are encouraged to self-select books to read recreationally. And what happens when we ask reluctant readers to choose reading material? They often pick the easiest books they can find. This is why I have high school students who read at grade level still spinning their wheels reading *A Child Called "It"* (Pelzer 1995) or *Diary of a Wimpy Kid* (Kinney 2007). Reading books that are too easy can have the same deleterious effect on young readers as asking them to read books that are too hard: interest is soon lost and reading becomes a bore.

I have come to believe that most of the reading done in our schools is either too easy or too hard. This is different from the reading that occurs outside the walls of the school building, where most people read somewhere in that zone between "too easy" and "too hard." This zone is where you and I do most of our reading. And it is in this zone between "too easy" and "too hard" where I propose that most of our students' reading should be occurring. So how do we move our kids into this new zone of reading?

A New Shift: From 50/50 to 20/80

My attempt to move students into the zone of reading between "too easy" and "too hard" begins by replacing the 50/50 Approach I advocated in *Readicide* with a 20/80 Approach. In short, I am striving for the following kinds of reading for my students (Figure 8.3):

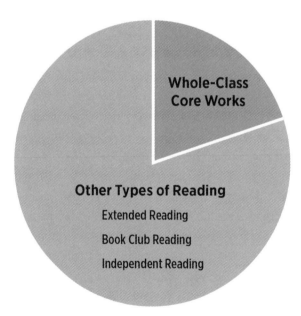

Figure 8.3 The 20/80 Approach

Let's take a closer look at each section of the 20/80 Approach reading pie.

20 Percent: Whole-Class Core Works

There is a lot of shifting going on right now around the topic of teaching the whole-class core work. Some people I respect a lot are advocating a severe limiting of, or, in some cases, a complete removal of whole-class core works from the curriculum. Their arguments are many:

- Different students have different interests. One book does not speak to the same thirty students.
- Requiring students to read books that are too hard for them is the central contributing factor in turning kids off to reading.
- Choice is a key motivating factor for young readers. When the teacher chooses the text, motivation suffers.
- Hard reading often shuts down readers and leads to fake reading. "SparkNotes reading" replaces real reading.
- Hard reading often leads to slow reading. If all reading is hard, fluency, and thus, comprehension, will suffer.
- There are tons of worthy books to read. Isn't it presumptuous of the teacher to decide which one is worthy for all students to read?
- Choosing a classic for students to read perpetuates racism and/or sexism, as most of the canon is made up of dead, white, European, male writers; students need to read more culturally relevant authors and books.

Each of these concerns speak to me, but I remain steadfast in believing that whole-class core work instruction remains an important part (20 percent) of my classroom. Here are my responses to each of the preceding concerns:

Different students have different interests. One book does not speak to the same thirty students.

Though I agree that my students' interests are varied, I do believe some works are so rich that they merit a whole-class reading. *Hamlet,* for example, is one of these works. Its themes cut across time, across cultures, across generations. There is something rich to think about in this play for every one of my students. *Hamlet* explores some pretty serious and relevant questions: What happens to us when we die? What are the ramifications of your actions (or inactions)? What are the consequences of misogyny? How are nations led to ruin? Is revenge ever worthwhile? Is suicide ever a reasonable option? What happens when we are guided by lust instead of by reason?

All students, not just a select few, should have the opportunity to wrestle with the questions embedded in *Hamlet*. Some works are grand enough to speak to all. *Hamlet* is one of them.

Requiring students to read books that are too hard for them is the central contributing factor in turning kids off to reading.

First, I have always been a little queasy determining if a book is too hard for my students. Readability formulas are sometimes unreliable and are often affected by so many factors— motivation, genre, prior knowledge, syntax—that I sometimes struggle with telling my students they can only read within a predetermined band. That said, it is clear that there are books that are truly too hard for my students to read on their own, and asking them to do so would amount to, as some have suggested, educational malpractice.

But when I teach a whole-class work, I am not asking my students to read hard works on their own. I am asking them to read them *alongside me* and *alongside their classmates*. If the work, like *Hamlet*, is too hard for them to read independently, then I have to design lessons that help fill the gaps created by their reading deficiencies. When teaching *Hamlet* to students far below reading level, for example, I give them copies of *No Fear Shakespeare* (SparkNotes 2003), which translates Shakespearean language into modern language. My goal is not to enable students to be able to decipher 400-year-old language; my goal is that my students understand the play well enough to think deeply about what they've read. If need be, I provide some students with professional audio recordings so they can listen along as they read. In addition, I show several different film interpretations of key scenes. When deep confusion continues, we stop and revisit key passages in the text, pausing for students to discuss and to write about their thinking. I don't assign *Hamlet*; I teach it.

It is counterintuitive, but I think students—with expert guidance from the teacher— should read a few books (and poems and short texts) that are a bit too hard for them. This is how young readers stretch and grow. There are lines in *Hamlet* I still do not understand, and I have read the play countless times. Does this mean I never should have attempted to read it?

Choice is a key motivating factor for young readers. When the teacher chooses the text, motivation suffers.

I agree that students are often demotivated when the teacher selects the text that everyone will read. I can remember the trepidation I felt in high school when *Hamlet* became my required reading. It was hard and confusing, and I am sure I would have rather read something else. But I love *Hamlet* today because someone *made me* read it. This is not a bad thing, as there is a greatness in *Hamlet* that I needed to "discover"—a greatness I never would have encountered had I not been required to read it. This is my job as a teacher of deep literature—to design lessons so that my students can discover this greatness as well. (My thinking here is not simply about *Hamlet*. I am using that work as a placeholder for all great works of literature.)

That said, there will always be some students who do not like the whole-class text. This also does not concern me, as my job is not to get every student to like the work; my job is to get every student to recognize the value of reading the text. Not every student will adore *Hamlet*, but I do want every student to take thinking away from the reading of the play that will make him or her smarter about the world in which we live. Or to take another example, you don't have to like science fiction to get some value from reading science fiction. Some students don't like reading *1984*, but all who read Orwell's novel learn to understand propaganda techniques and language manipulation—skills they can apply well beyond high school. There is a lifelong value to studying *1984*, even if it is not your favorite book or genre.

Hard reading often shuts down readers and leads to fake reading. "SparkNotes reading" replaces real reading.

Asking kids to read hard books is not the problem. Asking them to read *only* hard books is the problem. If everything they read is hard, eventually they will shut down or resort to fake reading. But remember, in the approach I am advocating here, hard reading makes up only 20 percent of the reading I want my students to do over the course of the year. Most of the reading I will ask them to do is much more likely to be found in the zone between "too easy" and "too hard."

And one last thought about "SparkNotes reading": It does not bother me in the least that my students read SparkNotes. I have read them as well over the years, and I have learned from them. I don't mind if a student reads the *To Kill a Mockingbird* SparkNotes while concurrently reading the novel. In fact, reading SparkNotes *may help the student to enjoy the novel.* This lesson was reinforced to me this year when I went to see a production of *Twelfth Night* on Broadway. Since I had not read the play in many years, can you guess what I did before attending? That's right. I went online and read the complete synopsis of the play. This "cheating" did not detract from the play I was to see later that evening; on the contrary, it made my "reading" of the play much better.

The reading of SparkNotes does not bother me; what bothers me is when students read *only* the SparkNotes. These notes should augment the reading of major literary works, not replace the reading of them.

Hard reading often leads to slow reading. If all reading is hard, fluency, and thus, comprehension, will suffer.

Slow reading is an important skill to cultivate, especially in an age when students are doing a lot of "click and go" reading. All of the scanning and skimming while reading digitally has cognitive neuroscientists worried that humans "seem to be developing digital brains with new circuits for skimming through the torrent of information online. This alternative way of reading is competing with traditional deep reading circuitry developed over several millennia" (Rosenwald 2014).

Maryanne Wolf, a Tufts University cognitive neuroscientist and the author of *Proust and the Squid: The Story and Science of the Reading Brain*, worries "that the superficial way we read during the day is affecting us when we have to read with more in-depth processing" (Rosenwald 2014). Wolf warns of an "eye byte" reading culture where students risk losing the ability to read deeply, and she suggests that educators work hard to cultivate "biliterate" reading brains—brains that can scan and skim as well as read slowly and deeply over extended periods of time. This second skill set—the ability to read slowly and deeply over extended periods of time—is only developed one way: by having students read slowly and deeply over extended periods of time. There are no shortcuts to developing that skill set. Hard reading is the place where the deeper half of the biliterate brain is developed, and the vast majority of my students—most of whom spend most of their reading lives skimming and scanning—need more practice reading cognitively challenging, extended texts.

I am not concerned that the kind of slow, deep reading I am advocating here will have deleterious effects on my students' overall reading fluency. In fact, I am arguing just the opposite: Students need practice slowing down and really wrestling with text. But it is also important to remember that this kind of deep, slow reading makes up only 20 percent of my students' proposed reading diet. They will still be reading lots of other kinds of texts at a much brisker pace (more on this later in this chapter). Certainly enough of this other kind of reading will occur so that both their fluency and their comprehension will steadily improve.

There are tons of worthy books to read. Isn't it presumptuous of the teacher to decide which one is worthy for all students to read?

If I were a social science teacher teaching an American history class, I certainly would not try to teach every major event in this nation's history. Doing so would flatten out the curriculum into a coverage approach, and would lead my students into becoming memorizers instead of thinkers. Instead, I would make sure that my students studied in depth specific events that I had selected. For example, I would certainly spend a great deal of time on the Civil War because I believe that students who do not deeply understand the Civil War do not deeply understand American history. I would not leave it to chance that my students would choose the Civil War as a unit of study. On the contrary, an in-depth study of the Civil War would be a nonnegotiable requirement, and I would design a unit that would take *all of my students* into a deep examination of this seminal event.

Likewise, if I were an art teacher teaching a sculpture class, I would have students study Michelangelo's *David,* and we would continue to develop an appreciation of greatness by studying other influential works of sculpture (chosen by me, the teacher). Students would also be given opportunities to branch out and explore other sculptors who they felt were worthy of study, but these explorations would be intertwined with whole-class study of sculptors who had greatly influenced the field.

If I want my students to gain a deeper understanding and appreciation of my content area (in this case, the study of literature), I must select some works that are worthy of whole-class study. Is it presumptuous for me to select which titles are worthy of whole-class attention? Yes, of course! But this is no more presumptuous than the history teacher who selects the Civil War to be studied in depth, or the art teacher who decides that the unit of study will start with Michelangelo's *David* and work outward from there. My job is to bring greatness into the classroom and set it in front of the students, and to do this, I have to make a judgment call on what defines "greatness." Doing so *requires* me to be presumptuous. In fact, teachers in all content areas are presumptuous, because no teacher can teach everything in his or her content area in one year (or semester). All teachers make serious decisions on what to leave in and what to leave out. All teachers are presumptuous (whether they know it or not).

One last note on this point: I am not advocating that individual teachers be empowered to decide which core books are worthy of whole-class instruction. I have seen too many teachers pick books that are too "light" or, in some cases, books that are inappropriate for the entire class to read. What I am advocating is that members of English departments sit down together and have serious discussions as to what books are worthy of whole-class instruction. These decisions should be team decisions. (For what makes a book worthy of whole-class instruction, read Carol Jago's *With Rigor for All* [2011].)

Choosing a classic for students to read perpetuates racism and/or sexism, as most of the canon is made up of dead, white, European, male writers; students need to read more culturally relevant authors and books.

Not all whole-class novels need to emanate from the traditional canon. In my school in California, where my students are predominantly Latino, we studied Rudolfo Anaya's (1972) *Bless Me, Ultima* as a whole-class read. In the school where I taught in New York, the students are predominantly African-American, which is one reason they read Toni Morrison's *The Bluest Eye* (1994). Again, I would never teach a whole-class novel by *any* author unless the book was worthy of a deep study, but there are many books outside the traditional canon worthy of whole-class reading.

That said, I am also a proponent of teaching the classics, and there is no denying that a literature class steeped in teaching the classics will favor dead, white, European, male writers. This is another reason why the classics only compose 20 percent of the reading my students will do in a school year. The rest of the reading my students do will give them plenty of opportunity to dive into more culturally relevant authors and books.

80 Percent: The Other Types of Reading

The whole-class novel approach discussed in the preceding section still represents reading that is very hard for my students. The goal, however, behind the shift to the 20/80 Approach is to give my students a lot more experience reading in the zone found between "too easy" and "too hard." This targeted zone comprises three different kinds of reading—extended reading, club reading, and independent reading—which are defined as follows.

Extended Reading

"Extended reading" extends a core work and branches students into related readings. If students had just completed *1984*, for example, I might put them in groups and suggest one of the following dystopias as their next read. Each group then decides which book it wants to read.

Suggested Extended Reads

Awaken by Katie Kacvinsky (2011)

The Book Thief by Markus Zusak (2006)

Divergent by Veronica Roth (2012)

The Last Book in the Universe by Rodman Philbrick (2000)

Little Brother by Cory Doctorow (2008)

Matched by Ally Condie (2010)

Snow Falling in Spring: Coming of Age in China During the Cultural Revolution by Moying Li (2010)

Escape From Camp 14 by Blaine Harden (2012)

The extended list is suggested: Students have the right to propose other titles they feel would also extend a big idea found in the core work. (For this and other text sets built around core works, search my name at Booksource.com and use "KellyG" as a code to receive a discount. Please note that I do not personally profit from my association with Booksource—all of my proceeds for the sale of these sets are paid in high-interest books, which are then donated to needy schools. I receive no payment.)

In extended reading, students choose what to read, but their choices are limited by the connection to the core work and by the teacher's recommended reading list (though students can propose other titles).

Club Reading

In club reading, students have choice when it comes to what they will read, but these readings will be done in small-group settings. Here are some central tenets of book club reading:

- *Students are grouped.* The teacher forms the book club groups after careful consideration of reading abilities and interests, student motivation, gender, and the personalities involved. Students are given some voice in grouping decisions as well, as they are given the opportunity to submit suggested partners (with rationales) to the teacher.
- *Choice is the centerpiece.* In their book clubs, students choose which books they will read. Sometimes the new selection may extend the reading of the previous selection; other times this is not the case. Often, students are encouraged to pick a book that "pushes back" or counters what they have just read. Sometimes the book chosen is completely disconnected to any previous readings. With these considerations in mind, the students in the small group decide what the next read will be.
- *Groups meet regularly.* Each group meets three times over the course of reading their book, and those meetings should occur when they have read one-third of the book, when they have read two-thirds of the book, and when they have finished reading the book. These are rough goals, for each group determines its own pacing and due dates. Some students will read faster than required by the due dates. When this happens they are encouraged to revisit and skim the section of reading before the discussion.
- *Groups meet over the long haul.* The book clubs are not formed until the reading culture of the classroom is established, and this usually does not occur until after the first couple of months of the school year. Once the groups are established, I want

students to build reading relationships with one another, which take time to develop. (One disclaimer: occasionally groups may have to be adjusted if a conflict arises that is not readily solvable.)

- *There is instruction attached to the book club meetings.* Even though students are self-selecting the books to be read, there is still instruction attached to book club meetings. Before each club meeting, a mini-lesson is conducted by the teacher. Some of the lessons may be tied to identifying big ideas in the books. Students might be asked to consider one or more of the following questions: What is worth talking about? What does the author want us to think about? What is a big idea that is hiding in this book? These questions, which can be asked at all three meetings, are designed to encourage students to track their thinking over time, and in doing so, to make them more discerning readers. Other mini-lessons might be designed to enable students to recognize the writer's craft—to notice the writer's "moves." Sometimes light is shined on these moves to help students understand how these moves help readers to uncover the big idea(s). Other times students look at a writer's moves because doing so leads them to adopt the same moves for their own writing. Recognizing good writing is foundational to creating good writing.

- *Student thinking should be made visible.* As they read, students capture their thinking in thought logs (composition books), and these logs are brought to each book club meeting to help spur meaningful conversation. Students are also asked to share sentences from the books that exhibit beautiful craft—some of which we will study later as a class.

- *Assessment comes in many forms.* How does the teacher know if the students are doing their reading and whether or not they are generating meaningful conversations? I recommend the following assessment tools:

  - Book club notes. The teacher sits in on the students' club discussions and takes notes, getting a sense of who is deeply contributing to the conversation.
  - One-on-one notes. The teacher confers with individual students, again measuring the depth of each student's participation and thoughtfulness. These conferences are built into SSR time and other times when students are working independently.
  - Student thought logs are collected and assessed.

Independent Reading

In independent reading, students select books to read on their own. Of course, I do many things to help students "discover" high-interest books. The first, and by far the most important, thing I do is to make sure there are high-interest books in the classroom library, which helps me to match students with the right books. Here are other strategies I use to generate interest in books:

- I begin each class with a Reading Minute—a brief commercial on a book I think my students might read. I read something interesting to them for one minute.
- Students get up in front of the class and share books they are enjoying. After the first month of school, students sign up and conduct the Reading Minutes.
- I keep a large three-ring notebook in the classroom titled "Books We Recommend." Inside the notebook, there are dividers labeled by genre (e.g., "sports," "science fiction"). Each section has notebook paper in it, and when a student really likes a book, she creates an entry that lists the author, title, and a brief explanation on why she recommends the book. When a student doesn't know what book he might read next, he can open the notebook, find his genre of interest, and look up book titles that other students have recommended.
- About once a quarter I conduct a book pass. When students walk in the door, there is a book placed on every desk. Each student reads that book for one minute, then passes it to the next student. In half an hour, each student is exposed to thirty good books. As they sample these books students write the titles of books that interest them in a "Books to Read" list. They can refer to their lists later in the year when they are at a loss on what to read next.

All my students like to read, but they don't all know it yet. Getting the right book to the right kid at the right time is the key to developing independent readers.

Nirvana High School: A Student's Reading Year

The 20/80 Approach I am advocating in these pages is built on work that came before me—most notably by Richard Allington (2001) in *What Really Matters for Struggling Readers* and by Penny Kittle (2013) in *Book Love*. Working from their thinking, I now visualize what a year in the life of a reader might look like in my dream secondary school. Here is a possible week-by-week breakdown of that vision:

SUGGESTED TIMETABLE FOR A STUDENT'S READING YEAR AT NIRVANA HIGH SCHOOL	
WEEK 1	Set up reading expectations/Why should you read?/Start looking at good books.
WEEKS 2–4	Read independent book #1.
WEEKS 5–7	Read independent book #2.
WEEKS 8–11	Read core work #1: *1984*.
WEEKS 12–14	Read extended reading book.
WEEKS 15–17	Read book club selection #1.
WEEKS 18–20	Read book club selection #2.
WEEKS 21–23	Read independent book #3.
WEEKS 24–27	Read book club selection #3.
WEEKS 28–32	Read independent book #4.
WEEKS 33–35	Read core work #2: *Hamlet*.
WEEKS 36–38	Read book club selection #4.
WEEKS 39–40	Write reading reflections/Create a reading portfolio.

Or to think about it in a different form, see the curriculum map depicted in Figure 8.4.

Breaking the year down into a week-by-week schedule brings good news and bad news. On one hand, it is very helpful to see an overview of what a reading year looks like, but, on the other hand, I share this knowing my students will not fit perfectly into a cookie-cutter schedule. (What happens, for example, to the kid who wants to read a really long book—a book that cannot be finished in a three-week time frame?) In reality, a one-size-fits-all schedule does not fit all. Obviously, adjustments have to be made based on interactions with students. Given these limitations, however, I still think it is important to begin the school year with the "big picture" roadmap of my students' reading journeys in mind.

WHAT MIGHT A 20/80 APPROACH LOOK LIKE OVER THE COURSE OF A HIGH SCHOOL YEAR?				
	20%	80%		
	WHOLE-CLASS CORE READING	EXTENDED READING	BOOK CLUB READING	INDEPENDENT READING
SEMESTER 1 WEEKS 1-20	Core work: *1984*. Read by all. Included would be auxiliary readings (e.g., close reading, poems, articles, other related readings)	After reading *1984*, students choose related books to read. They might choose one from this suggested list: *Awaken* *The Book Thief* *Divergent* *The Last Book in the Universe* *Matched* *Feed* *Snow Falling in Spring* *Escape From Camp 14* Or students may propose a title of their own.	These titles are selected by the groups. Each book club will be expected to read four books per semester (see suggested timetable).	Varies by student. Any reading done "on the side" is a bonus.
SEMESTER 2 WEEKS 21-40	Core work: *Hamlet*. Read by all. Included would be auxiliary readings (e.g., close reading, poems, articles, other related readings)	None	These titles are selected by the groups. Each book club will be expected to read four books per semester (see suggested timetable).	Varies by student. Any reading done "on the side" is a bonus.

Figure 8.4 A suggested reading curriculum map

For most secondary schools—and for many elementary schools as well—this proposed reading schedule is a very different paradigm for how to build readers. So different, in fact, that I suggest this school might be called Nirvana High School. To make this dream a reality, decision makers in our schools will have to think very differently. As I write this, for example, I am teaching at the Harlem Village Academies in New York, and I am fortunate enough to be in a school system that is willing and flexible enough to make sure it provides significant funding so that book clubs can occur. By the time you read this, however, I will be back teaching in a large urban district in California, and I anticipate that making the shift towards 20/80 reading will be much more problematic, if not initially impossible. Why? The obstacles are many:

- The philosophy behind the teaching of reading will need to change—for both teachers and administrators.
- Schools will have to rethink how money is allocated. It will be necessary to spend less on the acquisition of whole-class works; conversely, more money will have to be allocated for the purchasing of book club titles. At my school, for example, ELA only gets funding to buy books every five to seven years. If the money is not spent wisely, it is a long wait before the opportunity for reform returns.
- Money will need to be set aside so that teachers can build extensive classroom libraries.
- School librarians will need to rethink how they order books. Instead of buying one or two copies of a given title, multiple copies of specific titles will need to be ordered.

Given these obstacles, it is very likely that—due to the constraints of my school system—I will not be teaching this year in the 20/80 paradigm I am advocating in these pages. If, for example, I don't have immediate funding to purchase books for my students' book clubs, then book clubs will not immediately happen. Unfortunately, the way reading is taught in our schools is deeply entrenched and hard to change, but this doesn't mean we should accept the status quo. What this does mean is that *we should begin working diligently toward changing the paradigm*, which, as you read this, is what I am doing.

Staying True to Our Core Values

Remember, the 20/80 Approach to the teaching of reading comes from answering the first question posed on my four-question rubric for evaluating teacher effectiveness: *What percentage of your students can walk into a bookstore (or visit Goodreads.com) and know where to find books that interest them?* As this chapter has illustrated, thinking about this question has deeply changed my approach to the teaching of reading.

I now invite you to consider what other ways your practice would change if the other three questions posed on the proposed rubric of teacher effectiveness actually played a part in determining the level of your salary. In the left column of the following chart, you will find the three remaining questions; each of them, in turn, generate new questions worth thinking deeply about (found on the right).

REMAINING TEACHER-EFFECTIVENESS QUESTIONS	NEW QUESTIONS WORTH THINKING DEEPLY ABOUT
What percentage of your students write without being asked to do so by a teacher?	• If your salary were contingent on developing *independent* writers, how would this change your approach to the teaching of writing? • What would your students' writing journey look like over the course of the year? • What role would writing groups play in your classroom? • How would the use of models—from both professional writers as well as from you, their teacher—help your students to build their writing skills? • How would choice factor into your students' writing lives? • How would your grading practices change?
What percentage of your students can stand and speak effectively and confidently in front of a group of people?	• If your salary were contingent on developing effective and confident speakers, how would this change your approach to teaching speaking skills? • Would you create more opportunities for students to practice their speaking skills? If so, when? How? Where? • What would your students' public speaking journey look like over the course of the year? • How would the use of models—from both professional speakers as well as from you, their teacher—help your students build their speaking skills? • How would you assess a speaker's "effectiveness" in a way that motivates your students to want to continue to develop their public speaking skills?
What percentage of your students can actively listen to others— can carefully consider both what is said and what is not said?	• If your salary were contingent on developing students who were active listeners, how would this change your curriculum? • How would you deepen the active listening skills in your students? • When and where would you give your students more opportunity to strengthen their listening skills? • How would you get students to carefully consider what is *not* being said? • How would you assess a listener's "effectiveness" in a way that would encourage him or her to continue to sharpen his or her listening skills?

A Sample Unit

With the four-question rubric for evaluating teacher effectiveness in mind, let me share a sample unit from my classroom.

Poetry Unit

Length: Three weeks

Note: Though this is technically a three-week unit, it will not necessarily fit exactly into a three-week period. The unit might be woven around other things that are going on in the class. If, for example, my students meet in book clubs on Mondays and in their writing groups on Thursdays, this unit will take more than three weeks to complete, even though the total teaching time remains fifteen days.

This unit is centered on an essential question: What makes a poem great?

Days 1–5: Poetry Swim

If students are to gain an appreciation of poetry, they have to read a lot of poems. To ensure this, I begin by surrounding kids with numerous poetry books and I have them go on exploratory reading journeys. I want to make sure they are exposed to all kinds of poetry: narrative, haiku, free verse, elegies, ballads, epics, sonnets, spoken poetry, and so forth (for a list of high-interest poetry books, go to kellygallagher.org and click on "Kelly's Lists" under the "Resources" tab).

In this unit, students will be creating poetry logs that chart their discoveries and their thinking. I distribute small composition books, and as they read through a number of poems, I require them to collect some that spark an interest. I ask them to copy the poems into their logs. Alongside their selections I ask students to share their thinking in written reflections.

While students are reading and reflecting on their poems throughout the week, I start every class period with a brief mini-lesson that helps them to read poetry more critically. For example, I might do a mini-lesson on recognizing the author's use of metaphor, and how the use of metaphor deepens the reader's understanding of the poem. Or we might study a poet's decision making when it came to determining line breaks. Or we might study how punctuation is manipulated to create meaning. Mini-lessons are layered throughout the week to help my students become more discerning as they break out and read more poetry on their own.

By the end of the first week I want to see evidence that my students have gone on a deep poetry swim and that they have given rich thought to the poetry they have selected and studied.

Days 6-10: Poetry Study

After they've read poems for a week, I ask students to zero in on something worthy of deeper study. For example, one student might choose a genre of poetry worth delving deeply into (e.g., spoken poetry). Another student might latch on to a specific poet (e.g., Nikki Giovanni or Billy Collins) to study in greater depth. During this second week, students are asked to find something specific and to drill deeper.

As was the case in the first week, students continue collecting poems and writing reflections in their logs, but these collections and reflections now occur within the specific areas they've chosen to study. To prod my students to dig deeper, I may give them some of the following questions to consider: What makes this poet (or genre) worthy of study? Can you identify the "greatness" of this poet (or genre)? What makes this poet (or genre) distinct? Why has this poet (or poem) stood the test of time?

As students conduct this second week of deeper study, I continue to weave in mini-lessons to help deepen their understanding and appreciation.

Days 11-15: Poet Emulation

The emphasis now shifts into having my students emulate the excellent poetry they have encountered. If, for example, a student has studied spoken poetry, she is asked to write spoken poems. If another student studied narrative poetry, he is asked to write narrative poems. Emulation becomes the work of this week.

Of course, as the teacher, my mini-lessons shift this week into a modeling mode. I, too, pick a poet (or genre) and do some emulation in front of my students, thinking out loud as I do so. I go, and then they go.

Culminating Activities for the Poetry Unit

There are two culminating activities to the unit. First, we revisit the essential question ("What makes a poem great?"), and students consider the question through the lens of their three-week poetry study. And second, we end by placing the "author's chair" in the front of the room, and each student sits in front of the class and shares an original poem.

Staying True to What Is in the Best Interest of Our Students

Consider for a moment what I did in the poetry unit of study. I designed lessons that were student centered and in which kids did the exploring and the heavy lifting. I surrounded them with good books and mentor texts. I created an environment where students both read and wrote a lot of poems. I wove in a number of mini-lessons that deepened their understanding and appreciation of poetry. I built in lots of choice for the students, for I believe all students like to learn when given an opportunity to explore their own interests. And I made sure there was an oral component as well by creating an environment where lots of poetry was spoken and where lots of poetry was heard. Woven together, this poetry unit felt more like a celebration of poetry—a unit where kids left my class looking forward to reading poetry again later in life.

Now take a moment and consider what I did *not* do in this unit of study. I did not sit down and sweat over thirty-six Common Core anchor standards. I did not plan with any distant state test items in mind. I did not create a checklist to see which standards I covered. I did not distribute a single worksheet focused on strengthening my students' skills. I did not administer multiple-choice quizzes to prepare them for the exams in the spring (in fact, I didn't give them *any* quizzes). I did not, as Billy Collins (1988) warns, have them tie poems to chairs and torture confessions out of them. Most importantly, I did not drill the love of poetry out of them.

Did this poetry unit address many of the current Common Core ELA standards? Certainly. But it is also important to note that this unit moved *beyond* the current standards by asking my kids to do things that are not measured by CCSS-aligned exams. This unit was not designed with the CCSS (or other newly adopted standards) in mind. Instead, I designed the unit with one question in mind: What is in the best interest of my students? The answer to that question sometimes aligns with the latest standards and testing movements; often, however, it does not. So let me finish this book by reminding you that rich language arts instruction is steeped in what works—regardless of the current political winds—and what works is often found in the answer to the question I hope all of us will continue to ask: "What is in the best interest of my students?"

Appendices

Appendix A: Track Your Writing Chart

Below you will chart the pieces you write this year. Remember, for the end-of-the-year portfolio, you must have samples of writing for each of the categories listed below. Stretch yourself as a writer!

Narrative Writing	Titles of my narrative pieces: • • • • •	Dates Completed • • • • •
Informative Writing	Titles of my inform/explain pieces: • • • • •	Dates Completed • • • • •
Argument Writing	Titles of my argument pieces: • • • • •	Dates Completed • • • • •
Poetry	Titles of my poems: • • • • •	Dates Completed • • • • •

Appendix B: Conversation Chart

Speaking

C = Clear and convincing

U = Unclear/trails off

↑ = Too loud/disruptive

↓ = Too quiet/hard to hear

Evidence

A = Sophisticated, original, convincing argument

DR = Uses direct textual reference

DNQ = Alludes to text but doesn't quote it

O = Uses relevant outside evidence

EC = Evidence does not connect

Leadership

BLD = Refers to or builds on another student's comments

CQ = Asks a clarifying question of another student

Q = Poses a question to the class

S = Offers a summary/synthesis

L = Links one student's ideas to another's

— = Comment is disconnected to topic/listening?

* = Obvious leader of discussion

References

Adele. 2011. "One and Only." Musical recording from album *21*. Compact disc. London: XL Recordings.

Adler, R., Lawrence Rosenfeld, and Russell Proctor. 2012. *Interplay: The Process of Interpersonal Communicating*. New York: Oxford University Press. (Breakdown of communication percentages can be found at: http://www.skillsyouneed.com/ips/listening-skills.html#ixzz38DjINBpa.)

Allington, Richard L. 2001. *What Really Matters for Struggling Readers: Designing Research-Based Programs*. New York: Longman.

American Principles Project. 2013. "Dr. Megan Koschnick Presents on Common Core at APP Conference." https://www.youtube.com/watch?v=vrQbJlmVJZo&feature=youtu.be.

American Rhetoric. 2014. "Top 100 Speeches." http://www.americanrhetoric.com/top100speechesall.html.

Anaya, Rudolfo A. 1972. *Bless Me, Ultima*. New York: Warner Books.

Anderson, Laurie Halse. 2008. *Chains*. New York: Simon and Schuster Books for Young Readers.

Associated Press. 2013. "'Cal' Whipple, Who Helped Get WWII Photo Published, Dies at 94." March 18.

BirdLife International. 2014. "Species Factsheet: Kakapo *Strigops habroptila*." http://www.birdlife.org/datazone/speciesfactsheet.php?id=1492.

Boser, Ulrich, and Lindsay Rosenthal. 2012. *Do Schools Challenge Our Students?* Washington, DC: Center for American Progress. July 10. http://www.americanprogress.org/issues/education/report/2012/07/10/11913/do-schools-challenge-our-students/.

Bradbury, Ray. 1953. *Fahrenheit 451*. New York: Ballantine Books.

Cisneros, Sandra. 1991. *The House on Mango Street*. New York: Vintage Books.

Coleman, David. 2011. "Bringing the Common Core to Life." Full transcript of webinar. New York State Education Department. http://usny.nysed.gov/rttt/docs/ bringingthecommoncoretolife/fulltranscript.pdf.

Coleman, David, and Susan Pimentel. 2012. "Revised Publishers' Criteria for the Common Core State Standards in English Language Arts and Literacy, Grades 3–12." April 12. http://www.corestandards.org/wp-content/uploads/Publishers_Criteria_ for_Literacy_for_Grades_3-12.pdf.

College Board. 2013. "AP English Literature and Composition 2013 Free-Response Questions." College Board. http://media.collegeboard.com/digitalServices/pdf/ap/ apcentral/ap13_frq_eng_lit.pdf.

Collins, Billy. 1988. "Introduction to Poetry." Poetry Foundation. http://www. poetryfoundation.org/poem/176056.

Collins, Suzanne. 2009. *Catching Fire*. New York: Scholastic.

Condie, Ally. 2010. *Matched*. New York: Dutton Books.

Crane, Stephen. 2009. *The Red Badge of Courage*. Edited and introduction by Paul Sorrentino. Cambridge, MA: Belknap Press of Harvard University Press.

Daniels, Harvey, and Elaine Daniels. 2013. *The Best-Kept Teaching Secret: How Written Conversations Engage Kids, Activate Learning, and Grow Fluent Writers, K–12*. Thousand Oaks, CA: Corwin.

Dickinson, Emily. 1976. "I Heard a Fly Buzz—When I Died." In *The Complete Poems of Emily Dickinson*, edited by Thomas H. Johnson. New York: Back Bay Books.

Doctorow, Cory. *Little Brother*. 2008. New York: Tom Doherty.

Dodd, Jillian. 2012. *That Boy*. Flower Mound, TX: Bandit.

Fall Out Boy. 2013. "The Phoenix." *Save Rock and Roll*. CD. New York: The Island Def Jam Music Group.

Fasanella, Ralph. 1977. *Lawrence 1912—The Bread and Roses Strike*. Painting. http://www. breadandrosescentennial.org/node/17.

Fitzgerald, F. Scott. 1925. *The Great Gatsby*. New York: Scribner.

Fullen, Michael, and Katelyn Donnelly. 2013. *Alive in the Swamp: Assessing Digital Innovations in Education*. Nesta. July 16.http://www.nesta.org.uk/publications/alive-swamp-assessing-digital-innovations-education.

Gaiman, Neil. 2009. "100 Words." Available at http://kittysneverwear.blogspot.com/2009/11/new-neil-gaimanjim-lee-print-100-words.html.

———. 2013. "Why Our Future Depends on Libraries, Reading and Daydreaming." *Guardian*. October 15. http://www.theguardian.com/books/2013/oct/15/neil-gaiman-future-libraries-reading-daydreaming?CMP=twt_gu.

Gallagher, Kelly. 2004. *Deeper Reading: Comprehending Challenging Texts, 4–12*. Portland, ME: Stenhouse.

———. 2009. *Readicide: How Schools Are Killing Reading and What You Can Do About It*. Portland, ME: Stenhouse.

———. 2011. *Write Like This: Teaching Real-World Writing Through Modeling and Mentor Texts*. Portland, ME: Stenhouse.

Goldberg, Jeffrey. 2011. "Creating a Reverse Bucket List." *Atlantic*. October 5. http://www.theatlantic.com/national/archive/2011/10/creating-a-reverse-bucket-list/246003/.

Golding, William. 1962. *Lord of the Flies*. New York: Coward-McCann.

Gonchar, Michael. 2014. "200 Prompts for Argumentative Writing." *New York Times*. February 4. http://learning.blogs.nytimes.com/2014/02/04/200-prompts-for-argumentative-writing/?nl=learning&emc=edit_ln_20140206.

Greenwood, Barbara. 1994. *A Pioneer Sampler: The Daily Life of a Pioneer Family in 1840*. Boston: Houghton Mifflin.

———. 2007. *Factory Girl*. Toronto: Kids Can Press.

Halberstam, David. 1994. *October 1964*. New York: Villard Books.

Harden, Blaine. 2012. *Escape from Camp 14: One Man's Remarkable Odyssey from North Korea to Freedom in the West*. New York: Viking.

Harper's. 2013. "Harper's Index." September. http://harpers.org/archive/2013/09/harpers-index-353/.

Harwayne, Shelley. 2013. Interview by author. New York. October 9, 2013.

Hillocks, George. 2011. *Teaching Argument Writing, Grades 6–12: Supporting Claims with Relevant Evidence and Clear Reasoning*. Portsmouth, NH: Heinemann.

Hirsch, E.D., and Robert Pondiscio. 2010–2011. "There Is No Such Thing as a Reading Test." *American Educator* 34(4): 50–51. http://files.eric.ed.gov/fulltext/EJ909947.pdf.

Hoffelder, Nate. 2013. "Infographic: Who Spends the Most Time Reading in the World? (We Don't Actually Know)." The Digital Reader. July 1. http://the-digital-reader.com/wp-content/uploads/2013/07/Hours-Spent-Reading-Around-the-World1.jpg.

Hopper, Edward. 1942. *Nighthawks*. Painting. Art Institute of Chicago. http://www.artic.edu/aic/collections/artwork/111628.

Huffington Post. 2012. "25 of the Most Obvious Headlines Ever." May 24. http://www.huffingtonpost.com/2012/05/24/most-obvious-headlines-ever-photos_n_1542847.html.

ITE English. 2014. "Speaking and Listening at Key Stage 2 and Beyond."http://www.ite.org.uk/ite_topics/speaking_listening/002.html.

Jacoby, Tamar, and Tom Tancredo. 2012. "Does the U.S. Need Illegal Immigrants?" *The New York Times Upfront* 144(11).

Jago, Carol. 2011. *With Rigor for All: Meeting Common Core Standards for Reading Literature*. 2nd ed. Portsmouth, NH: Heinemann.

———. 2013. "What's With the Dog?" *IRA Secondary Reading Newsletter* 26(1).

Kacvinsky, Katie. 2011. *Awaken*. Boston: Houghton Mifflin.

Kain, Erik. 2011. "High Teacher Turnover Rates Are a Big Problem for America's Public Schools." *Forbes*. http://www.forbes.com/sites/erikkain/2011/03/08/high-teacher-turnover-rates-are-a-big-problem-for-americas-public-schools/.

Karimi, Faith, and Joe Sutton. 2014. "Magnitude 5.1 Earthquake Rattles Los Angeles Area." March 31. CNN. http://www.cnn.com/2014/03/29/us/california-earthquake/.

Kaye, Phil. 2011. "Repetition." YouTube. https://www.youtube.com/watch?v=EILQTDBqhPA.

KCRW. 2014. *Left, Right, and Center*. Radio program. http://www.kcrw.com/news/programs/lr.

Keys, Alicia. 2012. "Girl on Fire." *Girl On Fire*. CD. New York: RCA.

Kidd, David Comer, and Emanuele Castano. 2013. "Reading Literary Fiction Improves Theory of Mind." *Science.* http://www.sciencemag.org/content/342/6156/377. abstract.

King Jr., Martin Luther. 1963. *Letter from Birmingham City Jail.* TeachingAmericanHistory. org. http://teachingamericanhistory.org/library/document/letter-from-birmingham-city-jail-excerpts/.

Kinney, Jeff. 2007. *Diary of a Wimpy Kid: Greg Heffley's Journal.* New York: Amulet Books.

Kittle, Penny. 2013. *Book Love: Developing Depth, Stamina, and Passion in Adolescent Readers.* Portsmouth, NH: Heinemann.

Krashen, Stephen. 2004. *The Power of Reading: Insights from the Research.* 2nd ed. Westport, CT: Libraries Unlimited.

———. 2012. "How Much Testing?" Posted on Diane Ravitch's blog. July 21. http://dianeravitch.net/2012/07/25/stephen-krashen-how-much-testing/.

———. 2013. "The Common Core Only Prepares Students for Taking Tests." SKrashen. Blog. http://skrashen.blogspot.com/2013/08/the-common-core-only-prepares-students.html.

Kurtzleben, Danielle. 2014. "7 Charts That Show How Americans Spend Their Time." Vox. http://www.vox.com/2014/4/11/5553006/how-americans-spend-their-time-in-6-charts.

Langer, Judith A. 1995. *Envisioning Literature: Literary Understanding and Literature Instruction.* New York: Teachers College Press.

LaReau, Jamie. 2014. "Dealerships Settle Deceptive Advertising Charges in FTC Sweep." *Automotive News.* http://www.autonews.com/article/20140109/RETAIL07/140109857/dealerships-settle-deceptive-advertising-charges-in-ftc-sweep#.

Layton, Lindsey, and Emma Brown. 2012. "SAT Reading Scores Hit a Four-Decade Low." *Washington Post.* September 24. http://articles.washingtonpost.com/2012-09-24/local/35495510_1_scores-board-president-gaston-caperton-test-takers.

Lee, Harper. 1960. *To Kill a Mockingbird.* Philadelphia: Lippincott.

Li, Moying. 2010. *Snow Falling in Spring: Coming of Age in China During the Cultural Revolution.* New York: Square Fish.

Loveless, Tom. 2012. *How Well Are American Students Learning? The 2012 Brown Center Report on American Education* III(1). Washington, DC: The Brookings Institution. http://www.brookings.edu/~/media/Newsletters/0216_brown_education_loveless. PDF.

Lowry, Lois. 1993. *The Giver*. Boston: Houghton Mifflin.

Macklemore, and Ryan Lewis. 2012. "Can't Hold Us." *The Heist*. CD. Macklemore.

Marzano, Robert J., and John S. Kendall. 1998. *Awash in a Sea of Standards*. Denver, CO: Mid-Continent Research for Education and Learning.

Moore, Michael. 2002. *Bowling for Columbine*. DVD. Beverly Hills, CA: MGM Home Entertainment.

Morrison, Toni. 1994. *The Bluest Eye*. New York: Plume.

National Association of Colleges and Employers. 2012. "The Skills and Qualities Employers Want in Their Class of 2013 Recruits." October 24. http://www.naceweb. org/s10242012/skills-abilities-qualities-new-hires/.

National Center for Education Statistics. 2013a. "Fast Fact: SAT Scores." U.S. Department of Education. http://nces.ed.gov/fastfacts/display.asp?id=171.

———. 2013b. "Vocabulary Results from the 2009 and 2011 NAEP Reading Assessments: National Assessment of Educational Progress at Grades 4, 8, and 12." U.S. Department of Education. http://nces.ed.gov/nationsreportcard/pdf/main2011/2013452.pdf.

National Center for Public Policy and Higher Education/Southern Regional Education Board (SREB). 2010. "Beyond the Rhetoric: Improving College Readiness Through Coherent State Policy." June. http://www.highereducation.org/reports/college_readiness/CollegeReadiness.pdf.

National Geographic. 2014. "Wild Hawaii: Violence in the Deep." Video clip. http://channel.nationalgeographic.com/wild/wild-hawaii/videos/violence-in-the-deep/?videoDetect=t%252Cf.

Netburn, Deborah. 2014. "Even Cows Need Friends: Study Finds Calves Raised in Pairs Are Smarter." *Los Angeles Times*. February 28. http://www.latimes.com/science/sciencenow/la-sci-sn-calves-pairs-smarter-20140228,0,4628942.story#axzz2uiQryxIF.

Newkirk, Thomas. 2009. *Holding On to Good Ideas in a Time of Bad Ones: Six Literacy Principles Worth Fighting For*. Portsmouth, NH: Heinemann.

———. 2011. *The Art of Slow Reading: Six Time-Honored Practices for Engagement.* Portsmouth, NH: Heinemann.

Neyer, Janet. "Why Read?" Infographic. http://static.squarespace.com/static/52eec360e4b0c81c80749630/t/544fb9dbe4b0bf8d82cafce4/1414511067775/Why%20Read%20Infographic.pdf.

NGA/CCSSO (National Governors Association Center for Best Practices and Council of Chief State School Officers). 2010a. "English Language Arts Standards » Anchor Standards » College and Career Readiness Anchor Standards for Reading." Common Core State Standards Initiative. http://www.corestandards.org/ELA-Literacy/CCRA/R/.

———. 2010b. "English Language Arts Standards » Language » Grade 3: Vocabulary Acquisition and Use." Common Core State Standards Initiative. http://www.corestandards.org/ELA-Literacy/L/3/#CCSS.ELA-Literacy.L.3.5.

———. 2010c. "Appendix B: Text Exemplars and Sample Performance Tasks." Common Core State Standards Initiative. http://www.corestandards.org/assets/Appendix_B.pdf.

———. 2010d. "English Language Arts Standards » Anchor Standards » College and Career Readiness Anchor Standards for Writing." Common Core State Standards Initiative. http://www.corestandards.org/ELA-Literacy/CCRA/W/.

———. 2010e. "Common Core State Standards for English Language Arts & Literacy in History/Social Studies, Science, and Technical Subjects." Common Core State Standards Initiative. http://www.corestandards.org/assets/CCSSI_ELA%20Standards.pdf.

———. 2010f. "English Language Arts Standards » Speaking & Listening » Grade 9–10." Common Core State Standards Initiative. http://www.corestandards.org/ELA-Literacy/SL/9-10/.

Oatley, Keith. 2011. "In the Minds of Others." *Scientific American Mind* 22(5).

Obama, Barack. 2013. "Remarks by the President in the State of the Union Address." The White House Office of the Press Secretary. February 12. http://www.whitehouse.gov/the-press-office/2013/02/12/remarks-president-state-union-address.

Orwell, George. 1946. *Animal Farm.* New York: Harcourt, Brace.

———. 1949. *1984.* New York: Signet Classics.

Palmer, Erik. 2011. *Well Spoken: Teaching Speaking to All Students*. Portland, ME: Stenhouse.

———. 2013. *Teaching the Core Skills of Listening and Speaking*. Alexandria, VA: Association for Supervision and Curriculum Development.

———. 2014. "Effective Communication with Erik Palmer." Boston: Houghton Mifflin Harcourt. http://my.hrw.com/content/hmof/language_arts/hmhcollections/ resources/common/videoPlayer/index.html?shortvid=V_FLLIT_0303.

PARCC. 2012. *PARCC Model Content Frameworks: English Language Arts/Literacy, Grades 3–11*. Version 2.0. Partnership for Assessment of Readiness for College and Careers. http://www.parcconline.org/sites/parcc/files/PARCCMCFELALiteracyAugust2012_ FINAL.pdf.

Pearce, Matt. 2012. "Sandy Hook Teacher Victoria Soto Is Given a Hero's Farewell." *Los Angeles Times*. December 19. http://articles.latimes.com/2012/dec/19/nation/la-na-nn-sandy-hook-teacher-victoria-soto-hero-20121219.

Pearson, P. David. 2014. "Implementing the CCSS: Comprehension, Close Reading, and the Common Core." Webinar. March 26. https://www.youtube.com/watch?v=TP8qoi-1kuU.

Pelzer, David J. 1995. *A Child Called "It": An Abused Child's Journey from Victim to Victor*. Deerfield Beach, FL: Health Communications.

Perry, Susan. 2013. "Want to Identify More with Others? Reading Literary—Not Pop— Fiction May Help." MinnPost. http://www.minnpost.com/second-opinion/2013/10/ want-identify-more-others-reading-literary-not-pop-fiction-may-help.

Philbrick, Rodman. 2000. *The Last Book in the Universe*. New York: Blue Sky.

Pitts Jr., Leonard. 2014. "A Few Disclaimers on the 4th Amendment." *Miami Herald*. January 14. http://www.miamiherald.com/2014/01/14/3871014/a-few-disclaimers-on-the-4th-amendment.html.

Powers, Kevin. 2012. *The Yellow Birds: A Novel*. New York: Little, Brown.

Remarque, Erich Maria. 1929. *All Quiet on the Western Front*. Boston: Little, Brown.

Richman, Josh. 2013. "Field Poll: California Voters Favor Gun Controls Over Protecting Second Amendment Rights." *San Jose Mercury News*. February 26. http://www. mercurynews.com/ci_22666985/field-poll-california-voters-feel-new-gun-controls.

Rihanna. 2012. "Stay." *Unapologetic.* CD. New York: The Island Def Jam Music Group.

Robinson, Ken. 2006. "How Schools Kill Creativity." TED Talk available on YouTube. http://www.ted.com/talks/ken_robinson_says_schools_kill_creativity?language=en.

Rosenwald, Michael S. 2014. "Serious Reading Takes a Hit from Online Scanning and Skimming, Researchers Say." *Washington Post.* http://www.washingtonpost.com/local/serious-reading-takes-a-hit-from-online-scanning-and-skimming-researchers-say/2014/04/06/088028d2-b5d2-11e3-b899-20667de76985_story.html.

Roth, Veronica. 2012. *Divergent.* New York: Katherine Tegen Books.

Sapolsky, Robert M. 2013. "Another Use for Literature." *Los Angeles Times.* http://www.latimes.com/opinion/commentary/la-oe-sapolsky-theory-of-mind-20131229,0,5186627,print.story.

Scherer, Marge. 2001. "How and Why Standards Can Improve Student Achievement: A Conversation with Robert J. Marzano." *Educational Leadership* 59(1).

Schuster, Edgar Howard. 2003. *Breaking the Rules: Liberating Writers Through Innovative Grammar Instruction.* Portsmouth, NH: Heinemann.

Shakespeare, William. 1997. *The Tragedy of Hamlet, Prince of Denmark.* Champaign, IL: Project Gutenberg.

Silverthorne, Sandy, and John Warner. 2007. *One Minute Mysteries and Brain Teasers.* Eugene, OR: Harvest House. http://www.oneminutemysteries.com/samplechapters.pdf.

Smarter Balanced Assessment Consortium. 2014a. "Diamonds in the Sky." English Language Arts/Literacy sample items. Olympia, WA: Smarter Balanced Assessment Consortium. http://sampleitems.smarterbalanced.org/itempreview/sbac/ELA.htm.

———. 2014b. "Cell Phones in School—Yes or No?" English Language Arts/Literacy sample items. Olympia, WA: Smarter Balanced Assessment Consortium. http://sampleitems.smarterbalanced.org/itempreview/sbac/ELA.htm.

Smithsonian American Art Museum. 2014. "Education: Student Podcasts." http://americanart.si.edu/education/resources/guides/podcast.cfm.

Snodgrass, W. D. 2001. *De/Compositions: 101 Good Poems Gone Wrong.* Minneapolis, MN: Graywolf.

SparkNotes. 2003. *No Fear Shakespeare: Hamlet*. New York: Author.

Stein, Joel. 2012. "How I Replaced Shakespeare: And Why Our Kids May Never Read a Poem as Lovely as a Tree." *Time*. December 10. http://content.time.com/time/magazine/article/0,9171,2130408,00.html.

Steinbeck, John. 1939. *The Grapes of Wrath*. New York: Viking.

———. 1993. *Of Mice and Men*. New York: Penguin.

Stotsky, Sandra. 2013. "Literature or Technical Manuals: Who Should Be Teaching What, Where, and Why." Hoosiers Against Common Core. http://hoosiersagainstcommoncore.com/the-best-explanation-of-why-common-core-ela-standards-are-rubbish/.

Sullivan, Robert, ed. 2003. *100 Photographs That Changed the World*. New York: Life Books.

Tartt, Donna. 2013. *The Goldfinch*. New York: Little, Brown.

Taylor, Jill Bolte. 2008. "Jill Bolte Taylor's Stroke of Insight." TED Talk available on YouTube. www.youtube.com/watch?v=UyyjU8fzEYU.

Tennyson, Alfred. 1998. *The Works of Alfred Lord Tennyson*. Hertfordshire, UK: Wordsworth.

Toulmin, Stephen. 2003. *The Uses of Argument*. New York: Cambridge University Press.

Vocabulary.com. 2014. s.v. "Declamation." http://www.vocabulary.com/dictionary/declamation.

Wales, Jimmy. 2005. "The Birth of Wikipedia." TED. July. http://www.ted.com/talks/jimmy_wales_on_the_birth_of_wikipedia.html.

WebMD. 2012. "Piaget Stages of Development." http://www.webmd.com/children/piaget-stages-of-development.

Weiss, Elaine, and Don Long. 2013. "Market-Oriented Education Reforms' Rhetoric Trumps Reality." Broader, Bolder Approach to Education. April 22. http://www.epi.org/files/2013/bba-rhetoric-trumps-reality.pdf.

Wilson, Maja, and Thomas Newkirk. 2011. "Can Readers Really Stay Within the Standards Lines?" *Education Week*. December 14.

Wolf, Maryanne. 2007. *Proust and the Squid: The Story and Science of the Reading Brain.* New York: HarperCollins.

Zhao, Yong. 2012. *World Class Learners: Educating Creative and Entrepreneurial Students.* Thousand Oaks, CA: Corwin, a Joint Publication with the National Association of Elementary School Principals.

Zusak, Markus. 2006. *The Book Thief.* New York: Alfred A. Knopf.

Index